LANGUAGE AND TRAVEL GUIDE
TO SICILY

LANGUAGE AND TRAVEL GUIDE TO SICILY

Giovanna Bellia La Marca

*For Peggy and Jay
Another Italian
region to explore*

*Best Regards
Giovanna Bellia L.M.
Vienna July 10th 2017*

HIPPOCRENE BOOKS, INC.
New York

For information, address:
  Hippocrene Books, Inc.
  171 Madison Avenue
  New York, NY 10016
  www.hippocrenebooks.com

Library of Congress Cataloging-in-Publication Data

  La Marca, Giovanna Bellia.
    Language and travel guide to Sicily/Giovanna Bellia La Marca.
      p.   cm.
    Includes bibliographical references.
    ISBN-13: 978-0-7818-1149-1
    ISBN-10: 0-7818-1149-X
    1. Italian language—Conversation and phrase books—English.
  2. Italian language—Dialects—Italy—Sicily—Conversation and
  phrase books—English 3. Sicily (Italy)—Guidebooks. I. Title.

  PC1121.L33 2008
  914.5'80493—dc22   2007040644

Printed in the United States of America.

DEDICA DEDICATION

This book is dedicated to my brother Dr. Carmelo Bellia
and to the memory of our parents Felice Bellia and
Concettina Sirugo Bellia, who gave us our love for
the land of Sicily and our first language.

RINGRAZIAMENTI ACKNOWLEDGMENTS

I thank the Bellia, Sirugo, Biazzo, Muccio, and Cannizzaro families with whom I have the pleasure of speaking Sicilian.

I am grateful to our friend Dott. Nicola Spata for having proposed me for the "Ragusani Nel Mondo" award, and to President Giovanni Franco Antoci and Dott. Sebastiano D' Angelo for having presented the award to me in a nationally televised ceremony on August 28, 2004. I thank my Godparents Dott. Raffaele Cannizzaro, who has been a font of historic and cultural information, and Tina Cannizzaro Distefano for having given me a taste for prose and poetry in the Sicilian language. My thanks to Antonietta La Terra Bertini for always having time for my questions. My friends Padre Enrico Bommarito and Angela Pasqualetti for our explorations of Mount Etna. My husband Howard La Marca for his constant help and encouragement, to my daughter Nicoletta La Marca Sacco and son-in-law Steven Christopher Sacco for their affection and support and to my beloved grandchildren Felice and Francesca, who keep me in good spirits with their smiles, hugs and kisses.

My special thanks to Priti Gress, my wonderfully capable editor at Hippocrene, to Mary Tahan, who made the audio component of the book possible, and to my friend Dr. Salvatore Moltisanti, with whom I recorded the CD which accompanies this book in our native language of Ragusa and in Italian. A very special *Grazie* to my publisher, Dr. George Blagowidow, for his generous support of this project.

CONTENTS

Contents   ix

CD Track List

DISC 1

1. Chapter 1: The Land of Sicily—Dialogue
2. Helpful Phrases: Asking Travel Directions
3. Tickets and Reservations
4. Telling Time
5. At the Department Store/ Pharmacy
6. At the Movies/Theatre/ Concert Hall
7. At the Museum
8. Chapter 2: The Delectable Food of Sicily—Dialogue
9. Helpful Phrases: Where to Eat
10. At the Restaurant
11. At the Table
12. At the Market
13. Chapter 3: The Architecture of Sicily Spans the Centuries—Dialogue
14. Helpful Phrases: The Buildings of Sicily
15. At the Tourist Office
16. At the Train Station
17. Asking Street Directions

DISC 2

1. Chapter 4: The Arts of Sicily—Dialogue
2. Helpful Phrases: At the Bookstore/Gallery/ Craft Shop
3. Colors
4. Literature, Arts and Crafts
5. Fashion
6. Chapter 5: The Persistence of the Sicilian Language— Dialogue
7. "Lingua e Dialetti" by Ignazio Buttitta
8. Sicilian Proverbs
9. Chapter 6: Family and Customs—Dialogue
10. Helpful Phrases: At the Florist
11. At the Fruit Vendor
12. At the Pastry Shop
13. At the Wine Shop
14. Introductions
15. Greetings
16. Distances and Directions
17. Opposites
18. Emergencies
19. Telephone
20. Reservations at Restaurants
21. Reservations at Hotels
22. Reservations for Entertainment/Travel

CHAPTER 1

THE LAND OF SICILY

W elcome to Sicily!

Flying over Mount Etna, the fabled volcano of antiquity, travelers look forward to hearing and speaking the Italian they studied. But when they land in Catania, they hear a language that is familiar, yet hard to understand. Once the ear becomes attuned to the cadence and inflection of Sicilian, however, visitors begin to understand how it relates to Italian and are also able to appreciate its distinct character.

Sicilian pronunciation resembles Italian in that the vowels are always pronounced in the same way. Some Sicilian words have a double consonant, which indicates stress on the syllable where they occur.

The sounds of the vowels are: **a** as in <u>a</u>wait
    e as in <u>e</u>very
    i as in <u>i</u>gloo
    o as in <u>o</u>pen
    u as in d<u>u</u>et.

In **ce** and **ci**, the **c** sounds like the **ch** as in <u>ch</u>urch.
In **ca**, **co**, **cu**, **che**, and **chi**, the **c** sounds like the **ch** in chorus.
In **ge** and **gi**, the **g** sounds like the **g** in <u>ge</u>ntle.
In **ghe**, **ghi**, **ga**, **go**, and **gu**, the **g** sounds like the **g** in <u>ghe</u>tto.

Listen to the following dialogue between Giovanna and Salvatore as they speak each sentence or phrase—first in Sicilian and then in Italian.

1

DIALOGUE

In this and all dialogues throughout the book, Giovanna and Salvatore speak the first sentence in Sicilian and the second in Italian. The English translation follows; in some cases, the literal translation of the Sicilian and Italian phrases is provided in square brackets.

GIOVANNA: Ci sii mai statu sull'Etna?
GIOVANNA: Ci sei mai stato sull'Etna?
Have you ever been on Mount Etna?

SALVATORE: Comu no; è na scena ca nun si scorda mai.
SALVATORE: Come no; è una scena indimenticabile.
Certainly, it's an unforgettable experience.

G: Pari ri essiri 'nta luna e non in chistu munnu.
G: Sembra di essere sulla luna e non in questo mondo.
It seems as if you're on the moon and not on this earth.

S: Ci hai fattu casu ca nun c'è nenti ri vivu, mancu na fogghia ri erba?
S: Hai notato che non c'è niente di vivo, neanche una foglia d'erba?
Have you noticed that there's nothing living, not even a blade of grass?

G: Hai ragghiuni; ci voli cient'anni prima ca nasci na pianta duoppu na eruzioni.
G: Hai ragione; devono passare cento anni prima che nasca una pianta dopo una eruzione.
You're right; it takes a hundred years for a plant to grow [before a plant grows] after an eruption.

S: Però iu vitti tanti cuccinelli.
S: Però ho visto tante coccinelle.
But I saw lots of ladybugs.

G: **U truvirannu qualchicosa ri mangiri pi campari!**

G: Troveranno qualcosa da mangiare per vivere!

It must be that they find [they must find] something to eat to survive!

S: **Eppuri tutta sta petra ri lava è bedda e utili.**

S: Eppure tutta questa pietra di lava è bella e utile.

Yet, all this lava stone is beautiful and useful.

G: **A città ri Catania è cina cina ri beddi palazzi fatti ri petra ri lava.**

G: La città di Catania è piena di bei palazzi costruiti di pietra lavica.

The city of Catania is full of beautiful buildings made from lava stone.

S: **Certu; anche l'elefanti, simbulu ra città, è niuru pirchì fu fattu ri petra ri lava.**

S: Certo; anche l'elefante, simbolo della città, è nero perchè è stato fatto di pietra di lava.

Right; even the elephant, the symbol of the city, is black because it was made of lava stone.

G: **Ma i cosi ciù belli ri viriri sunu i mura naturali re Goli ri Alcantara.**

G: Ma le cose più belle da vedere sono le mura naturali delle Gole di Alcantara.

But the most beautiful things to see are the natural walls of the gorge, Gole di Alcantara.

S: **Faciennu na caminata 'nto sciumi, re Goli ri Alcantara, si virinu sceni ca sunu nu spettaculu.**

S: Facendo una passeggiata lungo il fiume delle Gole di Alcantara, si vedono scene spettacolari.

Walking along the river of the Gole di Alcantara, spectacular scenery can be seen [is seen].

G: Io ma firai a arrivari finu a cascata ri Alcantara.
G: Io sono stata capace di arrivare fino alle cascate di Alcantara.
I was able to make it up to the waterfalls of Alcantara.

S: Vale a pena arrivarici anche se l'acqua è sempri fridda, macari ri stati.
S: Vale la pena arrivarci anche se l'acqua è sempre fredda, anche in estate.
It's worth getting there even if the water is always cold, even in the summer.

G: I stivali luonghi luonghi aiutanu a varcari l'acqua fridda.
G: Gli stivali lunghi aiutano a varcare l'acqua fredda.
Hip-high boots help to wade through the cold water.

S: Pi davvero vali a pena irici.
S: Veramente vale la pena andarci.
It's really worth the trip.

SICILY: THE PEARL OF THE MEDITERRANEAN

The climate, with its constant sun, intense blue sky, brilliant light, and clear air, makes the land of Sicily a favorite tourist attraction. On a clear day you can truly see forever. From the enchanting medieval town of Erice on Sicily's western coast you can actually see majestic Mount Etna located clear across the island on the eastern coast. In *The Winter's Tale* (Act III, Scene I), William Shakespeare had this to say about Sicily:

> The climate's delicate; the air most sweet.
> Fertile the isle, the temple much surpassing
> The common praise it bears.

Most of the land area of Sicily is mountainous, and beautiful hill towns abound. Quaint houses with gray clay tiled roofs stack up endlessly along the mountainsides, offering unmatched photo opportunities. Typically, low walls made of unmortared white stones encircle the houses, delineating the fields, dotting the serene landscape, and forming a backdrop for the beautiful wildflowers filling every crevice of the white stone walls. Circles of the same white stone are used to create borders around the splendid carob trees, which, together with the century-old olive trees and the occasional farmhouse, accent the fields.

The sunshine that invigorates visitors also favors the growth of an amazing variety of flowers, rich in color and fragrance, which carpet the fields, hills, and mountains in the springtime. The brilliant light makes the color of the flowers even more intense.

The exuberance of nature is not only decorative, but it also provides an outlet for adventure, leading to delightful and unusual treats. Foraging for edible wild plants is a favorite pastime. Gathering **cicoria** (dandelions); looking for wild **finocchio** (fennel); finding **funghi selvatici** (wild mushrooms); picking **lassini** (a slightly bitter green), which is made into delectable **frittate** (omelets); harvesting **asparagi** (asparagus); digging for **patacchi** (jerusalem artichokes), crunchy when raw and sweet when cooked; and picking **capperi** (fresh capers) from plants that cling to and tumble from the walls make for a fun and productive afternoon.

The sun-ripened fruits and vegetables are the centerpieces of Sicily's wonderfully flavorful cuisine. Whether a plant is native to Sicily or was brought there, the climate and the rich volcanic soil work miracles on its rapid growth, abundance, and flavor. In this exceptionally fertile land, both native plants and those brought from afar grow with abandon. Plants that were brought from the Americas, such as the ubiquitous **fichi d'India** (prickly pear), prized for its flavor and sweetness, and **pomodori** (tomatoes), have not only adapted well all over the island over the centuries, but their quality, taste, and fragrance now surpass that of the original imports. It was the Spaniards who originally brought the prickly pears to Sicily from Mexico, an astonishing fact to this author when she first learned it. Sicily continues to produce, as it did in ancient times, the best wheat in the country. Its rich golden grains fed the Roman legions, and in ancient times Sicily became known as the granary of Rome.

The beaches of Sicily are second to none. Adults bury themselves in their fine golden sands to treat their aches and pains, while children build sand castles near the water. The beaches are made more attractive by the fact that they are seldom crowded. Although summer can be quite hot, it is always cooler in the shade, and the evening's breezes are delightfully comfortable.

A trip to **Mount Etna**, the volcano on the eastern coast, is a memorable event that never fails to impress. The mountains, bare of vegetation and snow topped in the distance, are like no other landscape on earth—a marvelous sculptural mass in warm tones of brown. Walking along the edge of one of the many inactive craters is truly an experience. Not to be missed is another miracle of nature, not far from Taormina, named **Gole di Alcantara**. This is a spectacular gorge defined by cliffs with extraordinary rock formations; they were created in antiquity when hot lava met the water of the river. Nature in all its splendor is the dramatic backdrop to the wonderfully rich and varied architecture of Sicily.

HELPFUL PHRASES

Asking Travel Directions

GIOVANNA: **Quali srata si pigghia p'arrivari all'Etna?**
GIOVANNA: Quale strada si prende per andare all'Etna?
                   Which road do we take [is taken] to go to Mount Etna?

SALVATORE: **Ma chi è piriculusu iri supra l'Etna?**
SALVATORE: È pericoloso andare sull'Etna?
                   Is it dangerous to go to Mount Etna?

G: **Finu a unni si po accianari ca machina?**
G: Fin dove si può salire con la macchina?
       How far up can you go by car?

S: Chi fa ci fussi na guida ri cca vicinu ca ni putissi purtari e Goli ri l'Alcantara?

S: Ci sarebbe una guida locale che ci potrebbe accompagnare alle Gole di Alcantara?

Would there be a local guide who could take us to the Gole di Alcantara?

G: Pi ghirici s'acciana, si cala, si fannu scali o si pigghia l'ascinzuri?

G: Per andarci, si sale, si scende, si fanno scale, oppure si prende l'ascensore?

To go there, do you go up, down, are there stairs, or do you take the elevator?

S: Vulissi na guida ca parra u 'nglisi.

S: Vorrei una guida che parli l'inglese.

I would like an English-speaking guide.

Tickets and Reservations

GIOVANNA: Quantu vinissi a custari u trenu, o u tassì?

GIOVANNA: Quanto costerebbe il treno, oppure il tassì?

How much would the train or a taxi cost?

SALVATORE: Quantu costa u bigliettu?

SALVATORE: Quanto costa il biglietto?

How much is the [admission] ticket?

G: U faciti u scuntu pe picciriddi e pi l'anziani?

G: Fate lo sconto per i bambini e per gli anziani?

Do you give a discount for children and senior citizens?

S: Se si vole iri ca guida comu si prinota u puostu?

S: Se si vuole andare con la guida come si prenota il posto?

If you want [one wants] to go with a guide, how do you reserve a place?

G: **Quannu si parti, ri matina, o ri vespiri? A chi ura?**
G: Quando si parte, di mattina, oppure di pomeriggio? A che ora?
When is the departure [does one leave], in the morning or in the
afternoon? At what time?

S: **E quannu si torna?**
S: E quando si torna?
And when is the [does one] return?

Telling Time

GIOVANNA: **Sunu i cincu e 'nquartu.**
GIOVANNA: Sono le cinque e un quarto.
It's 5:15 (five fifteen).

SALVATORE: **Sunu i siei e menza.**
SALVATORE: Sono le sei e mezza.
It's 6:30 (six thirty).

G: **Sunu i siei e tri quarti.**
G: Sono le sei e quarantacinque.
It's 6:45 (six forty-five).

S: **Sunu i setti menu 'nquartu.**
S: Sono le sette meno un quarto.
It's 6:45 (a quarter to seven).

G: **Matina, manzuornu, sira.**
G: Mattina, mezzogiorno, sera.
Morning, noon, evening.

S: **A nascita ro suli, a calata ro suli, a menzanotti.**
S: All'alba, al tramonto, a mezzanotte.
Sunrise, sunset, midnight.

G: È l'una, si stannu faciennu i rui, si ficinu i tri ri matina.
G: È l'una, si stanno facendo le due, si sono fatte le tre di mattina.
It's one o'clock, it's almost two, it's gotten to be three in the morning.

S: A vacanza ni sta faciennu fari l'uri nichi.
S: La vacanza ci sta facendo fare le ore piccole.
This vacation is keeping us up to the wee hours.

G: Sunu l'uottu, i novi, i reci, l'unnici, è manzuornu.
G: Sono le otto, le nove, le dieci, le undici, è mezzogiorno.
It's 8 a.m., 9 a.m., 10 a.m., 11 a.m., it's noon.

S: È l'una ri vespiri, i rui, i tri, i quattru, i cincu.
S: Sono le tredici, le quattordici, le quindici, le sedici, le diciassette.
It's 1 p.m., 2 p.m., 3 p.m., 4 p.m., 5 p.m.

G: Sunu i siei ri sira, i setti, l'uottu, i novi, i reci e l'unnici.
G: Sono le dicotto, le diciannove, le venti, le ventuno, le ventidue e le ventitré.
It's 6 p.m., 7 p.m., 8 p.m., 9 p.m., 10 p.m., and 11 p.m.

At the Department Store/Pharmacy

GIOVANNA: Cercu russiettu, borotalcu, smaltu pi l'ugna, cuttuni, e acitoni.
GIOVANNA: Cerco rossetto, borotalco, smalto per le unghie, cotone, e acetone.
I'm looking for lipstick, talcum powder, nail polish, cotton balls, and nail polish remover.

SALVATORE: Vulissi nu spazzolinu pe rienti, na crema pa varba, na colonia pi duoppu a varba.
SALVATORE: Vorrei uno spazzolino per i denti, crema per la barba, colonia dopobarba.
I would like a toothbrush, shaving cream, aftershave cologne.

G: Vulissi aspirina, antacidu, supposti, cerotti, crema antibiotica,
     gazza.
G: Desidero aspirina, antacido, supposte, cerotti, crema antibiotica,
     garza.
     *I would like aspirin, antacid, suppositories, band-aids, antibiotic
     cream, gauze.*

S: Chi fa, n'aviti rotolini pa machinetta fotografica o dischetti
     pa machinetta digitali?
S: Ne avete rullini per la macchina fotografica, dischetti per la
     macchina digitale?
     Do you have film for the camera, or disks for the digital camera?

At the Movies/Theater/Concert Hall

GIOVANNA: Vulissi rui biglietti po cinema, u teatru, o u
                cuncertu.
GIOVANNA: Vorrei due biglietti per il cinema, il teatro, oppure il
                concerto.
                *I would like two tickets for the movies, the theater, or
                the concert.*

SALVATORE: Quannu accumenza u spettaculu?
SALVATORE: Quando comincia lo spettacolo?
                When does the show start?

G: Accumenza e rui ri vespiri, all'uottu ri sira, e novi ri sira,
     all'unnici ri sira.
G: Comincia alle quattordici, alle venti, alle ventuno, alle ventitré.
     It starts at 2 p.m., at 8 p.m., at 9 p.m., at 11 p.m.

S: Ma chi faciti, scuntu pi l'anziani?
S: Fate sconto per gli anziani?
     Do you give a discount to seniors?

At the Museum

GIOVANNA: **Pi favuri, mi ricissi l'orariu ri apirtura e ri ciusura.**
GIOVANNA: Per favore, mi dica l'orario di apertura e di chiusura.
Please tell me the opening and closing time.

SALVATORE: **A mosra è o pian terrenu oppuri o primu pianu?**
SALVATORE: L'esibizione si trova al pian terreno oppure al primo
piano?
*Is the exhibition on the ground floor or on the first
floor?*

G: **Chi fa, c'è l'ascinzuri?**
G: C'è l'ascensore?
Is there an elevator?

S: **Ma unni sunu i gabinetti?**
S: Dove sono i gabinetti?
Where are the bathrooms?

G: **C'è nu risturanti o unni pigghiari un cafè?**
G: C'è un ristorante o dove prendere un caffè?
Is there a restaurant or somewhere to have coffee?

S: **Unni s'accattunu i riproduzioni ri arti?**
S: Dove si comprano le riproduzioni di arte?
Where can you buy art reproductions?

G: **Quantu costa na guida?**
G: Quanto costa una guida?
How much is a guidebook?

S: **Chi fa, accittati a carta ri creditu?**
S: Accettate carte di credito?
Do you accept credit cards?

CHAPTER 2

THE DELECTABLE FOOD OF SICILY

DIALOGUE

GIOVANNA: Pirchì si rici ca na pirsuna onesta e rispittusa è
bona comi u pani?

GIOVANNA: Perche si dice che una persona onesta e rispettosa è
buona come il pane?
*Why do they say that an honest and considerate person
is as good as bread?*

SALVATORE: Pirchì nun c'è nenti ch'è ciù buonu ro pani.

SALVATORE: Perche non c'è niente più buono del pane.
Because there's nothing as good as [better than] bread.

G: E allura guriemuci 'mpiezzu ri pani friscu friscu.

G: Allora godiamoci un pezzo di pane fresco fresco.
So, let's enjoy a very fresh piece of bread.

S: E chi ni manciamu pi cumpanagghiu?

S: Che cosa mangeremo per companatico?
What shall we eat with it?

G: Ti piacissi na 'nzalata ri lumia cu pipi ardienti?

G: Ti piacerebbe un'insalata di limone con peperoncino?
Would you like a lemon salad with hot pepper flakes?

13

S: Ma comu no! È perfetta pi spunzarici tanticcia ri pani.
S: Come no! Perfetto per inzupparci un po'di pane.
Why not! Perfect to dip a little bread in the juices.

G: U sai ca u furmientu ra nosra terra è unu re miegghiu comu
    qualità?
G: Lo sai che il frumento della nosra terra, come qualità è fra i
    migliori?
*Do you know that the quality of the wheat from our land is among
the best?*

S: Certu, u sapievunu anchi ai tiempi ri l'antichi Rumani.
S: Sì, si sapeva anche nei tempi degli antichi Romani.
Yes, this [it] was known even in the times of the ancient Romans.

G: Ca nosra farina siciliana u pani e a pasta 'mpastata vieninu
    gialli comu l'oru e annu un sapuri ca nun si po livari
    ra ucca.
G: Con la nostra farina siciliana il pane e la pasta fatti in casa
    risultano gialli come l'oro e hanno un sapore squisito (che non
    si smetterebbe di mangiare).
*With our Sicilian flour, the bread and homemade pasta come out
as yellow as gold, and they have such a delicious taste (that you
don't want to stop eating them.)*

S: Accettu cu tantu piaciri stu beddu spuntinu.
S: Accetto con piacere questo buono spuntino.
I accept this delicious snack with pleasure.

THE INTENSE FLAVORS AND FRAGRANCES OF SICILY

The food of Sicily is as rich and varied as its long history. This
ancient cuisine is as multicultural as the many people who have
inhabited this lovely island since antiquity. Its golden wheat is

of exceptional quality. The fragrant mountain honey is prized by gourmets. The cheeses, which are subject to strict quality control, match other famous Italian cheeses in the world market. The wines are also taking their place among Italy's best. The olive tree produces both olives for snacking and cooking and extra-virgin olive oil of exceptional quality. Native crops, as well as those that were brought to the island, found a favorable climate and fertile soil and continue to produce crops of incomparable flavor and fragrance.

Sicilian blood oranges are known all over the world. So are special crops such as the delicious **ciliegino** (cherry tomato) from Pechino in southeastern Sicily. Semidried and packed in extra-virgin olive oil, it is now available in gourmet shops in Sicily and abroad. The exceptional pistachios from the town of Bronte, located on the slopes of Mount Etna, are made into a delicious pesto for pasta as well as a sweet topping for desserts. Along with the pistachios, the honey from this region and from Monti Iblei to the south is prized among connoisseurs. The full-bodied caciocavallo cheese from Ragusa, known as Ragusano, is also widely available.

With such exceptional produce, the simplest vegetable soup, enriched with fragrant olive oil and enlivened by a shower of grated cheese, becomes a treat. The cooking of Sicily continues to depend on the freshness of ingredients in season and at the peak of their flavor. To release the fragrance of fresh vegetables, a quick stir-fry in cold-pressed olive oil and a sprinkle of salt and pepper is all that is needed. Indeed, extra-virgin olive oil is so basic to the cuisine that a bottle is always found at the table to properly finish soups, vegetables, and salads. Since olive oil loses much of its flavor after cooking, adding a drizzle at the table enhances even the simplest dish.

Sicilian cuisine has wonderful mixes of ingredients that are as surprising as they are delightful. The orange salads that are now served in many restaurants, enriched with celery, onion, or fennel and then sprinkled with salt and drizzled with extra-virgin olive oil, have been discovered by the home cook.

Adding raisins and **pinoli** (pine nuts) to meats and vegetables is a delicious combination that comes from the island's Arab ancestors. The taste for sweet and spicy is found in a tomato sauce that includes sweet onions, salted capers, and hot red pepper flakes. The author's grandfather used a special blend of spices for Sunday meat sauce that included nutmeg, allspice, and cloves, which, together with a spoonful of sugar, make a deliciously aromatic sauce.

Pasta con le sarde is a recipe typical of Palermo, combining sardines, wild fennel, raisins, and pine nuts in what many consider the classic dish of Sicily. Adding salted anchovies to sauces intensifies the taste and complexity of the dish. But since cheese is never added to a fish sauce, the inventive Sicilian cook tops fish dishes with **muddica** (fresh bread crumbs toasted with extra-virgin olive oil) to add fragrance, flavor, contrast, and crunch. The same breadcrumb topping crowns the famous **sfincione** (thick, deep-dish pizza) of Palermo. Trapani boasts a unique **cuscus** (couscous) dish made with a rich fish stew. **Arancini** (filled, deep-fried rice balls) take their name from little oranges that they resemble in shape and color. These delicious snacks are perhaps the most popular and best-known Sicilian food.

Unique to Sicilian cooking is the great variety of **scaccie** (savory pies) made with a bread crust enclosing fillings of vegetables, cheeses, or even meat, as in the case of the spectacular lamb **'mpanata**, which is made for Easter in Ragusa. Some scaccie are made with spinach, to which raisins and walnuts are added; some with broccoli, sometimes topped with Italian sausage; and some are made with eggplant layered with cheese within the double crust. Ricotta with onion or leek is another winning combination.

Another type of scaccia made like a savory strudel rewards with its delicious taste and enticing appearance. The thin layers of dough coated with sauce and cheese—or parsley, cheese, and oil—are stacked in a tasty and delightful-looking savory bread. Scaccie, which are not found in the average restaurant, can be enjoyed in many of the **Agriturismo** farms, which are working farms that are permitted by law to open to the public as long as they serve traditional homemade dishes. This is an attempt to preserve recipes, cooking techniques, and age-old culinary traditions at a time when they are being threatened by standardization.

Together, sweets are the triumph of Sicilian cooking. Chocolate confections, made famous by the **Antica Dolceria Bonajuto** of Modica, are created without butter, milk, or cream and are still made using the original Aztec recipe brought to Sicily by the Spaniards from America in the fifteenth century.

Impressive desserts such as **cassata** (sponge cake layered with sweetened fresh ricotta); **cannoli** (fried pastry tubes also filled with sweetened ricotta); cakes playfully named **minne ri vergini** (virgins' breasts) in honor of Saint Agatha; and **biscotti ai pinoli** (pignoli or pine nut cookies), crispy on the outside, soft on the inside and redolent of almond paste, are a sweet luxury. **Biscotti** in limitless varieties and for all occasions; **granite** (flavored ices), which make the most of the fragrant fruits, nuts, and berries; and **gelato** (ice cream) of exceptional smoothness, richness, and flavor are some of the treats that await the visitor.

The king of sweets combines art and good taste in the beautiful and delicious **pasta reale**, the marzipan fruits that abound all over Sicily and are easily available abroad. The variety of the marzipan is limited only by the artist's imagination. Almond paste is shaped into realistic-looking fruits, vegetables, nuts, and other goodies of every imaginable sort. These traditional sweets are perhaps the best-known Sicilian treats and are the showstoppers of Sicilian desserts.

HELPFUL PHRASES

Where to Eat

GIOVANNA: **Nu risturanti ri lussu.**
GIOVANNA: Un ristorante di lusso.
A deluxe restaurant.

SALVATORE: Na trattoria modesta.
SALVATORE: Una trattoria modesta.
A modest trattoria.

G: Nu bar vicinu accà.
G: Un bar vicino qua.
A bar near here.

S: Unni si mancianu arancini buoni?
S: Dove si mangiano delle buone arancine?
Where can you eat good arancini [rice balls]?

G: Qual è a miegghiu gilatiria?
G: Quale sarebbe la miglior gelateria?
Which is the best ice cream store?

S: Unn' è ca fanu i scacci buoni?
S: Dove fanno delle buone scaccie?
Where do they make good scacce [savory pies]?

G: Nu Agriturismo unni manciari a ricotta caura?
G: Un Agriturismo dove mangiare la ricotta calda?
An Agriturismo where you can eat [to eat] warm ricotta?

S: E na pasticceria tipica ri stu paisi?
S: Una pasticceria tipica di questo paese?
A pastry shop typical of this town?

At the Restaurant

GIOVANNA: Vulissi prinutari pi ruminicaria.
GIOVANNA: Vorrei prenotare per domenica.
I would like to make a reservation for Sunday.

SALVATORE: Chi siti apierti lunniria?
SALVATORE: Siete aperti lunedì?
Are you open on Monday?

G: Martiria siti apierti a manzuornu?
G: Martedì siete aperti a mezzogiorno?
On Tuesday, are you open at lunchtime [noon]?

S: Chi sirviti 'mpiattu speciali miercuriria?
S: Servite un piatto speciale il mercoledì?
Do you serve a special dish on Wednesday?

G: Na prinutazioni a pranzu pi iuoviria?
G: Una prenotazione a pranzo per giovedì?
A reservation for lunch on Thursday?

S: Chi ci aviti pisci friscu ri viniriria?
S: Avete pesce fresco il venerdì?
Do you have fresh fish on Friday?

G: Sabbatu sira a chi ura accumenza a musica?
G: Sabato sera a che ora comincia la musica?
On Saturday night, what time does the music start?

S: I iorna ra sumana si scrivunu ca minuscola in sicilianu e in italianu.
S: I giorni della settimana si scrivono con la minuscola in siciliano e in italiano.
The days of the week are written in lowercase letters in Sicilian and Italian.

G: Lunniria, martiria, miercuriria.
G: Lunedì, martedì, mercoledì.
Monday, Tuesday, Wednesday.

S: Iuoviria, veniriria, sabbutria, e ruminicaria.
S: Giovedì, venerdì, sabato, e domenica.
Thursday, Friday, Saturday, and Sunday.

G: Pi piaciri, vulissi apparicchiari pi na quinta pirsuna?
G: Per piacere, vorrebbe apparecchiare per una quinta persona?
Would you please set the table for a fifth person?

S: Chi ni cunsigghia?
S: Che cosa ci consiglia?
What do you suggest [to us]?

G: Sirviti specialità ri cca?
G: Servite specialità locali?
Do you serve local specialties?

S: U pisci è friscu oppuri scongilatu?
S: Il pesce è fresco oppure scongelato?
Is the fish fresh or frozen [defrosted]?

G: Pi primu pighiamu 'mpiattu ri pasta.
G: Per primo prendiamo un piatto di pasta.
As a first course, we'll take a dish of pasta.

S: Pi secunnu ni piacissi u farsumagru.
S: Per secondo vorremmo il farsumagru.
For the second course, we would like farsumagru [beef roll].

G: Primu, secunnu, tierzu, quartu, e quintu.
G: Primo, secondo, terzo, quarto, e quinto.
First, second, third, fourth, and fifth.

S: Sestu, settimu, ottavu, nonu, e recimu.
S: Sesto, settimo, ottavo, nono, e decimo.
Sixth, seventh, eighth, ninth, and tenth.

G: **Unnicesimu, ruricesimu, e triricesimu.**
G: Undicesimo, dodicesimo, e tredicesimo.
   Eleventh, twelfth, and thirteenth.

S: **Quattordicesimu, quinnicesimu, e siricesimu.**
S: Quattordicesimo, quindicesimo, e sedicesimo.
   Fourteenth, fifteenth, and sixteenth.

G: **Chi fa c'è u priezzu fissu?**
G: C'è il prezzo fisso?
   Is there a fixed price?

S: **Chi faciti u scuntu pe picciriddi e pi l'anziani?**
S: Fate lo sconto per i bambini e per gli anziani?
   Do you have a discount for children and seniors?

At the Table

GIOVANNA: **A tavula cunzata rapi l'appititu.**
GIOVANNA: La tavola apparecchiata apre l'appetito.
   A table which is set stimulates [opens up] the appetite.

SALVATORE: **Piattu, bicchieri, cucciara, furchetta e cutieddu.**
SALVATORE: Piatto, bicchiere, cucchiaio, forchetta e coltello.
   Dish, glass, spoon, fork, and knife.

G: **Tuvagghia e sirvietta.**
G: Tovaglia e tovagliolo.
   Tablecloth and napkin.

S: **U canniscieddu ro pani.**
S: Il cestino del pane.
   The bread basket.

G: **Acqua, vinu, e birra.**
G: Acqua, vino, e birra.
Water, wine, and beer.

S: **Pi antipastu, capunatina e pipi arrustuti.**
S: Per antipasto, caponata e peperoni arrostiti.
For an appetizer, caponata and roasted peppers.

G: **Accuminzamu cu pani cunzatu e tanticcia ri affettatu.**
G: Cominciamo con pane condito e salumi affettati.
Let's begin with bread drizzled with [dressed with] olive oil and cold cuts.

S: **Pi primu bruoru ri carni ca pastina, pastasciutta co ragù.**
S: Per primo brodo di carne con pastina, pastasciutta con ragù.
For a first course, beef bouillon [meat broth] with pastina, pasta with meat sauce.

G: **Pi secunnu manzu, maiali, iaddina, e pisci.**
G: Per secondo manzo, maiale, pollo, e pesce.
For a main course beef, pork, chicken, and fish.

S: **A carni o sangu o cotta buona.**
S: La carne al sangue o ben cotta.
Meat, rare or well done.

G: **Pi cuntuornu patatini fritti o vudduti.**
G: Per contorno patatine fritte o bollite.
A side of fried or boiled potatoes.

S: **Virdura cotta, cucuzzedda, e mulinciana.**
S: Verdura cotta, zucchini, e melanzana.
Cooked [leafy green] vegetables, zucchini, and eggplant.

G: **Pi ultimo, na 'nzalata.**
G: Per ultimo, l'insalata.
Lastly, the salad.

S: Uogghiu, acitu, lumia, sali, e pipi.
S: Olio, aceto, limone, sale, e pepe.
Oil, vinegar, lemon, salt, and pepper.

G: Caciu e frutta.
G: Formaggio e frutta.
Cheese and fruit.

S: Nu beddu cafè e quattru viscuttedda.
S: Un bel caffè e qualche biscottino.
A good [espresso] coffee and some cookies.

G: Duoppu manciari ci voli na bedda granita.
G: Dopo mangiare ci vuole una bella granita.
After dinner, a delicious granita hits the spot.

S: Vu puozzu offriri nu digestivu?
S: Vi posso offrire un digestivo?
May I offer you an after-dinner drink?

At the Market

GIOVANNA: Chi fa n'aviti cosicavaddu rausano o parmigianu?
GIOVANNA: Ne avete caciocavallo ragusano oppure parmigiano?
Do you have caciocavallo from Ragusa or parmesan cheese?

SALVATORE: Quantu costa mienzu chilu ri ricotta salata?
SALVATORE: Quanto costa mezzo chilo di ricotta salata?
How much is a half-kilogram of [dry] salted ricotta?

G: U latti, caciu, burru è friscu?
G: Il latte, formaggio, burro è fresco?
Is the milk, cheese, butter fresh?

S: 'Nta quali ripartu si trova a pasta/a frutta/a virdura/l'acqua/i
    bibiti?

S: In quale reparto si trova la pasta, frutta, verdure, acqua, bibite?

    *In which section can we find [is found] macaroni, fruit, vegetables,
    water, soft drinks?*

CHAPTER 3

THE ARCHITECTURE OF SICILY SPANS THE CENTURIES

DIALOGUE

GIOVANNA: 'Nta nosra Sicilia c'è tutta a storia ri l'architittura.
GIOVANNA: Nella nostra Sicilia c'è tutta la storia dell'architettura.
In our Sicily, there is the entire history of architecture.

SALVATORE: A Ispica ci sunu ancora abitazioni ri recimila anni addietru.
SALVATORE: A Ispica ci sono ancora abitazioni di diecimila anni fa.
In Ispica there are still ten-thousand-year-old dwellings.

G: E nun sulu, ma i tiatri Greci sunu ancora in usu 'nta Sicilia.
G: E non solo, ma i teatri Greci sono ancora in uso in Sicilia.
And not only that, but Greek theaters are still in use in Sicily.

S: I Rumani ri l'antichità ci facivanu bedde ville comu a chidda ri Piazza Armerina.
S: Gli antichi Romani ci costruivano belle ville come quella di Piazza Armerina.
The ancient Romans built beautiful villas like the one in Piazza Armerina.

G: Chi diri re Bizantini ca ficinu a meravigghia ri Murriale!
G: Che dire dei Bizantini che costruirono la meraviglia di Monreale!
And what can we say of the Byzantines who created the wonder of Monreale!

S: L'Arabi lassarru beddi palazzzi comu chiddu ca ora è San Giovanni degli Eremiti a Palermu.
S: Gli Arabi lasciarono dei bei palazzi come quello che oggi è San Giovanni degli Eremiti a Palermo.
The Arabs left beautiful buildings like the one that is today St. John of the Hermits in Palermo.

G: E puoi 'nta provincia ri Rausa e 'nta Valli ri Nuotu regna u Barocco.
G: E poi nella provincia di Ragusa e nella Val di Noto regna il Barocco.
And then, in the province of Ragusa and in the Val di Noto, the Baroque reigns.

AN ARCHITECTURAL WALK THROUGH THE AGES

Architecture comes to life in Sicily. The 10,000-year-old prehistoric dwellings of Ispica stand as awesome reminders of man's ingenuity. Indeed, upon entering these ancient dwellings, it is not difficult to imagine these ancient people having the same needs, concerns, and dreams as people today. Some of the caves that dot the landscape continued to be used until the early twentieth century for storage and shelter. The grottos, which are clearly visible from the road connecting Ragusa with Ragusa-Ibla, were used by families, including the author's own, for weeks and months during the bombings that took place during World War II. Today, these dwellings offer historic continuity with the past.

Greek temples and theaters, some of which are still in use, have been preserved in Sicily—a symbol of and tribute to one of Sicily's most ancient cultures. The theaters of Siracusa and Taormina are used for summer productions, while the Cathedral of Siracusa continues to be a place of worship after over two thousand years. Originally a Greek temple, the spaces between the columns were filled to create a church, so that what was once a pagan temple now serves a Christian community, while preserving its ancient identity. This beautiful and imposing cathedral integrates ancient Greek architecture and eighteenth-century Baroque, the style of its façade.

The city of Agrigento, the birthplace of the fifth-century philosopher Empedocles and the twentieth-century Nobel Laureate Luigi Pirandello, is situated high atop two adjacent hills and offers a vista of extraordinary beauty encompassing the Valley of the Temples and the Mediterranean Sea. The temple of Segesta, built high on a flat mountain slope and clearly visible from a distance, demonstrates Greek skill at choosing perfect locations for their elegant architecture. A short walk into the pine grove next to it affords a stunning view of the temple framed by the trees—a lovely contrast to the imposing white stone.

At Piazza Armerina there is an ancient imperial Roman villa intact in all its splendor. Its mosaics offer a glimpse of a luxurious lifestyle dating back to the third or fourth centuries. One of the most reproduced scenes depicts young Sicilian women gymnasts in what look like contemporary bikinis. The villa was in use until the eleventh century, when a flood and a landslide buried the vast building. The excavations that brought this extraordinary fourth-century complex to light began in 1929. Today it is a UNESCO (United Nations Educational Scientific and Cultural Organization) World Heritage Site. The mosaics are visible from walkways raised a few feet above the floor, providing a good view of the art while protecting it from wear.

Mosaics in the Byzantine tradition cover the interior walls of the spectacular Cathedral of Monreale. This church overlooks the Conca d'Oro, the valley below, which is planted with orange groves. It was built in 1174 and is intact. The richly decorated Byzantine mosaics of biblical scenes that cover the walls offer a striking contrast to the ceilings of intricately painted beams. The main apse is dominated by a spectacular mosaic of Christ the Creator on a gold background high above the altar. The cathedral is flanked by the cloisters of an ancient Benedictine convent, which is a superb example of Byzantine architecture. The columns, some ornamented with Arabic designs, others with mosaics, are covered with scenes from the Bible.

The town of Erice, high on top of Monte San Giuliano, takes the visitor back in time. This enchanting medieval village of stone houses, narrow lanes, and cobbled streets, each in a different pattern, hosts an annual international physics conference in its famous Centro Ettore Majorana, a former convent that now houses a scientific institute. It is also the home of the Maria Grammatico Pasticceria (pastry shop), which enjoys international renown. Maria learned the art of pastry making in a convent in Erice, where, as a young girl, she found refuge during World War II. After she began exporting her pastry to the United States, food editor Florence Fabricant raved about her marzipan creations in the *New York Times*.

San Cataldo in Palermo, with its three red domes over the central nave and original floor, was built in about 1160 and is a wonderful example of Arab architecture. San Giovanni degli Eremiti, another example of Muslim architecture, is topped by red domes that stand out against the intense blue sky.

The Palazzo dei Normanni in Palermo is a magnificent royal palace. Built in the ninth century, in the eleventh century it became the royal residence of both the Norman and the Swabian nobility. Its Cappella Palatina (Palatine Chapel) is one of the best examples of Norman art in Palermo. Richly decorated in spectacular Byzantine style mosaics, it shows Christ against a gold background looking down from the dome and giving a blessing above a procession of angels.

The Teatro Massimo, built in classical style, is the famous opera theater of Palermo. Recently reopened after extensive renovations, it remains one of the great opera houses and is reputed to have perfect acoustics. The Teatro Politeama, the top floor of which houses the Gallery of Modern Art, is another splendid example of classical architecture with its beautiful high reliefs surmounted by equestrian bronzes on its grand façade.

Piazza Archimede in Siracusa, which honors Archimedes—mathematician, physicist, and native son, as well as the most important scientist of ancient times—is a marvel of taste, perfect proportion, and grace. Every building surrounding the beautiful fountain is perfectly placed, and each enhances the beauty of this most elegant of city squares. Siracusa is a jewel of a city.

The Sicilian Baroque period, which is represented throughout the entire southeast region, is linear and elegant with movement created by the gentle curvature of a convex façade, such as that of the Duomo of San Giorgio in Ragusa Ibla, rather than through flamboyant decorative elements. Majestic staircases give a vertical thrust to the buildings and set them apart as places that seem to lend themselves to the enactment of dramatic scenes from opera or a wedding procession.

Ragusa, its province, and the Val di Noto are UNESCO World Heritage Sites. Ragusa and Ragusa Ibla were separated after the earthquake, with surviving residents of Ragusa Ibla choosing to rebuild their town in the same location, changing only the location of the duomo, while the others began building the new Ragusa farther up the mountain using the innovation of a grid to build the new city. Ragusa has thrived as the capital of the province. Ragusa Ibla, the historic section of the city, has seen a remarkable rebirth and has become a tourist center. The piazza in front of the church, lined with beautiful palm trees and cafés, where visitors can stop for espresso coffee, granite, or gelato, has become the destination for the evening *passeggiata* (stroll). The university has brought new life and vigor to the town. The old houses have been restored and renovated. Hotels and restaurants have become favorite places to meet friends and spend a lovely evening.

In mid-summer, Ragusa Ibla hosts an important international music competition, known as the Ibla Grand Prize, in which hundreds of musicians from all over the world compete in public. The founder and director of the competition, Dr. Salvatore Moltisanti, a native of Ragusa and a piano virtuoso, then brings the winners to Carnegie Hall in New York the following year. During the rest of the year, the concerts continue in other cities of the United States, as well as in Canada, Russia, Norway, and Japan; each year more venues are added for these talented musicians to be seen and heard.

The town of Noto, which was also destroyed by the earthquake of 1693, voted, after much municipal discussion, to rebuild in a totally new location. Noto is truly a planned town where jewels of Baroque architecture designed by the most prominent architects of the time can be seen in a well-integrated town plan and design unique in the history of architecture. The building plan with anti-seismic features was realized through the financial commitment of the local aristocracy and the church as well as the vision of the most prominent architects and city planners of the time, among them Vincenzo Sinatra, Paopo Labisi, and the famous Rosario Gagliardi, who was the chief architect of the city of Noto. The many innovations of the seventeenth-century reconstruction earned the eight towns the UNESCO title of World Heritage Site.

The variety and richness of architectural styles going back thousands of years give the visitor to Sicily a unique possibility for the study and enjoyment of this most important art form.

HELPFUL PHRASES

The Buildings of Sicily

GIOVANNA: 'Nta Sicilia e 'nta l'Italia pi ghiri o primu piano s'accianinu i scali.

GIOVANNA: In Sicilia ed in Italia per andare al primo piano bisogna salire le scale.

In Sicily and in Italy, to get to the first floor you have to climb stairs.

SALVATORE: Chiddu c'americani ciamunu u primu piano 'nti niautri è u pian terrenu.

SALVATORE: Quello che gli americani chiamano il primo piano da noi è il pian terreno.

What Americans call the first floor is for us the street floor.

G: I mura attuornu re casi, i ciusi, e i macci sunu una re biddizzi ra nosra terra.

G: Le mura a secco intorno alle case, prati, ed alberi sono una bellezza della nosra terra.

The dry stone walls around the houses, fields, and trees are one of the beautiful sights of our land.

S: I *dammusi* ri Pantelleria sunu na cosa speciali ri viriri.

S: I *dammusi* di Pantelleria sono una cosa speciale da vedere.

The dammusi *[typical houses] of Pantelleria are a special thing to see.*

G: I mosaici ra Sicilia sunu tra i ciù beddi ro munnu.

G: I mosaici della Sicilia sono fra i più belli del mondo.

The mosaics of Sicily are among the most beautiful in the world.

S: I chiesi barocchi che beddi scalinati parunu scene ri tiatru.

S: Le chiese barocche con le belle scalinate sembrano scene di teatro.

The Baroque churches with beautiful staircases look like stage sets.

G: I paisi ca parunu 'mpiccicati 'nte muntagni sunu na meravigghia.

G: I paesi che sembrano attaccati alle montagne sono una meraviglia.

The hill towns hanging off the mountains are wonderful.

At the Tourist Office

GIOVANNA: Quannu u fanno u festival ro cinima a Taormina?
GIOVANNA: Quando lo fanno il festival del film a Taormina?
            When is the film festival in Taormina?

SALVATORE: Chi accittati carti ri creditu?
SALVATORE: Accettate carte di credito?
            Do you accept credit cards?

G: Mi rassi informazioni su u festival ri Ibla.
G: Mi dia informazioni sul festival di Ibla.
      Give me information about the Ibla Festival.

S: Ogni annu a fini i giugnu fanno un cuncursu internazionali ri
      musica a Ibla.
S: Ogni anno a fine giugno fanno una competizione internazionale
      di musica a Ibla.
      Every year at the end of June there is an international music competition in Ibla.

G: Ci si po ghiri e concerti?
G: Ci si pò andare ai concerti?
      Can anyone go to the concerts?

S: Sunu tutti franchi e apierti o pubblicu.
S: Sono tutti gratis ed aperti al pubblico.
      They are all free and open to the public.

At the Train Station

GIOVANNA: Quannu parti u trenu pi Piazza Armerina?
GIOVANNA: Quando parte il treno per Piazza Armerina?
            When does the train for Piazza Armerina leave?

SALVATORE: Quantu costa u bigliettu ri prima o secunna classi?
SALVATORE: Quanto costa il biglietto di prima o seconda classe?
How much is a first- or second-class ticket?

G: Quannu arriva?
G: Quando arriverà?
When does [will] it arrive?

S: Ci voli a prinutazioni ro puostu?
S: È necessario prenotare il posto?
Is it necessary to reserve a seat?

G: Ci sunu autobus ca fannu a stissa srata?
G: Ci sono pullman che fanno la stessa strada?
Are there buses that go to the same place?

S: Unni sunu a stazioni ri l'autobus e a firmata re tassì?
S: Dove sono la stazione degli autobus e la fermata dei tassì?
Where are the bus station and the taxi stand?

Asking Street Directions

GIOVANNA: Pi piaciri, unn'è u Tiatru Massimu?
GIOVANNA: Per piacere, dove si trova il Teatro Massimo?
Please, where is the Teatro Massimo?

SALVATORE: Pi favuri, unn'è u telefunu pubblicu?
SALVATORE: Per favore, dove si trova il telefono pubblico?
Please, where is the public telephone?

G: Pi piaciri, unn'è a buca ra posta?
G: Per piacere, dov'è la cassetta della posta?
Please, where is the mailbox?

S: **Mi scusassi, ma unn'è a banca, l'ufficiu postali, a cattidrali?**
S: Mi scusi, ma dove si trova la banca, l'ufficio postale, la
   cattedrale?
   Excuse me, but where is the bank, the post office, the cathedral?

G: **Ravanti, rarrieri, dassutta, dassupra, a manu ritta, a manu
   manca.**
G: Davanti, dietro, giù, su, a destra, a sinistra.
   *Straight ahead (in front of), behind, down, up, to the right, to
   the left.*

CHAPTER 4

THE ARTS OF SICILY

DIALOGUE

GIOVANNA: L'arti ra puisia Siciliana avi milli anni ri storia.
GIOVANNA: L'arte della poesia Siciliana ha un millennio di storia.
The art of Sicilian poetry has a one-thousand-year history.

SALVATORE: U sai ca u sunettu fu 'nvintatu 'nta corti ri Fidiricu secunnu?
SALVATORE: Lo sai che il sonetto è stato inventato nella corte di Federico secondo?
Do you know that the sonnet was invented in the court of Frederick the Second?

G: Puri Dante Alighieri fici unuri o pueta Jacupu ri Lintini.
G: Anche Dante Alighieri fece onore al poeta Jacopo da Lentini.
Even Dante Alighieri paid homage to the poet Jacopo from Lentini.

S: A Sicilia si vanta r'aviri rui scritturi ca vincierru u premiu Nobel.
S: La Sicilia si vanta di avere due scrittori che hanno vinto il premio Nobel.
Sicily takes pride in having two writers who won the Nobel Prize.

G: U primu fu Luigi Pirandello, e u secunnu fu Salvatore Quasimodo.

G: Il primo è stato Luigi Pirandello, e il secondo è stato Salvatore Quasimodo.

The first was Luigi Pirandello, and the second was Salvatore Quasimodo.

S: 'Nta musica aviemu u maisru ranni comu Vincienzu Bellini, ca scrissi l'opira a *Norma*

S: E in musica abbiamo il grande Vincenzo Bellini, compositore dell'opera *Norma*

And in music we have the great composer Vincenzo Bellini, who wrote the opera Norma.

G: 'Nta l'arti aviemu u pitturi Antonellu ri Messina.

G: Nell'arte abbiamo il pittore Antonello da Messina.

In art we have the painter Antonello da Messina.

S: A ceramica ri Cartagiruni a statu culliziunata ri tanti seculi.

S: La ceramica di Caltagirone è collezionata da tanti secoli.

The ceramics of Caltagirone have been collected for many centuries.

G: L'arti folcloristica ro carrettu sicilianu fa parti ra nosra storia e ra nosra cultura.

G: L'arte folcloristica del carretto siciliano fa parte della nostra storia e della nostra cultura.

The folk art of the Sicilian cart is part of our history and our culture.

S: I raccami o cincucientu fatti a manu valunu comu l'oru e si tramannanu 'nte famigghie.

S: I ricami al cinquecento fatti a mano valgono come l'oro e si tramandano nelle famiglie.

The handmade Cinquecento *(sixteenth-century drawn thread) embroideries are worth their weight in gold and are passed down in families.*

FLOURISHING OF A TRADITION OF LITERATURE AND CREATIVE ARTS

Sicily's long literary tradition includes a number of distinguished writers who have left their mark on the rich literature of Italy. In *The Divine Comedy*'s *Purgatory*, Dante paid homage to the best-known poet of the Sicilian School, Jacopo da Lentini, and acknowledged the invention of the sonnet in the court of Frederick the Second in the thirteenth century. Frederick was a patron of the Sicilian School of poetry, and it was in his court that the first use of a literary form of Sicilian appeared. In the nineteenth and twentieth centuries, Sicily produced great writers such as Giovanni Verga, known for inventing the style of literary realism (*verismo*), and whose short story was the basis of the libretto for the well-loved opera *Cavalleria Rusticana* by Pietro Mascagni. Elio Vittorini, Leonardo Sciascia, Gesualdo Bufalino, and Vincenzo Consolo are among the most well-known contemporary writers. Perhaps the most important modern literary figure outside Italy is Giuseppe Tomasi di Lampedusa, who made *The Leopard* an international bestseller. Ignazio Buttitta was a poet who celebrated the language of Sicily in his poetry.

This long and distinguished literary tradition has also given the world two Nobel Prize winners, dramatist Luigi Pirandello, author of *Six Characters in Search of an Author*, who was awarded the prize in 1934, and poet Salvatore Quasimodo, who was awarded it in 1959. This rich literary output continues into the present. For example, the Sicilian words and phrases used by contemporary writer Andrea Camilleri have now become part of standard Italian.

The Sicilian language's thousand-year-old literary tradition is preserved by people who continue the ancient oral tradition by reciting epic poems by memory in Sicilian. The famous cantastorie (storyteller) and collector of the now rare decorated Sicilian carts, Giovanni Virgadavola, can still be heard reciting long epic poems in Sicilian at the Castle of Donnafugata near Ragusa. My husband and I heard Ignazio Buttitta's heartfelt poem "Lingua e Dialetti" (Language and Dialect) recited by him there in 2004.

The famous traditional Sicilian puppet theater, *u teatru re pupi*, presents historic epic poems, which give faces and voices to the ancient characters. The creation of the puppets is an art form in itself and has been handed down by families who maintain this ancient tradition.

The colorfully painted Sicilian cart also tells the history of Sicily. Once a common sight throughout Sicily, the striking images and colors are now relegated to handcrafted miniature reproductions. They often adorn the homes of Sicilians, particularly those living abroad. To the delight of happy spectators, authentic old carts are still brought out and paraded on holidays and feast days. Wrought iron is another local handicraft. It is used to adorn the Sicilian cart, as well as the beautiful Baroque balconies of South Eastern Sicily, and is still an important craft in the area of Taormina.

Another art form that originated in the fourteenth century but is still produced and admired today is the *sfilato siciliano*, a special embroidery technique made with fine thread, often on linen; it is prized both for its beauty and for its investment value. Indeed, during World War II many families survived by selling pieces of this work, which is known as *Cinquecento* (literally, the 500s) because of the historical provenance of the sixteenth-century designs. Cinquecento linens are still part of a bride's trousseau, and they continue to be used, treasured, and passed down in every family. The Museo dello Sfilato (The Embroidery or Thread Museum) in the enchanting hill town of Chiaramonte Gulfi, in the province of Ragusa, is very much worth a detour.

The city of Caltagirone is the home of a ceramic industry that is centuries old. An imposing, long staircase ascending the adjacent mountain has risers that are each made of a different ceramic pattern. Caltagirone boasts the famous Luigi Sturzo School of Ceramic Art, the important Museum of Ceramic Art, and one of the most beautiful city parks in the region. Hundreds of studios are open to the public and offer a vast array of beautiful and distinctive designs.

There is a great deal in Sicilian history that is a source of both pride and pleasure, not only to Sicilians but to the world. Today we all delight in the music of Sicilian bel canto composer Vincenzo Bellini, who wrote the opera *Norma,* which is still in the repertoire of most opera companies. How delightful—and delicious— that we can celebrate his genius every time we enjoy the classic dish *pasta alla Norma,* named for this beloved opera.

We still admire the works of Renaissance painter Antonello da Messina, but we also enjoy those of contemporary artists, such as painters Renato Guttuso and Piero Guccioni and sculptor Giovanni Cappello, whose impact has been felt well beyond their birthplace of Sicily. One of the finest photographers in Sicily is the internationally known native of Ragusa, Giuseppe Leone, who has illustrated countless books on Sicily with his superb photographs, and who exhibits his photographs all over the world.

Travelers to Sicily are well rewarded by what they discover in both the fine arts and traditional crafts, which are still admired and enjoyed as they continue to play a role in the everyday life of the people.

HELPFUL PHRASES

At the Bookstore/Gallery/Craft Shop

GIOVANNA: Unn'è a biblioteca?
GIOVANNA: Dov'è la biblioteca?
            Where is the public library?

SALVATORE: Unn'è na libreria?
SALVATORE: Dove sarebbe una libreria?
Where would a bookstore be?

G: Mi piacissi cumprari nu libru scrittu in sicilianu.
G: Mi piacerebbe acquistare un libro scritto in siciliano.
I would like to buy a book written in Sicilian.

S: Quantu costa: stu libru, stu discu, stu piezzu ri ceramica, sta fotografia, sta stampa?
S: Quanto costa: questo libro, questo disco, questo pezzo di ceramica, questa fotografia, questa riproduzione?
How much is this: book, record, piece of ceramic, picture, print?

G: Stu beddu piattu mu putissi 'mpaccari e mannari pi posta ?
G: Questo bel piatto me lo potrebbe impaccare e spedire per posta?
Can you pack and mail this plate for me?

S: Mi piacissi 'n fazzulittieddu, 'n centrinu, na tuvagghia, e rurici sirvietti sfilati e raccamati o cincucientu.
S: Mi piacerebbe un fazzolettino, un centrino, una tovaglia, e dodici tovaglioli sfilati e ricamati al cinquecento.
I would like a handkerchief, a doily, a tablecloth, and twelve napkins with finely drawn thread and Cinquecento embroidery.

Colors

GIOVANNA: Nu cappieddu niuru, na sciarpa bianca, na machina russa.
GIOVANNA: Un cappello nero, una sciarpa bianca, una macchina rossa.
A black hat, a white scarf, a red car.

SALVATORE: **Celesti comu o cielu, giallu comu nu girasoli, russu comi nu ialofru.**

SALVATORE: Celeste come il cielo, giallo come il girasole, rosso come un garofano.

Blue like the sky, yellow like the sunflower, red like the carnation.

G: **Virdi comu na ciusa, aranciu comu na mannarina, viola comu na mulinciana.**

G: Verde come un prato, arancio come un mandarino, viola come una melanzana.

Green like a field, orange like a tangerine, purple like an eggplant.

Literature, Arts, and Crafts

G: **Scritturi, pueta, cantastorie.**
G: Scrittore, poeta, cantastorie.
Writer, poet, storyteller.

S: **Romanzu, novella, puisia.**
S: Romanzo, novella, poesia.
Novel, short story, poem.

G: **Libriria, biblioteca, nicuoziu.**
G: Libreria, biblioteca, negozio.
Bookstore, public library, store.

S: **Libru, rivista, giurnali.**
S: Libro, rivista, giornale.
Book, magazine, newspaper.

G: **Pitturi, sculturi, ciramista.**
G: Pittore, scultore, ceramista.
Painter, sculptor, ceramist.

S: **Quadru, statua, statuetta, scutedda artistica.**
S: Quadro, statua, statuetta, scodella artistica.
Painting, statue, figurine, artistic bowl.

G: **Atturi/attrici, musicanti, ballerinu/ballerina**
G: Attore/attrice, musicista, ballerino/ballerina.
Actor/actress, musician, dancer.

S: **Carrettu sicilianu, sceccu, cavaddu.**
S: Carretto siciliano, asino, cavallo.
Sicilian cart, donkey, horse.

G: **Raccamu sfilatu, fierru battutu, travagghiu a manu.**
G: Ricamo sfilato, ferro battuto, lavoro fatto a mano.
Drawn-thread embroidery, wrought iron, hand-crafted work.

S: **Opira re pupi, cinima, teatru.**
S: L'opera dei pupi, cinema, teatro.
Puppet show, movie, theater.

Fashion

G: **U vistitu, a giacca, e u golfinu.**
G: Il vestito, la giacca, ed il golfino.
The suit, the jacket, and the sweater.

S: **A vistina, a camicetta, e a gonna.**
S: La veste, la camicetta, e la gonna.
The dress, the blouse, and the skirt.

G: **I causi, a cammisa, e u cappieddu.**
G: I pantaloni, la camicia, ed il cappello.
The trousers, the shirt, and the hat.

S: A sciarpa, a bursetta, e i scarpi.
S: La sciarpa, la borsetta, e le scarpe.
The scarf, the handbag, and the shoes.

G: U pigiama, i pantofuli, e a burritta.
G: Il pigiama, le pantofole, ed il berretto della notte.
The pajamas, the slippers, and the nightcap [a traditional cap once worn in bed].

S: U costumi ri bagnu, i sannali, e u siccitieddu.
S: Il costume da bagno, i sandali, ed il secchiello.
The bathing suit, the sandals, and the pail.

CHAPTER 5

THE PERSISTENCE OF THE SICILIAN LANGUAGE

DIALOGUE

GIOVANNA: Quannu i nuosri paisani s'innierru ra Sicilia ci lassarunu u cori.

GIOVANNA: Quando i nostri paesani partirono dalla Sicilia ci lasciarono il cuore.

When our countrymen left Sicily, they left their hearts there.

SALVATORE: Ma l'affettu po paisi u resinu e figghi.

SALVATORE: Ma l'affetto per il paese lo diedero ai figli.

But they gave their children their love for their land.

G: E quannu i picciuotti vieninu ccà trasinu comu si fossiro a so casa.

G: E quando i giovani vengono qua entrano come se fossero a casa loro.

And when the young people come here they feel at home.

S: Annu 'ntisu parrari re biddizzi nuosri, e quannu i virunu restunu 'ncantati.

S: Hanno sentito parlare delle nostre bellezze, e quando le vedono rimangono incantati.

They've heard about our beautiful sights, and when they see them they are enchanted.

G: I picciuotti ca nascierru a Merica, 'nto Canadà, all'Ausralia
annu 'ntisu parrari re nuosri beddi paisi.

G: I ragazzi nati in America, in Canada, ed in Australia hanno sentito
parlare dei nostri bei paesi.

*The young people born in America, Canada, and Australia have
heard about our beautiful towns.*

S: S'arriuordinu i cunti re ginituri e re nanni, e torninu 'nta
nosra terra pirchì ci porta u cori.

S: Si ricordano le storie dei genitori e dei nonni, e tornano nella
nostra terra perche li porta il cuore.

*They remember the stories of their parents and grandparents, and
they return to our land because their hearts bring them (back).*

G: E quannu parrinu a nosra lingua, ni fa tantu piaciri.

G: E quando parlano la nosra lingua, ci fa tanto piacere.

And when they speak our language, it gives us great pleasure.

AN OLD LANGUAGE WITH A DISTINGUISHED LITERARY TRADITION

The author's generation spoke Sicilian from birth, but in school
the instruction was in standard Italian. All Italians were at one
time bilingual. Unfortunately, the dialects are no longer spoken
in every home, which means that a rich cultural and linguistic
patrimony has been lost. Although Sicily has a wonderful literary
tradition, Sicilians were not taught to read and write their first
language. Those who learned to read and write Sicilian did so on
their own out of personal interest.

Sicilian, like any dialect, is a more intimate means of com-
munication and self-expression. Growing up in the United States,
my experience was not unusual: I spoke Sicilian to my parents,
English to my brother, Italian to friends from Italy and even to
Sicilians whom I did not know intimately. After marrying and
having a child, I spoke Italian to my daughter, whom I wanted to
be bilingual, and English to my husband.

The dialects of Sicily, like the architecture and the cuisine, were influenced by the island's many occupants—Greek, Latin, Arabic, French, Lombard, and Spanish—making it a very rich language indeed. In addition to how words have been absorbed into the language, there are sub-dialects on the island that have remained isolated and have been handed down through the generations. In Piana degli Albanese they still speak the Greek of the original settlers. In San Fratello they speak a Gallo/Italic dialect. In Ragusa people pronounce many words as if there were no letter *H* and are teased that the letter was stolen. Below are some examples (see pronunciation guidelines in Chapter 1).

Ragusano	*Sicilian*	*Italian*	*English*
ciavi	chiavi	chiave	key
ciuso	chiusu	chiuso	closed
cianciri	chiagniri	piangere	to cry

Interestingly, Sicilian is being preserved in seemingly unlikely places. Indeed, in the Bronx in New York; in Toronto, Canada; or in Melbourne, Australia, an authentic, though archaic, Sicilian can still be heard. In these places the twentieth-century Sicilian immigrants, particularly those who came before World War II, spoke only the dialect in the home, so that many children learned English only after entering first grade. The Sicilian that these second- and third-generation children learned remained frozen in time, whereas the dialect spoken in Sicily, particularly as it was spoken toward the end of the twentieth century, continued to change and grow ever closer to standard Italian.

When Sicilian Americans go to Sicily they find that most Sicilians do not speak the dialect at home and that the language they learned abroad is an older, authentic form of Sicilian, not—as some may think—an inferior form of Italian. Born in Manhattan's East Harlem, a Sicilian enclave in the early part of the twentieth century, Joseph F. Privitera learned Sicilian as his native language and, after earning his Ph.D. in Romance languages from New York University in 1934, became a leading expert on it. The thesis of his book entitled *Sicilian, the Oldest Romance Language*, is that Sicilian derived from Latin, not Italian, making it the oldest Romance language.

The many books that continue to be published in Sicilian, as well as the numerous theater and music companies that present dramas, comedies, and song recitals in Sicilian, traveling the world to give their presentations, continue to stimulate interest in learning Sicilian.

The following organizations may be of interest to those wishing to deepen their knowledge of Sicilian:

L'Associazione Teatrale Angelo Musco di Catania, Sicily
    Program: "Gatta ci cova"
Gli Amici del Teatro di Chiaramonte Gulfi, Sicily Program: "U
    ruppu ra cravatta"
Al Qantarah—Promo Music of Bologna, Italy Program:
    Medieval Sicilian

Music
I Canterini di Ortigia, Siracusa, Sicily Program: Traditional
    Sicilian Music

The love for the Sicilian language is expressed in one of Ignazio Buttitta's best known poems, "Lingua e Dialettu." Fiercely proud of being Sicilian, Buttitta (1899–1997) speaks of the survival of the language as the most significant factor in the Sicilian identity as he implores his *paesani* (countrymen) to preserve the language and not allow anyone to steal this irreplaceable treasure.

"Lingua e Dialetti"
by Ignazio Buttitta
from *La Mia Vita Vorrei Scirverla Cantando*

Un populu,	Un popolo
mittitulu a catina,	mettetelo in catene
spugghiatulu,	spogliatelo
attuppatici a vucca,	tappategli la bocca
è ancora liburu	è ancora libero
Livatici u travagghiu,	Toglietegli il lavoro
u passaportu,	il passaporto
a tavula unni mancia,	la tavola sulla quale mangia
u lettu unni dormi;	il letto sul quale dorme
è ancora riccu.	è ancora ricco
Un populu	Un popolo
diventa poviru e servu	diventa povero e servo
quannu ci arrubbanu a lingua	quando gli rubano la lingua
addutata di patri:	adottata dai padri:
è persu pi sempri.	allora è perduto per sempre.

"Language and Dialect"
by Ignazio Buttitta

A people
Can be put in chains,
Be undressed,
Have their mouths sealed,
And they're still free.
Deprive them of work,
A passport,
The dining table,
The bed on which to sleep,
And they're still rich.
However, a people
Becomes poor and servile
When their language
Passed down by the fathers is stolen:
Then it's lost forever.

Sicilian Proverbs

GIOVANNA: A casa capi quantu voli u patruni.
GIOVANNA: La casa può accomondare tanta gente quanto vuole
il padrone.
*A house can hold as many people as the host or
owner wishes.*

SALVATORE: Quannu si ammitatu 'nta casa ri quarcarunu ha
tuppuliari co peri.
SALVATORE: Quando sei invitato a casa di qualcuno, devi bussare
con il piede (perché le mani sono ingombre di
regali e non sono libere).
*When you're invited to someone's house, you must
knock with your foot (because your hands are laden
with gifts and aren't free).*

G: Luntanu ri vista, luntanu ri cori.
G: Lontano di vista, lontano di cuore.
Out of sight, out of mind.

S: 'Nta paisi nuovo comu viri fari fai.
S: In un paese nuovo come vedi fare fai.
In a new town, do as you see others do.

G: Fai beni e scordatillu; fai mali e pensici.
G: Fai bene e dimenticalo; fai male e pensaci.
Do a good deed and forget about it; do ill and think about it.

S: Acqua e fuocu racci luogu.
S: Acqua e fuoco dateci luogo.
Give space to water and fire (because they can't be held back).

G: A passioni nun senti ragghiuni.
G: La passione non sente ragione.
Passion doesn't listen to reason.

S: Natali chi tuoi e Pasqua cu chiddi ca vuoi.
S: Natale con i tuoi e Pasqua con chi vuoi.
Christmas with your family and Easter with whomever you want.

G: Cu cerca trova.
G: Chi cerca trova.
He who seeks, finds.

S: Metti pani o renti ca fami si risente.
S: Metti pane al dente che la fame si risente.
Start eating and you'll develop an appetite.

G: Amuri nuovu trasi, amuri viecciu nesci.
G: Amore nuovo entra, amore vecchio esce.
New love enters, and the old love departs.

S: Ogni prumissa è debbitu.
S: Ogni promessa è debito.
Every promise is a debt.

G: Mazze e panelle fannu i figghi beddi, panelle senza mazze fanno i figghi pazzi.
G: Mazze e panelle fanno i figli belli, panelle senza mazze fanno i figli pazzi.
Discipline and treats make good children, but treats without discipline make crazy children.

S: Mischinu cu avi bisuognu.
S: Misero chi ha bisogno.
Woe to the person in need (if he has not provided for himself).

G: Cu avi i figghi si l'annaca.
G: Chi ha i figli se li dondola.
Whoever has children rocks them.

S: Nun ti vagnari prima ca ciovi.
S: Non ti bagnare prima che piova.
Don't get wet before it rains.

CHAPTER 6

FAMILY AND CUSTOMS

DIALOGUE

GIOVANNA: Iu mi ciamu Giovanna.
GIOVANNA: Io mi chiamo Giovanna.
My name is Giovanna.

SALVATORE: Iu mi ciamu Salvaturi.
SALVATORE: Io mi chiamo Salvatore.
My name is Salvatore.

G: Ma matri si ciama Cuncittina.
G: Mia madre si chiama Concettina.
My mother's name is Concettina.

S: Ma patri si ciama Iancilu.
S: Mio padre si chiama Angelo.
My father's name is Angelo.

G: Ma suoru si ciama Tina.
G: Mia sorella si chiama Tina.
My sister's name is Tina.

S: Ma frati si ciama Sergiu.
S: Mio fratello si chiama Sergio.
My brother's name is Sergio.

G: **Ma nanna si ciamava Carmela.**
G: Mia nonna si chiamava Carmela.
My grandmother was named Carmela.

S: **U ma nannu si ciamava Salvatore.**
S: Mio nonno si chiamava Salvatore.
My grandfather was named Salvatore.

G: **A ma figghia si ciama Nicoletta.**
G: Mia figlia si chiama Nicoletta.
My daughter's name is Nicoletta.

S: **U ma figghiu si ciama Iancilu comu a ma patri.**
S: Mio figlio si chiama Angelo come mio padre.
My son's name is Angelo like my father.

G: **A ma zia si ciama Lucia.**
G: Mia zia si chiama Lucia.
My aunt's name is Lucia.

S: **U ma ziu si ciama Vannuzzu.**
S: Mio zio si chaiama Giovannuzzu.
My uncle's name is Giovannuzzu.

G: **A ma cucina si ciama Carmela.**
G: Mia cugina si chiama Carmela.
My cousin's name is Carmela.

S: **U ma cuscinu si ciama Emanuele.**
S: Mio cugino si chiama Emanuele.
My cousin's name is Emanuele.

G: **A ma cugnata si ciama Costanza.**
G: Mia cognata si chiama Costanza.
My sister-in-law is named Costanza.

S: **U ma cugnatu si ciama Micheli.**
S: Mio cognato si chiama Michele.
My brother-in-law is named Michael.

G: **A ma nora si ciama Giuseppina.**
G: Mia nuora si chiama Giuseppina.
My daughter-in-law is named Giuseppina.

S: **U ma eneru si ciama Stefanu.**
S: Mio genero si chiama Stefano.
My son-in-law is named Stefano.

G: **A ma sogghira si ciama Nicoletta.**
G: Mia suocera si chiama Nicoletta.
My mother-in-law is named Nicoletta.

S: **U ma sogghiru si ciama Pippinu.**
S: Mio suocero si chiama Peppino.
My father-in-law is named Peppino.

G: **A ma cummari si ciama Rusina.**
G: Mia comare si chiama Rosina.
My godmother is named Rosina.

S: **U ma cumpari si ciama Turiddu.**
S: Mio compare si chiama Turiddu.
My godfather is named Turiddu.

THE CENTER OF SICILIAN LIFE

Sicilians are proud, naturally reserved, and influenced by centuries of occupation that has created a truly multiethnic society with a huge gene pool. Blue-eyed blondes, redheads, and olive-skinned, curly-haired types are a reflection of this diversity.

Although the saying "Natale con i tuoi, e Pasqua con chi vuoi" means "Christmas with your family, and Easter with whomever you want," social life still revolves around the family with regular get-togethers, often for Sunday dinner. The family is the most important entity for Sicilians. With the father, whose word is generally law, at the head and the mother as primary nurturer and educator, power is well balanced. Parents are supportive in dealing with the children and do not contradict each other. Sicilians are superlative hosts who make their guests feel completely at home, giving them the best accommodations in the house. Their hospitality is legendary, as is their generosity in bestowing gifts. Gift giving is a highly refined art form. When Sicilians receive a gift, they in turn give one of equal or greater value and importance. The nature of the gift is related to the importance of the person and the occasion. Because wedding gifts are traditionally silver, wonderful silver can be found in even the smallest shop, as each silversmith creates his unique designs for a people who truly appreciate, give, receive, and treasure such luxuries.

Here are some tips for visiting in Sicilian households. If you are a guest for an extended stay, bring an important gift. If there are children in the family, they too should receive gifts. For dinners with your host family, flowers are always appropriate, but you could also offer a bottle of wine or cordial, chocolates, or some fruit. For Sundays or for special-occasion dinners, a dessert, whether it is a tray of cookies, pastries, a tart, or a cake, is always welcome; local pastry shops can be counted on to make the presentation festive with attractive wrapping and ribbons. Before you end your stay you should arrange with the local florist to deliver an arrangement of flowers or a potted plant together with a thank-you note. In gift giving, nothing succeeds like excess!

Even though you are being entertained, the host family will also give you lovely presents. Do not be surprised if you are given the master bedroom while your hosts sleep in the guest room or on the pull-out sofa, not considered good enough for guests. The table will be set with a tablecloth and matching napkins for every meal, and you will always be served a *primo* (first course), which is a pasta or a soup, a *secondo* (main dish) with *contorni* (side dishes), usually ending the meal with fruit and cheese, followed by espresso afterward. A festive dinner, including the Sunday dinner, would include a rich and varied antipasto and a sweet dessert. If your hosts invite you to a restaurant or to a café for coffee or ice cream, they will not allow you to pay the bill. But, having accepted their generous hospitality, you will invite the family out to dinner, making it very clear beforehand that this is your treat. Beware, because they will intercept the bill with great skill so that it is not brought to the table. Of course, you will be expected to do the same if and when your hosts visit you.

A word about flowers: if you bring or send flowers to a native-born Italian or Sicilian living abroad, remember that chrysanthemums are reserved for the dead and are never brought into the house. In the United States, second-generation Italian or Sicilian Americans may not be aware of this custom. In Sicily, many people pay quick visits to the local cemetery on Sunday. In Ragusa the piazzetta near the cemetery entrance is filled with florist shops and stalls where crowds of people buy beautiful flowers to freshen up the graves and tombs. Because the cemetery itself is ablaze with the color and fragrance of the fresh flowers, it does not seem at all like a sad place, but one filled with people who visit regularly and take pride in its upkeep. Each grave has a vase for fresh flowers next to the photo of the deceased. There are fountains nearby where visitors can get water for the vases before filling them with flowers and replacing them in their stands. These cemetery visits and offerings give people a sense of continuity with the lives of the departed.

Fare bella figura, or making a good impression, is of paramount importance, whether it has to do with gift giving, hospitality, entertaining, reciprocating for having been entertained, or simply being seen in public. This also means taking great care in dressing, the rule being understated elegance with spare but excellent jewelry, well-fitting and fashionable clothing, and good-quality or name-brand accessories. The afternoon *passeggiata* (stroll) is a time of relaxation and socialization with friends, and being elegantly, even if modestly, dressed is very important. Although the little black dress is still preferred by many women, gone are the days when women over the age of fifty wore only black as a sign of mourning. The author's grandmother's generation would wear black for several years (the number ordained by custom or tradition) upon the death of a member of the immediate family. If in the meantime another family member died, the time would be extended, with the result that black might be worn forever more.

The loyalty that gives such cohesiveness to the Sicilian family is also lavished on friends who become part of the extended family. Good friends who are asked to be *compare* (godfather) or *commare* (godmother) for a baptism, confirmation, or wedding become as dear as blood relatives. I still have my compare and commare because my parents chose a fourteen-year-old cousin and his nine-year-old sister to be my godparents when I was born. Being godparents to a child is taken very seriously. Both of my godparents have been loving guides and mentors, continuing their attention and interest in me and my activities even after my family immigrated to the United States.

All cousins are considered close relations whether they are first, second, third, or even generations removed. For what English speakers collectively call in-laws, there are specific names in Sicilian and in Italian, with the exception of grandchildren and nieces and nephews, which, oddly, are not differentiated. When a relative or even a distant cousin comes to Sicily, even if there has been no previous contact, they are welcomed and given the royal treatment. The tradition of naming children gives continuity to a family, as first names are repeated and handed down from generation to generation. Generally, the first-born male child is named after the paternal grandfather and the first-born female child after the paternal grandmother. The second-born male child is named after the maternal grandfather, and the second-born female is named after the maternal grandmother. But, since these days Sicilians tend to have two children at most, the number of names has dwindled. This tradition of bestowing names makes it possible to identify even distant relatives as members of an extended family.

Sicilians are very formal, often addressing each other as Signor or Don before the last name, even if they are old friends, as a sign of mutual respect. It is also said that Sicilians speak with their eyes. As children we always understood our mothers or grandmothers from across the room when a simple glance communicated approval, disapproval, or another message. Rarely was there a need to scold in public, because a look immediately told children to mind their manners.

HELPFUL PHRASES

At the Florist

GIOVANNA: **Vulissi ordinari nu mazzu ri fiuri.**
GIOVANNA: Vorrei ordinare un mazzo di fiori.
I would like to order a bouquet of flowers.

SALVATORE: **Mu putissi mannari a stu indirizzu?**
SALVATORE: Lo potrebbe mandare a questo indirizzo?
Would you deliver it to this address?

G: **Ci mittissi quattro rosi, quattro ialofra, e quattro lillà.**
G: Ci metta quattro rose, quattro garofani, e quattro lillà.
Give me four roses, four carnations, and four lilies.

S: **Ci mittissi stu bigliettu.**
S: Ci metta questo biglietto.
Include this note.

G: **Grazie tantu; è veramente beddu.**
G: Grazie tanto; è veramente bello.
Thank you very much; it's really beautiful.

At the Fruit Vendor

GIOVANNA: **Mi putissi fari 'n cestinu ri frutta?**
GIOVANNA: Mi potrebbe confezionare un cestino di frutta?
Can you put together a basket of fruit?

SALVATORE: **Ci mittissi puma, aranci, piersichi, e kiwi.**
SALVATORE: Ci metta mele, arance, pesche, e kiwi.
Give me [put in] apples, oranges, peaches, and kiwi.

G: **Ci mittissi puri pompelmi, banane, ficu, racina, e n'ananas.**
G: Ci metta anche pompelmi, banane, fichi, uva, ed un ananas.
Also include [put in] grapefruits, bananas, figs, grapes, and a pineapple.

S: **Chi fa cinn'avi ficupali?**
S: Ha per caso dei fichi d'India?
Do you by any chance have prickly pears?

At the Pastry Shop

GIOVANNA: **Mi putissi priparari na bedda guantiera ri cosi aruci?**
GIOVANNA: Mi potrebbe preparare un bel vassoio di dolci?
Would you prepare a lovely tray of sweets?

SALVATORE: **Ci mittissi macari siei cannuoli ri ricotta, quattru pasticcini, e dui cucciddati.**
SALVATORE: Ci metta pure sei cannoli di ricotta, quattro pasticcini, e due cucciddati.
Also add [put in] six ricotta-filled cannoli, four pastries, and two cucciddati [cookies].

G: Ci iuncissi rui etti di viscotta, rui etti ri torroncini, e rui etti ri frutta ri pasta reali.

G: Ci aggiunga due etti di biscotti, due etti di torroncini, e due etti di frutti di pasta reale.

Add eight ounces of cookies, eight ounces of nougats, and eight ounces of marzipan fruits.

S: Chi ci aviti cioccolattu senza latti e burru?

S: Avete cioccolata senza latticini?

Do you have dairy-free chocolate?

G: A Muorica fanu u cioccolattu tuttu cacau e zuccuru.

G: A Modica fanno la cioccolata tutta cacao e zucchero.

In Modica, they make chocolate entirely of cocoa and sugar.

S: Pari ca usunu na ricetta ri l'aztechi, na tribù antica ri l'indiani americani.

S: Usano la ricetta degli aztechi, un'antica tribù di indiani americani.

They use the recipe of the Aztecs, an ancient tribe of American Indians.

G: E comu ci arrivau 'nta Sicilia sta ricetta?

G: E come arrivò in Sicilia questa ricetta?

How did this recipe get to [arrive in] Sicily?

S: Pari ca ci'a purtarru i spagnuoli quannu turnaru r'America e occuparunu a Sicilia.

S: La portarono gli spagnoli dall'America dopo che occuparano la Sicilia.

It was brought from America by the Spanish after they occupied Sicily.

At the Wine Shop

GIOVANNA: **Chi vinu mi cunsigghia pi fari nu rialu?**
GIOVANNA: Che vino mi consiglia per fare un regalo?
Which wine would you suggest for a gift?

SALVATORE: **Iu ci cunsigghiu u Biancu ri Alcamo, u Russu ri Avola, e u Cerasuolu ri Vittoria.**
SALVATORE: Le consiglio un Bianco di Alcamo, un Nero d'Avola, ed il Cerasuolo di Vittoria.
I suggest a white from Alcamo, a red from Avola, and a [red] Cerasuolo from Vittoria.

G: **Allura mi rassi nu Corvo ri Salaparuta biancu, unu ri Ronnafugata, e uno ri Regaleali.**
G: Allora mi dia un Corvo di Salaparuta Bianco, uno di Donnafugata, e uno di Regaleali.
So, give me a Corvo di Salaparuta white, one Donnafugata, and one from Regaleali.

S: **Mi rassi 'na buttigghia ri Marsala e quarchi autru vinu aruci.**
S: Mi dia una bottiglia di Marsala e qualche altro vino dolce.
Give me a Marsala and some other sweet wine.

G: **Aiu nu Muscatu ri Pantelleria e Malvasia ri Lipari.**
G: Ho un Moscato di Pantelleria ed un Malvasia di Lipari.
I have a Moscato from Pantelleria and a Malvasia from Lipari.

S: **Grazi tantu; mi ricissi quantu costa.**
S: Grazie tanto; mi dica quanto costa.
Thank you very much; tell me how much it costs.

Introductions

GIOVANNA: **Iu mi ciamu Giovanna.**
GIOVANNA: Io mi chiamo Giovanna.
          My name is Giovanna.

SALVATORE: **Ci presentu u miu amicu Nunziu.**
SALVATORE: Le presento il mio amico Nunzio.
           Meet my friend Nunzio.

G: **Tantu piaciri ri fare a so cunuscenza.**
G: Piacere di conoscerla.
    Glad to meet you.

S: **Comu sta?**
S: Come sta?
    How are you?

G: **Buonu, grazie; e lei?**
G: Bene, grazie; e lei?
    Well, thank you; and you?

S: **Ni viriemu rumani.**
S: Ci vedremo domani.
    We'll see each other tomorrow.

Greetings

GIOVANNA: **Bon giornu, signora.**
GIOVANNA: Buon giorno, signora.
           Good day/good morning, Madam.

SALVATORE: **Bona sera, signurina.**
SALVATORE: Buona sera, signorina.
           Good evening, Miss.

G: **Bona notti, signor Dutturi.**
G: Buona notte, signor Dottore.
Good night, Doctor.

S: **Buon riposu, bedda mia.**
S: Buon riposo, mia cara.
Sleep [rest] well, my dear.

G: **Grazi tantu, amicu.**
G: Grazie tanto, amico.
Thank you very much, [my] friend.

S: **Pregu.**
S: Prego.
You're welcome.

G: **Mi scusassi.**
G: Mi scusi.
Excuse me.

S: **Pi piaciri./Pi curtisia.**
S: Per piacere./Per cortesia.
Please.

Distances and Directions

GIOVANNA: **L'ufficiu re posti è vicinu o luntanu?**
GIOVANNA: L'ufficio postale è vicino o lontano?
The post office is nearby or far away?

SALVATORE: **Camina rittu e furria a manu ritta/manca.**
SALVATORE: Cammina dritto e gira a destra/sinistra.
Walk straight and turn right/left.

G: **Quannu arriva o semafuru si ferma e u risturanti e 'nfacci.**
G: Quando arriva al semaforo si fermi, il ristorante si trova
   dirimpetto.
   *When you get to the traffic light, stop, and the restaurant is across
   the street.*

S: **Pi ghiri a stazioni ti attocca accianari/scinniri sti scali.**
S: Per andare alla stazione bisogna salire/scendere queste scale.
   To go to the station, you have to climb/descend those stairs.

G: **U bar è ravanti/rarrieri ro teatru.**
G: Il bar si trova davanti/dietro il teatro.
   The bar is in front of/behind the theater.

S: **U nicuoziu è dassupra/o dassutta o terzu piano.**
S: Il negozio è su/giù al terzo piano.
   The store is up/down on the third floor.

Opposites

GIOVANNA: **Ri iuornu fa cauru; ri sira fa friddu.**
GIOVANNA: Di giorno fa caldo; di sera fa freddo.
   During the day it's hot; in the evening it's cold.

SALVATORE: **U picciriddu è ranni, e a picciridda è nica.**
SALVATORE: Il bambino è grande, e la bambina è piccola.
   The boy is big, and the girl is little.

G: **A porta è ciusa, e a finestra è aperta.**
G: La porta è chiusa, e la finestra è aperta.
   The door is closed, and the window is open.

S: **U pani è buonu, e u tiempu è tintu.**
S: Il pane è buono, ed il tempo cattivo.
   The bread is good, and the weather is bad.

G: U giornali è supra a tavula, e u iattu è sutta a tavula.
G: Il giornale è sopra il tavolo, e il gatto è sotto il tavolo.
The newspaper is on top of the table, and the cat is under the table.

S: A trasuta è a manu ritta, a nisciuta è a manu manca.
S: L'entrata è a destra, e l'uscita è a sinistra.
The entrance is on the right, and the exit is on the left.

Emergencies

GIOVANNA: Mi lori a testa; unn'è a farmacia?
GIOVANNA: Mi fa male la testa; dove si trova la farmacia?
I have a headache; where is the pharmacy?

SALVATORE: Chi ci voli a ricetta?
SALVATORE: Bisogna avere la ricetta?
Do you need a prescription?

G: Mi sientu tinta; pi favuri, ciamati autoambulanza o u dutturi.
G: Mi sento male; per piacere, chiamate l'autoambulanza o il dottore.
I feel sick; please call the ambulance or the doctor.

S: Aiuto, ciamati i carrabbinieri.
S: Aiuto, chiamate la polizia.
Help, call the police.

Telephone

GIOVANNA: Prontu. Cu è ca parra?
GIOVANNA: Pronto. Chi parla?
Hello. Who's this [Who is speaking]?

SALVATORE: **Cu cuè vulissi parrari?**
SALVATORE: Con chi vorrebbe parlare?
With whom would you like to speak?

G: **Un momentu, pi favuri.**
G: Un momento per favore.
Hold on [one moment], please.

S: **Chi fa, u puozzu lassari 'n messaggiu?**
S: Posso lasciare un messaggio?
May I leave a message?

G: **Pi favuri, putissi parrari ciù forti?**
G: Per favore, potrebbe parlare più forte?
Please, could you speak louder?

S: **Mi scusassi, ma chi parra u 'nglisi?**
S: Mi scusi, ma parla inglese?
Excuse me, but do you speak English?

G: **Vulissi parrari cu l'agente ri viaggi.**
G: Vorrei parlare con l'agente dei viaggi.
I would like to speak to the travel agent.

S: **Vulissi parrari cu meccanicu.**
S: Vorrei parlare con il meccanico.
I would like to speak to the mechanic.

Reservations at Restaurants

GIOVANNA: **Vulissi fari na prinutazioni.**
GIOVANNA: Vorrei fare una prenotazione.
I would like to make a reservation.

SALVATORE: **Na prinutazioni po pranzu a manzuornu.**
SALVATORE: Una prenotazione per pranzo a mezzogiorno.
    A reservation for lunch at midday [noon].

G: **Na prinutazioni pi cena e setti ri sira.**
G: Una prenotazione per cena alle diciannove.
    A reservation for dinner at 7 p.m.

S: **Chi ci aviti u menù vegitarianu?**
S: Avete un menù vegetariano?
    Do you have a vegetarian menu?

G: **Aviti u menù a priezzu fissu?**
G: Avete un menù a prezzo fisso?
    Do you have a fixed-price menu?

S: **Chi ci aviti comu piattu ro iornu?**
S: Cosa avete come piatto del giorno?
    What is the plat du jour [dish of the day]?

G: **A carne mi piaci o sangu/ben cotta.**
G: La carne mi piace al sangue/ben cotta.
    I like meat rare/well done.

S: **Mi purtassi a lista re vini.**
S: Mi porti la lista dei vini.
    Bring me the wine list.

Reservations at Hotels

GIOVANNA: **Prinutari na cammira all'albergu.**
GIOVANNA: Prenotare una camera all'albergo.
    Reserve a room in the hotel.

SALVATORE: **Na cammira cu na bedda vista.**
SALVATORE: Una camera con una bella vista.
A room with a nice [beautiful] view.

G: **Na cammira pi na pirsuna.**
G: Una camera singola.
A single room.

S: **Na cammira duppia.**
S: Una camera doppia.
A double room.

G: **Na cammira co liettu matrimoniali.**
G: Una camera con letto matrimoniale.
A room with a double bed.

S: **Na cammira cu ru letta.**
S: Una camera a due letti.
A room with two beds.

G: **Na cammira cu bagnu/doccia.**
G: Una camera con bagno/doccia.
A room with a bath/shower.

S: **Chi fa c'è a piscina/spiaggia?**
S: C'è la piscina/spiaggia?
Is there a swimming pool/beach?

Reservations for Entertainment and Travel

GIOVANNA: **Nu bigliettu pi concertu ri musica classica/partita ri calciu/museu.**
GIOVANNA: Un biglietto per un concerto di musica classica/partita di calcio/museo.
A ticket for a classical music concert/soccer game/ museum.

SALVATORE: Nu bigliettu po night club/po teatru grecu/pi l'opera.
SALVATORE: Un biglietto per il night club/il teatro greco/l'opera.
A ticket for the night club/the Greek theater/the opera.

G: Nu bigliettu ri iri e viniri cu trenu.
G: Un biglietto di andata e ritorno in treno.
A round-trip ticket by train.

S: Nu bigliettu pi l'aereo ri Catania e Palermu.
S: Un biglietto aereo tra Catania e Palermo.
A plane ticket between Catania and Palermo.

RAGUSA: Characteristic view of the city.

RAGUSA: Cathedral of Saint John the Baptist.

RAGUSA IBLA: The rebuilt Baroque Duomo of Saint Giorgio completed in 1775.

RAGUSA IBLA: Portal of the original Duomo of Saint Giorgio destroyed by the earthquake of 1693.

CALTAGIRONE: Endless steps with beautiful decorative ceramic tiles as facings.

CATANIA: Fontana dell'Elefante in Piazza del Duomo.

CATANIA: The port and harbor of the city with Mount Etna in the background.

CATANIA: The Badia di Sant'Agata with part of the cathedral on the right which houses the tomb of Vincenzo Bellini.

MOUNT ETNA: Volcano crater and lava from an eruption.

MESSINA: The Church of Christ the King.

PALERMO: Piazza Pretoria.

PALERMO: The Cathedral houses the tombs of the Norman Kings and the Hohenstaufen emperors including Frederick the Great, his mother Constance, and her father Roger II.

MONREALE:
Cathedral.

CEFALÙ: View of the Cathedral and town square with the lush palms of Sicily.

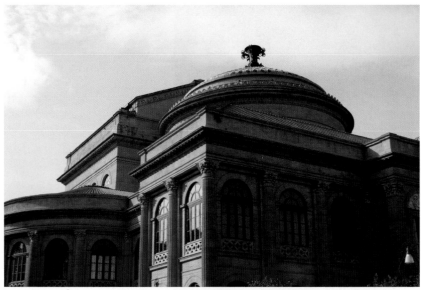

PALERMO: Teatro Massimo, the Opera Theatre of Palermo.

PALERMO:
Golden interior
of the Palatine
Chapel in the
Norman Palace.

TRAPANI: Windmills used to pump water into the salt ponds with sunset in the background.

ERICE: The Torretta Pepoli, built as a hunting lodge, is a symbol of the city.

AGRIGENTO: The Temple of Concord in the Valley of the Temples.

AGRIGENTO : The four columns of the Temple of Castor and Pollux, erected in 1836, are a symbol of the city of Agrigento.

GULF OF CASTELLAMMARE: Zingaro Natural Preserve is a stretch of magnificent natural and unspoiled land with one of the most beautiful beaches in Sicily.

STROMBOLI: The steaming active volcano seen through naturalized prickly pear plants.

SICILIAN COAST: A magnificent setting for an enchanting house.

LIPARI: A spectacular view of the town of Lipari seen from a castle above the harbor.

MARZIPAN: The remarkable artistry of hand-made almond paste fruits and vegetables.

The ubiquitous Prickly Pear Cactus, which found a fertile home in Sicily after it arrived from Mexico.

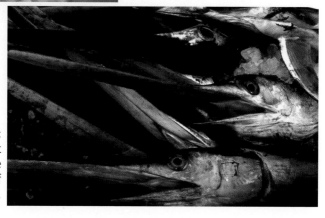

DONNALUCATA: Freshly caught swordfish in the market of Donnalucata.

Baroque balcony in Sicily.

SANTA CROCE CAMERINA: A 5th century Byzantine Chapel awaiting excavation.

DONNAFUGATA: The Castle of Donnafugata now open as a museum near Ragusa.

PIAZZA ARMERINA: Mosaics of Sicilian athletes in the 3rd-4th century Imperial Roman Villa of Casale.

SIRACUSA: The gleaming white marble of the still-used Greek Theatre.

ENNA: Medieval gold, jeweled crown on exhibit at the Alessi Museum.

PALERMO: View of the city and the harbor.

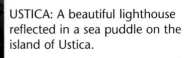

USTICA: A beautiful lighthouse reflected in a sea puddle on the island of Ustica.

CHAPTER 7

RAGUSA

The countryside around Ragusa is characterized by well-crafted, white dry-stone walls enclosing fields and beautiful old farmhouses, some of which are now open as restaurants or bed-and-breakfasts. In spring, the countryside is carpeted with wildflowers in a profusion of colors growing with abandon in the fields, along the walls, and out of every crevice.

Ragusa's economy has traditionally revolved around agriculture and the asphalt mines. Although oil was discovered in the 1950s, it did not become a major industry, and agriculture once again became dominant. The fertile land is used productively for grazing, grapes, as well as the production of vegetables and flowers. The **mucche di razza modicana** (a breed of Modica cows) produce excellent milk for cheese-making and are now a protected species. Perfect, showpiece crops, such as tomatoes, peppers, and asparagus, together with the magnificent local flowers, head for the gourmet shops of Europe. The famous local products, including **caciocavallo**, a cheese also known as **Ragusano; pomodori salati** (sun-dried tomatoes); and **miele dei Monti Iblei** (honey from the local Hybleian Mountains), are also in great demand for export.

The tourist industry is becoming important to this off-the-beaten-path southern tip of Sicily. In addition to the picturesque mountain towns with their magnificent views, the region is surrounded by some of Sicily's most beautiful sandy beaches, which are still uncrowded and unspoiled.

RAGUSA

The city of Ragusa is built on twin mountain peaks joined by three elegant bridges that span the gorge between the two mountains. The ancient part of the city, Ragusa Ibla, is built on a lower mountain east of and at the foot of the other two mountains. The two towns are connected by road and have long staircases for those who wish to take a lovely walk with beautiful views at every turn. Ragusa was settled by the Greeks in ancient times and has had continued habitation for well over two thousand years.

Ragusa and seven other towns near it were named World Heritage Sites by UNESCO in 2000. They were chosen for this distinction because after this area of Sicily was destroyed by a devastating earthquake in 1693, not only were the towns rebuilt in record time, but modern techniques of urban planning were applied to the reconstruction, which took fifty years. The rebuilding was planned so that Ragusa's streets form a grid; the main north/south streets are parallel to each other, and the east/west ones, which include the main street, Via Roma, are perpendicular. This was a novel approach in the seventeenth century.

Ragusa, with its location in the Monti Iblei (Hyblean Mountains), stands about 1,600 feet above sea level. From Corso Italia and Via Ecce Homo, two of the main streets affording views all the way up or down the hill, and from the Belvedere at the end of Via Roma, which crosses the first two, there are beautiful vistas of the surrounding mountains.

The **Cattedrale di San Giovanni Battista** (Cathedral of Saint John the Baptist) stands on a piazza that is actually a terrace with porticoes beneath it. It was created to take advantage of the incline of the land for the base of the new church built after 1693. San Giovanni is Baroque in design and has a graceful linear façade, with four columns framing the main entrance and two lateral doors. The bell tower and the dome dominate the panorama and can be seen from many parts of the city.

Via Roma 134. Tel: (0932) 621-658.

A short walk from the **Stazione di Ragusa** (Ragusa train station) leads through **Piazza Libertà** across the **Ponte Nuovo** (New Bridge) to the main street of **Via Roma**. From the Ponte Nuovo, no longer the "New" Bridge, the other two bridges, **Ponte Vecchio** (Old Bridge) and the most recent one, **Ponte San Vito**, can be seen. The view of the bridges themselves and the gorge with the river below, full of lush vegetation, is very beautiful.

At the left side of the beginning of **Via Roma** stands a modern building that houses the **Museo Archeologico Ibleo** on the first three floors and the newly renovated **Hotel Mediterraneo Palace** on the upper floors. The museum collection is a treasure trove of Greco-Roman artifacts that have been found in the various archeological sites in the province. The collection ranges from prehistoric through Greek, Roman, and Byzantine times. The exhibit includes a reconstruction of a potter's workshop, complete with period kilns. The well-displayed and clearly documented collection includes a large photo of a **Byzantine chapel** still to be excavated near the town of **Santa Croce Camerina**. The actual site is currently a farm, but it is possible to enter the **cupola** of this fifth-century church through a window that is now just above ground level at the base of the dome, which emerges from the ground. It is now a question of time before this treasure will be freed from its ancient burial site.

Museo Archeologico, Palazzo Mediterraneo. Tel: 39 (0932) 622-963.

Via Roma is a beautiful tree-lined street with elegant shops of all types and many cafés where one can sit to enjoy a delicious granita or espresso. Crossing **Via Sant'Anna**, **Corso Vittorio Emanuele**, and **Corso Italia** and climbing the hill provides good aerobic exercise while shopping. There are many excellent silver shops in the city, each with its own unique collection. For beautiful silver or jewelry, stop at **Orafo Franco** in Via Sant'Anna 170, just a half a block up from Via Roma. Franco Di Franco is an Old World gold and silversmith who designs many of the pieces he sells and who can usually be seen working at his bench behind the counter.

Across the street, in the **Sartoria La Terra** (La Terra Tailor Shop) in Via Sant'Anna 143, you will find another old world craftsman, Pippo La Terra, who still creates magnificent custom-made men's suits in one of the few tailor shops still making perfectly fitted handcrafted garments. For another kind of treasure, stop at **L'Arte del Ricamo**, Via San Filippo 91, for the exquisite traditional **sfilato** (drawn-thread embroidery) of Ragusa. It is expensive, but as an important art form, it is considered an investment.

In the evening all the cafés remain open as the *Ragusani* (inhabitants of Ragusa) enjoy their **passeggiata** along Via Roma, which is flat and makes for an easy walk, or in the **Piazza** in front of the cathedral, which is the *salotto* (living room) of the city. At the end of Via Roma, there are lovely views of the surrounding mountains.

RAGUSA IBLA

Descending on foot from Ragusa to Ragusa Ibla (over three hundred steps connect the two towns) affords the first beautiful panorama of **Ragusa Ibla** from the Church of **Santa Maria delle Scale** (Saint Mary of the Stairs). The fourteenth-century church, although damaged by the 1693 earthquake, was rebuilt with its original Gothic portal and bell tower. This imposing church, with its stairs, beautiful iron railings, and stone retaining walls dotted with occasional caper plants emerging from the crevices, and with the view of Ragusa Ibla in the background, has become the most well-known and representative panorama of the city. At night, when the city is illuminated, this view is spectacular. Sometimes you can hear the church choir rehearsing, as we did one evening. We were not only treated to the sight of Santa Maria delle Scale seen from above with the illuminated city and framed by the church's wrought iron railings, but also to the sounds of Beethoven's *Ode to Joy*.

Whereas Ragusa was rebuilt according to modern techniques of urban planning after the earthquake of 1693, Ragusa Ibla retained its medieval town plan with the streets still following the contour of the natural terrain. The **duomo** (cathedral), which was destroyed except for the beautiful medieval portal that stands to this day and has become a symbol of the city, was reconstructed in a new location. The new **Duomo di San Giorgio** (Cathedral of Saint George), designed by Rosario Gagliardi and considered his masterpiece, was built high at the end of the Piazza atop a very imposing staircase, in the then-contemporary Baroque style. The tall façade of the duomo has three tiers of columns and two side wings that, accentuated by its placement atop the grand staircase, give it a vertical thrust, placing into prominence the bell and the clock at the very top and standing out against the perennially blue sky. Completed with a neoclassical cupola designed by Carmelo Cutrano in 1820, encircled by a magnificent iron enclosure and gate topped with a small and exquisite sculpture of San Giorgio, the duomo dominates the Piazza and is both elegant and imposingly theatrical. The façade of San Giorgio was used as the setting for one of the four stories by Luigi Pirandello in the film *Kaos,* directed by Paolo and Vittorio Taviani. The entire panorama of Ragusa Ibla has been endlessly reproduced because of its compactness, its location in the midst of the Monti Iblei, and its great charm.

Piazza San Giorgio is where the inhabitants of Ragusa and Ragusa Ibla congregate in the evening. It is now a pedestrian area, lined on both sides with huge, lush palm trees and with the beautiful Duomo of San Giorgio surveying the scene. The cafés and restaurants surrounding the Piazza set up outdoor tables for excellent eating, people watching, and even an occasional concert *all'aria aperta* (in the open air). There are shops where you can buy the traditional crafts of pottery and embroidery and also local products such as *frutti di pasta reale* (marzipan, or almond paste sweets), the famous *miele dei Monti Iblei* (honey from the Hyblean Mountains), and *cioccolata di Modica* (chocolate from Modica).

Near the duomo in Via Capitano Bocchieri is the **Palazzo La Rocca**, which is among the city's beautiful aristocratic mansions; this one is open to the public during the day as the Tourist Office. Its previous owner, Dr. Raffaele Cannizzaro, a local historian and connoisseur, scrupulously restored it over a period of several decades. His daughter, Carolina Cannizzaro, raised in the exquisite palazzo, studied restoration and is now an expert restorer who works professionally in the city of Lucca, where she lives, spending her summers in Sicily.

Tourist Office, Via Capitano Bocchieri 33, Ragusa Ibla. Tel: 39 (0932) 221-511. www.ragusaturismo.com.

Next door to the Tourist Office is **Il Duomo**, an innovative Sicilian restaurant that has been singled out by the *New York Times* and whose chef Ciccio Sultano has been included in "Europe's Rising-Star Chefs." Via Capitano Bocchieri 31. Tel: (0932)651-265. This **quartiere** (neighborhood or district), with its picturesque narrow winding streets and even narrower alleyways, is enjoying a renaissance as houses are being restored and artisans return to practice their trades. Craft shops catering to locals, students, and tourists are also making a comeback. A local entrepreneur has been preserving this unspoiled historic district by connecting a number of the old houses, preserving their charming characteristics, and turning them into what will eventually be a hotel and restaurant complex. His vision is to preserve the Old World charm, while creating comfortable modern hotels to serve the emerging tourist industry. Interestingly, this working-class area, which is making its twenty-first-century comeback, was once the quarter of the Jewish artisans of Ragusa Ibla. The vitality of the town is due in part to Ragusa's university and its vibrant population of young people and to the inhabitants' appreciation for the historic look and feel of the town.

Day or night, a delightful oasis of tranquility can be found in the **Villa**, which is what the locals call the **Giardino Ibleo** (Ragusa Ibla garden). Its cobbled walks, with well-tended flowerbeds, and rows of grand and beautiful palm trees, have always been a favorite spot for photo opportunities. Near the Villa is the **Portale di San Giorgio**, the medieval gate, or portal, which is the symbol of the city.

MODICA

South of Ragusa is the city of **Modica**, a mountain town whose characteristic buildings appear to be stacked one on top of the other. Full of charm, it is also a vibrant modern city. You enter it from a spectacularly high bridge, one of the highest in Europe, which spans two peaks. Founded by the Romans, Modica gained importance in medieval times and gradually expanded down the mountain to fill the valley. Of course, grand staircases abound. The eighteenth-century **Cattedrale di San Giorgio** (Cathedral of Saint George), another masterpiece by architect Rosario Gagliardi, is set atop a monumental staircase. Climbing the steps provides an interesting vantage point and a chance to slowly approach the marvelous cream-colored Baroque façade and the cathedral's elegant lines.

The **Church of San Pietro** also dominates a majestic staircase in Modica's main street, which is named **Corso Umberto I**. The wide steps are enlivened by life-sized statues of the twelve apostles flanking and standing watch over the entrance. **Teatro Garibaldi**, also on Corso Umberto I, has been newly restored and is once again open to the public. In 2004, noted restorer Carolina Cannizzaro restored and re-mounted the wonderful ceiling painting by **Piero Guccioni**. Near the **Piazza del Municipio** is the site of the Jewish neighborhood that thrived in Modica until 1474, after which it was decimated when Sicily's Spanish occupiers expelled the Jews through the Inquisition. There was organized resistance to the expulsion of the Jews of Sicily from the Camera Regia, the Sicilian Parliament, because Jews had been integrated in the society for centuries. Despite economic, social, and moral objections to their expulsion, Sicily did not prevail, and Sicilian Jews were forced to leave their home, many of them settling elsewhere in the Italic peninsula long before Italy existed as a nation.

The **Museo Civico** (Town Museum) in Largo Merce is an interesting municipal museum that showcases typical local crafts and explains how they were made. Each workshop, with all its tools, occupies a room in a former monastery. The exhibits are well documented, showing the production and fine examples of the various traditional crafts.

Open daily 10 a.m. to 1 p.m. and 4:30 p.m. to 8 p.m. Tel: 39 (0932) 945-081.

The highest point of the city is the nineteenth-century bell tower of **San Giovanni Evangelista**, a church which was rebuilt in 1839 in **Via Regina Margherita** after its destruction in the earthquake of 1693. The church, which is dedicated to the city's patron saint, is a masterpiece of Baroque art. A magnificent view of the entire city of Modica can be seen from the **Belvedere Pizzo**, reached by walking on the road to the left of the staircase.

Justly famous for its sweets, Modica excels even by Sicilian standards. The shop, **Vecchia Dolceria Bonajuto**, prides itself on still making chocolate according to the original Aztec recipe brought by the Spaniards to Sicily from the Americas. In this very special treat, the cacao and sugar are heated until only the cacao, but not the sugar, melts, giving the chocolate a lush intense flavor and a crunchy texture. One of the most unusual flavors is a chocolate spiced with hot pepper. Equally exceptional **pasticcini** (pastry), **gelati**, and **granite** may be found in the many **pasticcerie** (pastry shops) of Modica.

Antica Dolceria Bonajuto, Corso Umberto I 159, Modica. Tel: 39 (0932) 941-225.

Modica is the birthplace of lyric poet and 1959 Nobel Laureate **Salvatore Quasimodo** (1901–1968), whose house is now open as a museum filled with personal objects and memorabilia. A staircase brimming over with flowers leads to the poet's second-floor living space. The museum's young docent, immensely proud of this great poet, is happy to let you hear the voice of Quasimodo reading his own poetry.

Parco Letterario Salvatore Quasimodo, Corso Umberto I #242, Modica. Tel: 39 (0932) 753-864.

CAVE D'ISPICA

West of Modica are the extraordinary Cave d'Ispica (Ispica caves). These caves, which were formed by the erosion of old rivers, go back ten thousand years and are located in a thirteen-kilometer-long valley carved out of limestone. They were used as dwellings during the Neolithic, Greek, Byzantine, Christian, and medieval periods, and there are also a large number of Sicilian and Byzantine necropoli and Christian catacombs. The **Larderia**, for example, is a necropolis with 464 early Christian catacombs. Near the entrance is a very small museum.

Open 9 a.m. to 5 p.m. Tel: 39 (0932) 951-884.

ISPICA

The town of Ispica is located south of the Cave d'Ispica. The church of Santa Maria Maggiore on Via XX Settembre, dating to the early 1700s, has an elegant façade and rich frescoes. It is also noteworthy for its high, exceptionally beautiful wrought-iron fence facing an elliptical portico that encloses the piazza in front of the church. It is a space that attracts by its sheer magnificence and is an integral part of the inhabitants' daily lives, as evidenced by the scenes of cheerful children playing ball in this spectacular piazza. The **Palazzo Bruno di Belmonte** on Corso Umberto I houses the *municipio* (town hall). This is a twentieth-century art nouveau building designed by Ernesto Basile. It has lovely majolica decorations, and equally impressive wrought iron grates, an architectural element typical of the town of Ispica.

SCICLI

A road from Ispica leads west to the town of **Scicli**, which owes its name to its Arab founders. The town has a charming appearance, rising up the hill with curved roadways and houses interspersed with stone outcroppings, all of which creates a unique panorama of harmony, form, and warm color. Along the way there are many hillside caves dotting the landscape before the road ends at the church of **San Matteo**, which stands on a medieval site just above the Baroque town center. The center of town is Piazza Italia, where the seventeenth-century **Chiesa Matrice Di Sant'Ignazio** is located. Destroyed by the earthquake of 1693, Sant'Ignazio was rebuilt, with the date, 1751, inscribed in the imposing central door of the Baroque façade. The nearby **Palazzo Beneventano** built in the early eighteenth century is famous for its unusual and uniquely flamboyant baroque decorations. The fifteenth-century **Chiesa di San Bartolomeo**, the only church that survived the earthquake of 1693, is worth visiting for its beautiful sixteenth-century wooden *presepio* (crèche). The twenty-nine figures in the display come from an original set of sixty-five. Because they vary in size, there is an illusion of distance between the foreground and the background, creating a realistic perspective. The caves, which are so much a part of the town of Scicli, supposedly have secret passageways that allowed the townspeople to hide during ancient invasions and to survive for long periods because of the underground stream that supplied them with water. The caves are also an interesting and ingenious ancient defense system.

Pozzallo

Southeast of Scicli is the fishing village of **Pozzallo**, which became an important commercial center when loading docks for the transportation of Sicilian wheat, known since Roman times for its superior quality, were built in the fourteenth century. Still dominated by the **Torre Cabrera**, originally built in the sixteenth century as part of the island's defense system and to protect the warehouses, Pozzallo was rebuilt after the earthquake of 1693. The town boasts a lovely, wide, uncrowded sandy beach. To spend a beautiful afternoon, indulge in a passeggiata on the **lungomare** (seafront promenade) along the beautiful port and enjoy a lunch of pasta with black sauce made with the ink of freshly caught squid in one of the local restaurants.

MARINA DI RAGUSA

Up the coast, west of Pozzallo, is **Marina di Ragusa**, the shore of the city of Ragusa, with its incomparable golden sand beach, lovely shops, and a lively summer nightlife. Since this is a favorite place for the Ragusani to have their summer homes, there are many fine restaurants and take-out establishments that make delicious traditional dishes for a picnic on the sand dunes. For naturalists, the **Riserva Naturale Macchia Foresta del Fiume Irminio**, a natural preserve, provides a wonderful respite from the vacationers.

PUNTA SECCA

This charming summer resort has yet another beautiful uncrowded beach, a lovely piazza overlooking the sea for the evening passeggiata, many cafés and gelaterie for a refreshing stop, and a beautiful white lighthouse. This perfect little town is part of the Andrea Cammilleri literary trail. Cammilleri's books featuring Inspector Montalbano are set in Sicily. The now famous stone building on the piazza of Punta Secca is familiar to all Italians as the home of Inspector Montalbano in the very popular film series about his adventures and investigations.

KAMARINA

Northwest along the beautiful coast is the **Parco Archeologico di Kamarina** (Archeological Park of Kamarina), which was an ancient Greek settlement founded in the sixth-century BCE and destroyed by the Romans in the third century BCE. The extensive site includes ancient city walls, many tombstones, and a number of sarcophagi, all within view of the **Museo Regionale di Kamarina**, a former stone farmstead with a beautiful walk outlined by a low dry-stone wall leading to the entrance. This excellent museum holds well-documented Greco-Roman treasures and an extensive collection of ancient Greek vases. The site now shares the still-beautiful and uncrowded coast with an upscale Club Mediterranée.

The complex is open daily from 9:00 a.m. to sunset.

CASTELLO DI DONNAFUGATA

West and inland from Kamarina is the serenely beautiful **Castello di Donnafugata**, a Venetian-style palace in the midst of Sicilian palms and prickly pears. Baron Corrado Arezzo inherited it in the nineteenth century and added the lovely loggia to the façade, landscaped the gardens, and created the famous maze in the garden. The castle remained in private hands until the 1970s and was purchased by the city of Ragusa in 1982. With restorations completed in the castle, attention is being turned to the restoration of the gardens. The historic house, its rooms furnished with period furniture, is now open as a museum, and guided tours explain the history. The courtyards and the surrounding rooms, once used by the craftsmen who served the complex, are now used for meetings and musical programs. The ground-floor kitchens have unfortunately been eliminated to create the extensive space needed for changing exhibits. The lovely chapel is still used for public services on Sunday morning. Giovanni Virgadavola, resident **cantastorie** (storyteller), continues the oral tradition by reciting historic epic poems in Sicilian dialect from memory at this site.

Open Tuesday to Friday 8:30 a.m. to 1:30 p.m. and Saturday and Sunday 9:30 a.m. to 5:30 p.m.

VITTORIA

Northwest of Donnafugata is **Vittoria**. Founded as an agricultural town in the early seventeenth century by Vittoria Colonna, wife of Count Luigi of Modica, it was built on the fertile **Monti Iblei** (Hyblean Hills). It continues to grow local produce and remains a wine-producing center. **Cerasuolo di Vittoria**, for example, is an excellent dry red wine of note and bears a label stating that it is DOC (Denominazione di Origine Controllata). The center of town is the **Piazza del Popolo**, which is dominated by the beautiful 1754 Baroque church of **Santa Maria delle Grazie** with the elegant neoclassic **Teatro Comunale** next to the church. Rebuilt after the 1693 earthquake, it has valuable altars in polychrome marble. The city's high elevation allows a view of the fertile valley reaching as far as the sea.

COMISO

The city of **Comiso**, located east of Vittoria, is an agricultural town set in a fertile valley. It became a center of political activism in the 1980s because of opposition to the NATO military base that had been installed against the wishes of the local population, which eventually forced its closing in 1991 and with it brought about the removal of the last cruise missiles in Europe. The military airport, which has been in use since World War II, is now being transformed into a commercial airport to help the development of the tourist industry in the Ragusa region. The cathedral of **Santa Maria delle Stelle**, which was built in the seventeenth century where an earlier church had once been, dominates the town, which sprawls into the valley. The **Museo Civico di Storia Naturale** (Town Museum of Natural History) displays a whale's skeleton and other interesting exhibits, including a marine diorama of a Caretta Caretta turtle laying eggs. The protected Caretta Caretta turtle, which still lays its eggs on the beaches of Comiso, appears on the United States Federal Fish and Wildlife Service and Wildlife Worldwide Endangered Species list. Museum Tel: 39 (0932) 722-521.

CHIARAMONTE GULFI

Northeast of Comiso is the charming town of **Chiaramonte Gulfi**, which was originally colonized in the twelfth century, destroyed before the end of that same century, and rebuilt and fortified in the thirteenth century by Manfredi Chiaramonte. Although it was destroyed once again in the earthquake of 1693, it was rebuilt, preserving the medieval plan of the town. The majestic stone **Arco dell'Annunziata** (Arch of the Annunciation) remained miraculously intact and is the only one remaining of the original four gates. The town has five small but very interesting museums. Four of them are housed in Palazzo Montesano on Via Montesano and include the following:

The **Museo dell'Olio** (Museum of Olive Oil) displays the tools and implements of the trade and shows how oil is extracted. A wooden press dating back to 1614 is also on exhibit. The **Casa Museo Liberty**, a museum unique in all of Sicily, includes eight beautifully appointed Art Nouveau rooms in the Palazzo Montesano. The excellent furniture, textiles, and decorative arts, including jewelry, Lalique glass, and other period objects, comprise the personal collection of Signora Emiliana Figliuoli, a local art collector and connoisseur who resides in Ragusa. **Il Museo degli Strumenti Etnico Musicali** (Museum of Ethnic Musical Instruments) contains instruments collected from all over the world by Duccio Belgiorno. Housed in the splendid **Palazzo Montesano**, the **Museo De Vita**, the collection of 51 works by Giovanni De Vita, a native son who won international fame for his paintings, is beautifully integrated into the elegant architecture of the Palazzo. The works, donated by the De Vita family, are a collection of impressionistic and beautifully evocative tempera, watercolors and oil paintings by the famous Maestro Giovanni De Vita.

A short walk away, near the **Scalinata di San Giovanni** in the medieval section of the city, is the **Museo del Ricamo e dello Sfilato**, a museum dedicated to *ricamo* (embroidery) and to the traditional **sfilato** (drawn-thread embroidery on linen) for which this region is justly famous. There is a group of **ricamatrici** (embroiderers) who get together once a month to keep the traditional sfilato alive by teaching and sharing ideas and techniques; their beautiful handmade pieces are for sale in the gift shop.

One ticket gives access to all five museums. Open weekdays from 9 a.m. to 1 p.m., Saturday from 3:30 p.m. to 7 p.m., and Sunday from 10:30 a.m. to 1 p.m. and 3:30 p.m. to 7 p.m. Information: 39 (0932) 922-3930.

The most famous restaurant in town is **Majore**, Via Martiri Ungheresi 12, which specializes in typical pork dishes, including the traditional **gelatina di maiale** (pork in aspic). Tel: 39 (0932) 928-019.

CHAPTER 8

SIRACUSA

Siracusa was founded as a Greek colony in 733 BCE. In its most glorious period, when it surpassed the power and importance of Athens, it was ruled by Dionysius.

From nearby Via Paolo Orsi, an ancient Roman road leads to the **Archeological Park of Neapolis**. This area, known as **La Città Greca** (Greek city), includes the **Teatro Greco** (Greek theater) and the **Latomie** (quarries)—**Latomie del Paradiso** (quarries of heaven) and **Latomia dell'Intagliatella**, a rocky arch that leads to **Latomia Santa Venera**, a quarry dotted with votive niches— **L'Orecchio di Dionisio** (Dionysius's ear), the **Grotta dei Cordari** (the rope makers' cave or grotto), the **Anfiteatro Romano** (Roman amphitheater), the **Necropoli Grotticelli**, (Grotticelli necropolis), and the **Tomba di Archimede** (Archimedes' tomb).

On the way to the Teatro Greco, the base of the **Ara di Ierone II** (the altar of Hieron II), the largest altar surviving from Hellenistic times, can be seen. The Teatro Greco is a magnificent relic from antiquity and an ancient monument that is not only preserved but still in use. Every two years (in May and June of even-numbered years), the ancient Greek dramas of Aeschylus, Sophocles, and Euripides are performed in this extraordinary theater, which has survived to our times. Carved entirely of living stone, this theater originally staged the tragedies of Aeschylus, who lived both in Greece and Sicily and died tragically in the city of **Gela**. It is said that an eagle trying to break the shell of a tortoise dropped it on the playwright's bald head, mistaking it for a rock.

From the Teatro Greco the path leads to the Latomia del Paradiso, a once-protected quarry, which is now open and lush with vegetation. The ubiquitous prickly pear grows there. Latomia del Paradiso is linked by a passage to the Latomia Intagliatella, which leads in turn to Latomia Santa Venera through a natural stone arch.

L'Orecchio di Dionisio has a small chamber above it where the acoustics are such that a mere whisper on the ground can clearly be heard; it was supposedly used to listen to prisoners' conversations and spy on them. A knock sounds like a small explosion in this strange ancient cave. The nearby **Grotta dei Cordari** was used well into the twentieth century by local rope makers who, in the cave's humid environment, pulled, twisted, and plied the damp fibers to make ropes.

The Anfiteatro Romano, another monument surviving from antiquity, is a theater carved partly out of living rock, in a large elliptical shape. It has a **piscina** (cistern) that is still visible and was used to flood the arena when sea battles were being enacted for the public, evidence that special effects in staging are nothing new.

The Grotticelli Necropolis, filled with ancient Greek and early Christian tombs, includes what is said to be the tomb of **Archimedes**. The **Catacombe di San Giovanni** (Catacombs of Saint John), with galleries covered in ancient frescos, mosaics, symbols, and decorations, give an idea of the early Christian survival from persecution.

The Museo Archeologico Regionale Paolo Orsi is named for the famous archaeologist who headed the museum's antiquities department in the nineteenth century and was responsible for many important archeological excavations and personal discoveries. It is divided into three sections, which feature the geology and the prehistory of Sicily, the Greek colonies, and artifacts from the colonies of Siracusa in the interior of the island.

Viale Teocrito. Tel: 39 (0931) 464-022.

Along Viale Teocrito, the **Museo del Papiro** (Papyrus Museum) exhibits parchments and shows ancient paper-making techniques. Art studios offer papyrus crafts for sale as souvenirs of the city.

Via Teocrido. Tel: 66 (0931) 61616.

ORTIGIA

Piazza Archimede is one of the most elegant squares of any Italian city. It has at its center a grand fountain with Diana, goddess of the hunt, encircled by sirens and tritons. The exceptionally beautiful buildings that surround the square give it balance and grace. Noteworthy among them is the magnificent fourteenth-century Palazzo Montalto.

The ancient site of **Fonte Aretusa** (Aretusa Spring) is the symbol of Siracusa. Lush with papyrus plants, which grow vigorously in the fertile soil of Sicily, and populated with frolicking ducks, it still celebrates the mythical love of **Aretusa** and **Alfeo** (Alpheus, the river god). The beauty of the spot continues to fascinate modern tourists as it did the ancients.

The duomo, true to its beginnings as a Greek temple, stands on the highest elevation of **Ortigia** and is characteristic of the locations that the Greeks chose to build their temples. Over 2,500 years of historical change is reflected in the Greek, Roman, Byzantine, Norman, and Baroque styles. It has been in continued use as a place of worship since its inception for these many civilizations. Originally a Greek temple to Athena, the goddess of wisdom, the space between the columns is now closed, but the previous structure is still apparent. On the outside, twenty-four of the original thirty-six columns still remain, as do the beautiful fluted Doric columns from the original temple in the interior. Now dedicated to Santa Lucia, the patron saint of Siracusa, it has a distinctly Sicilian Baroque façade which stands majestically atop an imposing staircase.

The beautiful thirteenth-century **Palazzo Bellomo** houses the **Galleria Regionale** (Regional Art Gallery), which contains among its treasures the fifteenth-century *Annunciation* by Antonello da Messina and seventeenth-century masterpiece *The Burial of Saint Lucy* by Michelangelo Merisi, also known as Caravaggio. Caravaggio painted this masterpiece during his stay in Sicily, thought to have been less than a year. The museum also houses a collection of furnishings, silver and gold objects, majolica, and illuminated manuscripts.

Via Capodieci 16, open Monday to Friday 9 a.m. to 2 p.m. (and from 3 p.m. to 7 p.m. on Tuesday and Friday) and 9 a.m. to 7 p.m. on Sunday. Tel: 39 (0931) 69617.

The city pays homage to Elio Vittorini, the twentieth-century writer from Siracusa, by implementing programs related to his life and work. The Parco Letterario Elio Vittorini was inaugurated in 2003 with the film *Viaggio sentimentale—Il garofano rosso* (*Sentimental Journey—The Red Carnation*), named for his novel *The Red Carnation*, written in the 1940s and highlighting the places in Siracusa that were important to Vittorini's life and writings.

Parco Letterario Elio Vittorini: Via San Sebastiano 14, Siracusa. Tel: 39 (0931) 481-200.

AVOLA

The town of **Avola** is unique for two culinary delights. It produces what are commonly called **mandorle pizzute** (pointed almonds), fragrant, well-flavored almonds that are prized throughout Sicily. The other very special local product is the wonderful full-bodied **Nero d'Avola** wine, one of the best Sicilian wines. But Avola is unique also for its town plan. When Avola was rebuilt after the earthquake of 1693, it was designed to center on an unusual hexagonal plan, with a square in the middle around which the new town developed in a radiating pattern.

NOTO

Noto was totally rebuilt in an entirely new location after the original old city was completely destroyed in the earthquake of 1693. The important innovations in the rebuilding of Noto include a plan that it has been said represents one of the first documented efforts to create a design in specific response to seismic disaster. Famed architect **Rosario Gagliardi** and his disciple **Vincenzo Sinatra** were responsible for creating the new city of Noto, which was rebuilt in the local golden limestone. The Sicilian eighteenth-century Baroque comes to life in Noto as in no other town. Noto offers an integrated whole of unsurpassed stylistic beauty and integrity.

The eighteenth-century reconstruction of Noto was spearheaded by the ambitions of the local aristocracy, who built impressive **palazzi** (elegant mansions) in the new town, and by the wealth and vision of the church, which engaged prominent architects for the rebuilding. This unequaled cluster of Baroque invention, visual excitement, and unified design represents one of the most singular accomplishments in the history of architecture, urban planning, and social interaction. This remarkable concept of urban development has been recognized by UNESCO as a World Heritage Site. There is an elegant theatricality in this city, where majestic staircases set off three churches in as many nearby squares. Start on Corso Vittorio Emanuele, where the Church of **San Francesco** designed by Galiardi stands atop a beautiful staircase. In Piazza XXX Ottobre, we reach **Santa Chiara**, another Gagliardi church, before we arrive at the **Duomo** in Piazza del Municipio. The linear and elegant style of the Cathedral of **San Nicolò**, also designed by Gagliardi, is set off by a staircase which glorifies the beautiful façade. Next to the cathedral is the nineteenth-century **Palazzo Vescovile** (bishop's palace) with the **Palazzo Trigona** and its beautiful curved wrought iron balconies behind it. On the other side is the **Palazzo Landolina**, the residence of the Sant'Alfano, a noble family of Norman origin. **Palazzo Nicolaci Villadorata** is enlivened with fabulous sculptures that hold up the six balconies together with magnificent wrought iron—pure Baroque delight. Across the street from the duomo is the stunning eighteenth-century **Palazzo Ducezio**, now the municipio (town hall), which is a symphony of beautifully proportioned arches and columns.

Continuing to Piazza XXIV Maggio is the church of **San Domenico**, also designed by Gagliardi. Across the square is the noteworthy nineteenth-century **Teatro Comunale**. Next to it is **Villa d'Ercole**, a beautiful park that has as its centerpiece a seventeenth-century fountain, a relic of Noto Antica (Old Noto).

The main street was planned in an east/west direction so that the beautiful buildings would be bathed in light. Noto is grand and elegant yet compact, and almost every part of the city is visually harmonious, providing soul-satisfying enjoyment. Although the town center was clearly designed and built for the aristocracy and the clergy, the **quartiere popolare** (neighborhood where the common people live) was not neglected by Gagliardi, who built the beautiful **Chiesa del Crocefisso** in **Piazza Mazzini**. The portal of the church incorporates two Romanesque lions from Old Noto, which stand at the sides of the entrance.

On the third Sunday of May, visitors flock to Noto to see the famous **Infiorata** on Via Corrado Nicolaci, which is carpeted with a long series of magnificent "paintings" made out of multi-colored flower petals. One of the most eagerly awaited events of the year, people also line up to see the work in progress, enjoying both the process and the finished presentation of these unique works of art.

PACHINO

South of Noto, almost at the tip of Capo Passero, is **Pachino**, a quiet agricultural town that produces what are considered by local **buongustai** (gourmets) some of the most flavorful tomatoes in Sicily. The semi-dried **ciliegini** (cherry tomatoes) of Pachino, packed in extra-virgin olive oil, are now available in gourmet shops all over Sicily—an excellent ready-made condiment for pasta or topping for bruschetta. Bring some back to enjoy the fragrance of Sicily at home. Pachino also produces excellent red wine.

CAPO PASSERO

Capo Passero, at the southernmost tip of Sicily, is a lovely uncrowded, unpretentious seaside fishing village with deep golden sandy beaches lining the coast. It has a tranquil and picturesque beach area for swimming and relaxation.

MEGARA IBLEA

North of Siracusa are the remains of **Megara Iblea**, an early Greek city settled by colonists from Crete. The inhabitans of Megara Iblea eventually left their settlement to escape war with Siracusa, crossed Sicily, and founded the colony of Selinunte on the western part of the island. Ancient walls are still visible at the site of Megara Iblea, together with the **agorà** (meeting place), the baths, and some of the foundations of the ancient structures, including a Hellenistic house with rooms typically arranged around two court-yards and with some actual remnants of the original floors. The initial excavations were done under the direction of the famous anthropologist Paolo Orsi at the end of the nineteenth century. Some of the treasured pieces that were unearthed are on exhibit at the Museo Archeologico in Siracusa, but the study of the complex continues to this day. The site is unfortunately near the industrial oil refining area of Augusta, which contrasts with the tranquility of the ancient ruins, but it merits a trip because it gives a good idea of life in this ancient city.

Open 9 a.m. to 6 p.m. Tel: 39 (0931) 67710.

CHAPTER 9

CATANIA

Catania is also known as **La Città Nera** (the black city) because of the prevalence of black volcanic stone used in as building material. It has ancient Greco-Roman beginnings with important monuments still standing in the middle of the city. Because it is located at the foot of Mount Etna, it has experienced dramatic and destructive lava flows and earthquakes throughout history. Yet it is the lava that has given the city the stone used so extensively for construction and made the countryside so fertile. Indeed, Mount Etna has shaped Catania's entire history.

Catania is a beautiful and vibrant modern city with an international airport, a thriving economy, an important university, and a lively cultural life. Frederick II had the **Castello Ursino** built in the thirteenth century on a promontory by the sea as an important fortification isolated and protected by a moat filled by the lava flow of 1669, which changed the coastline, giving the castle its present inland location. The Castello Ursino, housing the Museo Civico and the Pinacoteca, boasts magnificent collections of archeological treasure as well as an outstanding art collection. The earthquake of 1693 destroyed the city and decimated the population, but Catania was rebuilt with a plan for straight roads and large squares to which people could flee in the event of another earthquake. The present city has expanded beyond the original center of the seventeenth-century reconstruction. The nineteenth century saw major growth in population and construction of public works; the port was enlarged to meet the needs of commerce, and the **Teatro** (theater) and the **Giardini Pubblici** (public gardens) were built for the growing population. The sense of style which Giovanni Battista Vaccarini established as chief architect following the seventeenth-century reconstruction gives Catania a handsome unified look.

Catania at one point had lost its nightlife to fear of crime, whether real or perceived. But, like Palermo, it largely rid itself of criminality, whose cycle seems to have been broken. The Catanesi have reclaimed their beautiful city, and pedestrian areas are bustling with people enjoying themselves in cafés and restaurants.

Via Vittorio Emanuele and **Via Etnea**, the two main streets, intersect in **Piazza Duomo**, which is the **centro** (town center) of Catania. The focal point of the square is the eighteenth-century **Fontana dell'Elefante** (Elephant's Fountain) designed in 1736 by Giovanni Battista Vaccarini, who used the sculpture of the elephant to create a symbol for Catania. The elephant, which dates back to ancient Roman times, was combined with a dramatic Egyptian obelisk atop an imposing base. Vaccarini headed the reconstruction of the city as its chief architect, giving it a rational plan, a unity of purpose, and an integration of design that continue to serve it well.

Vaccarini reconstructed the eleventh-century duomo in the Baroque style. Incorporating the three apses and the transept of the original Norman church, he completed the church with an ornate Baroque façade, further enlivened by decorative sculptures. Constructed of volcanic stone and using thick walls to strengthen the building, it was designed to be anti-seismic. Inside is the **Tomb of Vincenzo Bellini** (1801–1835), the renowned bel canto composer and one of Catania's famous sons, who was honored by having **Teatro Bellini** and **Villa Bellini** named in his memory.

The **Palazzo Biscari**, just east of the duomo, fittingly has a magnificent **salone della musica** (music hall). The palazzo, a Baroque masterpiece, is still owned in part by a noble family, but the **salone** is open to the public for concerts, which are well attended by the Catanesi, as well as by audiences from other cities.

The ancient remains of classical Catania are in the middle of the city. The ancient ruins, in protected sites, peek through the surrounding buildings. The **Teatro Romano**, situated between Piazza San Francesco and Via Vittorio Emanuele, was probably built on the foundations of an earlier Greek theater, although today's remains are exclusively Roman. The marble facing of the ancient theater and some of the limestone blocks were removed and used in the construction of the cathedral. Nearby are the remains of the **Odeon**, a small theater that was used for rehearsals and competitions.

The house where Vincenzo Bellini was born in Piazza San Francesco is today the **Museo Belliniano**. It honors the memory of this great composer by preserving a collection of signed scores, musical instruments, and personal memorabilia, including his death mask. The grand Teatro Bellini, a short walk from the museum on Via Perrotta 12, was inaugurated on May 31, 1890, with Bellini's opera *Norma*. This beautiful and impressive theater continues to draw music lovers from Catania and environs. **Pasta alla Norma** is a delicious dish combining pasta with tomato sauce and fried eggplant, topped with grated ricotta salata. What better place to eat it than in the city of its origin?

Via Etnea, the beautiful and lively main street of Catania, which is equally delightful any time of day or night, leads to the Anfiteatro Romano (Roman Amphitheater). Like other classical remains in Catania, the amphitheater's remains are visible, although modern construction has taken place around them.

Continuing north on Via Etnea is Villa Bellini, a large, beautifully landscaped public park that is a welcome haven after shopping and busy city streets. The lovely paths, set among beautiful trees, offer refreshing views of snow-capped or smoking Mount Etna. On the other side of **Viale Regina Margherita** is l'**Orto Botanico** (the botanical park).

Baroque Catania, with its noteworthy palazzi and churches, can be seen along elegant **Via Cruciferi**, all the way to Via Antonino di San Giuliano. A right turn leads to the church of **San Nicolò all'Arena**. This massive church, which was planned as the

largest in Sicily and built in 1703, was unfortunately never completed. Its sundial is one of Europe's largest and still keeps correct
time; it marks the time when the sun comes through a hole in
the roof. Next to the church is the imposing former Benedictine
monastery of San Nicolò, which now houses the Art Department
of the University of Catania. Catania's famous university provides
vitality to the city, which is justly proud of its learning center,
reputed to have one of the finest libraries in Sicily.

The home of **Giovanni Verga** in Via Sant'Anna 8 is where that
writer lived and worked until his death in 1922. Now a museum,
it brings Verga to life with its displays of things that were dear to
him, in particular his extensive personal library.

Parco Lettrerario Giovanni Verga via Provinciale 27 Acitrezza
CT. Tel: 39 (095)-7116950.

MOUNT ETNA

Mount Etna, a peak over 10,000 feet high, is the largest active
volcano in Europe, with slopes that resemble a moonscape. Spectacular displays of smoke, ash, and fire can often be seen from
the steps of the Passionist Monastery in Mascalucia. In 2003, a
photo taken from outer space shows the plume of smoke from
Mount Etna reaching the continent of Africa, while the ash from
the volcano covered the balconies and the streets of Ragusa, the
southernmost city in Sicily. Hiking up the many hills and walking
along the spent craters is a memorable experience. The well-worn
curved paths spiraling up some of the craters are a symphony of
light and color. Despite the lack of vegetation, the landscape is
richly colored in earth tones, which, together with the lush brown
of the mountains, creates an unforgettable picture against the
intense blue sky. Even though many towns are located at the foot
of Mount Etna, their residents appear to be philosophical about
the danger of living near an active volcano.

The River Aci lends its name to a group of charming beach
towns, each with its own characteristics. Named after the shep-
herd Acis, the river was said to have surged after his death. The

three best-known towns on the coast east of Mount Etna are Aci Castello, Aci Trezza, and Acireale. During his Italian sojourn in the early 1700s, Georg Friedrich Handel wrote a serenata called *Acis and Galatea, A Pastoral Entertainment*, which he set in Sicily.

ACI CASTELLO

Aci Castello is dominated by its beautiful eleventh-century Norman Castle. Built of lava stone, it now houses the Museo Civico with natural history and marine archeology exhibits. Located in a spectacular spot, the cliff holding the castle drops off dramatically into the sea, making the castle seem one with the rocks on which it stands. There are magnificent views from the castle of the beginning of the **Riviera dei Ciclopi**, the area where the savage one-eyed giants of mythology descended from their home in Mount Etna. The imposing **Chiesa Madre** is also built of the typically black lava stone.

ACI TREZZA

Aci Trezza, the coastal town to the north of Aci Castello, is among the places, along with Vizzini and Catania, important to the life and work of the great verismo writer, Giovanni Verga. Aci Trezza was the setting of Verga's famous 1881 novel *I Malavoglia* (*The House by the Medlar Tree*), about the Malavoglia family, and for the 1948 Luchino Visconti film *La Terra Trema* (*The Earth Trembles*) based on the novel. From the harbor the **Isole dei Ciclopi** (the Isles of the Cyclops), a nature reserve can be seen. The **faraglioni** (huge craggy boulders), rising from the sea, are a well-known landmark. According to Homer, after being blinded by Ulysses, the cyclops Polyphemus hurled one of the boulders at the boat in which Ulysses was escaping.

Parco Letterario Giovanni Verga, Via Provinciale 27, Aci Trezza. Tel: 39 (095) 711-7147.

ACIREALE

Acireale is the largest of the three towns. After the 1693 rebuilding following the devastating earthquake, it emerged as a Baroque town of both substance and great charm. **Corso Vittorio Emanuele**, the main thoroughfare, has elegant stores and a choice of **pasticcerie** (pastry shops) and **gelaterie** (ice cream parlors), which tempt passersby with their delicious pastries, pasta reale (marzipan), and refreshing fresh fruit or almond granite. **Piazza Duomo** is the site of the beautiful **Cattedrale**, dating back to the beginning of the sixteenth century, the **Palazzo Comunale** (town hall), the traditional and especially Sicilian **Teatro dei Pupi** (Puppet Theater), and the **Biblioteca e Pinacoteca dell'Accademia Zelantea** (library and art gallery). The seventeenth-century library has an outstanding collection of books, and its gallery features an ancient bust of Julius Caesar, the famous **Busto di Acireale**. Acireale has one of the most elaborate and imaginative **carnevale** (carnivals) in Sicily; a good time to visit and take part in the festivities is just before the beginning of Lent. The spa of **Santa Venera**, named for the patron saint of the city, has been used since ancient times and still attracts visitors, who come for a rest and to benefit from its sulphur baths.

GIARRE

On the coast north of Acireale are the two nearby towns of **Giarre** and **Riposto**. These towns date from Roman times and were, as the names indeed suggest, storehouses. Foods, olive oil, and goods from inland were stored in Giarre, which also means jars, and Riposto, which means repository. Giarre's main street, **Via Calliopoli**, is lined with handsome palazzi and enticing souvenir shops that sell locally crafted **ceramiche** (pottery), including wonderful cache pots in the shape of heads in all sizes. Planting herbs or flowers in them give the heads their "hair." The **pupi** are dressed like the historical characters that are so much a part of Sicilian craft, history, and folklore. Giarre is also famous for its handmade wrought iron designs. The centro (town center) is in **Piazza Duomo**, where the majestic white stone neoclassical eighteenth-century duomo defines the evident well-being of this lovely town.

GIARDINI NAXOS

Giardini Naxos is striking for the beautiful shape of its shoreline and brilliant light. The transparent water changes in color from aquamarine to turquoise to deep blue. It is easy to understand why, when the Greeks landed here 2,700 years ago, they stayed on to colonize Sicily. A lovely late-twentieth-century monument sculpted in the form of a winged victory commemorates the founding of Naxos, the first Greek settlement in Sicily. From the monument, the view toward the sea is spectacular; uphill to the west, the lovely city of Taormina can be seen with its equally irresistible panorama.

TAORMINA

Perched high on the slopes of **Monte Tauro**, the beautiful town of **Taormina** has beckoned travelers since antiquity. The Greeks, coming up from Naxos, chose this appealing spot to build the **Teatro Greco** (Greek Theater), which is still in use today. On the way up to Taormina, spectacular views abound. Enhanced by the bright light, the architectural beauty, and the flower displays and lush vegetation along the steep slopes, there are memorable scenes just about everywhere. Photo opportunities abound, offering cliffs with profusely growing prickly pears, palms, cacti, and orchids, historic buildings, and spectacular panoramas of the coast with the deep hue of the sea. From the views of the majestic snow-capped Mount Etna, to the many quaint little alleyways, to the balconies overflowing with geraniums and pastry shop windows filled with fruits and vegetables expertly made of marzipan, to the heady fragrance of the flowering trees, this gem of a city is a thrill for the senses.

The Teatro Greco, with its tiered seats carved out of the living rock of the hill set with the natural backdrops of sea, sky, and snow-capped Mount Etna, is pure magic. The theater is used for the famous Taormina Art Festival, which presents theater, film, dance, and music shows. This magnificent setting was also featured in the Woody Allen movie *Mighty Aphrodite,* which won actress Mira Sorvino her Academy Award.

Greek Theater: Via Teatro Greco 40. Tel: 39 (0942) 23220.

Taormina Arte Tel: (0942) 21141.

From the Greek Theater, a walk to **Piazza Vittorio Emanuele** leads to the austere **Palazzo Corvaia**, a building of Moorish origins where the first Sicilian parliament met in the fifteenth century and that is now open to the public as the **Museo delle Arti Figurative Popolari della Sicilia.** The exhibitions include **carretti siciliani** (typical Sicilian mule-drawn carts) and the beautifully made decorative wrought iron pieces related to their construction, which are now sought after as collectibles; pupi (traditional puppets); ceramica (pottery); traditional costumes; magnificent sfilato (drawn-thread work embroidery); and other handicrafts. The building also houses the Tourist Office.

Piazza Vittorio Emanuele Tel: 39 (0942) 23243.

To the right is **Porta Messina**, the medieval gate to the city from which **Corso Umberto**, Taormina's main street and a wonderful pedestrian area, eventually reaches **Porta Catania**. A leisurely passeggiata along the way rewards the visitor with elegant shops and cafés. **Piazza IX Aprile** is like the living room of the town. Whether strolling or stopping for a caffè, aperitivo, delectable Sicilian granita, or gelato, sometimes served in a uniquely Sicilian fashion in a sweet bun, spectacular vistas of hills, terraces, and balconies overflowing with flowers spilling down the cliffs are all within view from the many wrought iron railed **belvedere** (overlooks). The view reaches into the enchanting bay of Giardini Naxos and Mount Etna to the south, sometimes providing natural fireworks on evenings when the volcano is awake. Across the piazza is the church of **San Giuseppe**; the top of its elegant double staircase provides a prime vantage point from which to survey the activity on the piazza. The stone architecture of the church stands in front of the hill's natural cliff, forming a backdrop to the façade and the **campanile** (bell tower), the man-made and natural beauty of the scene framed by flowering trees, set against the intense blue sky. It would be practically impossible to pick out the most beautiful spot in Taormina, but the integration of the natural cliffs and beautiful flowering trees, combined with the human genius that created the art and architecture, comes very close.

The **Cathedral of San Nicolò** in Piazza Duomo, with its stately and austere façade, contrasts with the lovely Baroque fountain in front of it. Built in the thirteenth century, the simple and elegant church, its crenellations outlined against the sky, dominates the piazza. San Nicolò hosts a well-attended winter concert series of classical music.

Palazzo Santo Stefano near Porta Catania in Via de Spuches is another magnificent example of medieval architecture. It is made of striking black lava with a white stone frieze. Its galleries exhibit the sculptures of Giuseppe Marzullo.

Open 9:30 a.m. to 12:30 p.m. and 4:30 p.m. to 7 p.m.

A short walk from Palazzo Santo Stefano is the famous **Palazzo San Domenico**, the former fourteenth-century Dominican monastery. Today it is the most famous hotel in all of Sicily and has preserved an atmosphere of class and dignity. This legendary hotel may not suit all budgets, but the hotel bar at night, when the gardens are romantically illuminated by torches, is a lovely spot to experience the hotel while enjoying a drink and live piano music.

The Anglican **Church of Saint George**, built in the 1920s, attests to the English presence in Taormina, which continues to this day. The 1999 book *A House in Sicily* by Englishwoman Daphne Phelps tells the story of her early twentieth-century family house, **Casa Cuseni**, of which she became proprietor upon her uncle's death in 1947 and which she turned into a kind of inn. She came to Taormina for the first time planning to sell the house and return to England, but she remained instead for over sixty years, becoming a force in the cultural and social life of the town. Over the years, Casa Cuseni has functioned as an intellectual salon; noted figures such as Tennessee Williams, Bertrand Russell, Roald Dahl, and William Faulkner stayed there, as did the famous Oxford historian Dennis Mack Smith, who wrote his *History of Sicily* there. Phelps's is a wonderful story and she tells it well.

Taormina is a town meant to be enjoyed on foot, but it is well served by public transportation, buses, taxies, and shuttles. Cable cars leaving from Via Pirandello cross citrus groves as they descend the cliffs, connecting Taormina to the nearby beach town of Mazzarò. This is truly a magnificent stretch of the Ionian Coast.

GOLE DELL'ALCANTARA

A short drive west of Taormina are the wondrous gorges **Gole dell'Alcantara**. These spectacular gorges, with a river flowing at the bottom and a waterfall at the end, have dramatic vertical cliffs rising sixty-five feet. They were formed in prehistoric times by hot lava reaching the water. As the lava cooled and contracted, it took on fantastic prismatic shapes that look like sculptured geometric shapes. These shapes have been further polished by the constant flow of water over millions of years. To visit the gorges, a visitor may rent hip boots as protection from the very cold water. There is a long flight of steps from the parking lot, but an elevator down to the river is also available. Hardy sportsmen can follow the shallow river for 490 feet to the waterfalls, but even without making the entire trek, it is worth the trip just to see the magnificent, absolutely unique, and unforgettable walls of the gorges.

LINGUAGLOSSA

West of the Gole di Alcantara is the town of **Linguaglossa**, an inland town on the northern slope of Mount Etna. The town is a base for hiking the trails to Mount Etna, as well as for excursions to the ski slopes of **Piano Provenzano**. The **Museo delle Genti dell'Etna** is an interesting museum well worth a visit to learn about the history, activities, and traditions of the area.

Museo delle Genti dell'Etna Tel: 39 (095) 643-094.

RANDAZZO

Continuing west on the northern slopes of Mount Etna is the town of **Randazzo**. Although Randazzo is closest to the craters, amazingly it has never had a lava flow within the town. Local artisans and craftsmen have exploited the easy availability of the natural lava stone for construction, street paving, and souvenir sculptures. The city has always enjoyed a lively trade of goods and services. Curiously, the town is divided into three ethnic areas, each headed by a church: Santa Maria for the Latins, San Nicolò for the Greeks, and San Martino for the Lombards. Each church had its turn at being the town cathedral until 1916, when Santa Maria was permanently designated as the Cathedral of Randazzo.

BRONTE

Turning south on the western slope of Mount Etna is the town of **Bronte**. Unlike Randazzo, it was devastated several times by eruptions, with some of the lava flows still visible. Bronte is a farming community that specializes in the cultivation of naturally green pistachios, prized for their incomparable flavor. Two delicious pistachio sauces can be found here, a pesto served on tiny gnocchi with grated cheese and a sweet version to top ice cream. Both sauces are available in jars in Bronte, as well as in gourmet shops all over Sicily.

ADRANO

Continuing south from Bronte is **Adrano**. Archeological finds date the origin of the town to the fifth century BC. The eleventh-century **Castello Normanno** (Norman Castle), which was recently restored and is open to the public from 9 a.m. to 1 p.m., houses the **Museo Archeologico** (Archeological Museum) containing artifacts that have been excavated in the area. The **Museo dell'Artigianato** (Crafts Museum) shows local crafts, including works in wrought iron for which the area is famous. This farming community produces and markets delicious honey from Mount Etna.

NICOLOSI

Nicolosi is a summer resort, but it also has access to winter ski slopes. From Nicolosi there is access to hiking trails to many of the spent cones from which the main, active crater of the volcano can be seen. Trails lead to the **Rifugio Sapienza**, a base camp halfway up Mount Etna. Information about hiking can be obtained from the **Gruppo Guide Alpine Etna Sud**, Tel: 39 (095) 791-4755.

For lunch or dinner, try **Il Cantuccio**—Via Torino 1, Nicolosi, Tel: 39 (095) 910-667—for delectable pastas and excellent antipasti.

TRECASTAGNI

Heading west from the coast is **Trecastagni**, a city known as La Città Della Lava (the Lava City). The **Chiesa Madre of San Nicola**, built from lava stones, is a national monument. From the front of the church there is a fabulous view of some of the towns that take their names from the Aci river such as **Aci Sant'Antonio, Aci San Filippo, Aci Catena**, as well as the better known ones. The **Santuario di Sant'Alfio, Cirino e Filadelfo**, is also worth a visit for its outstanding collection of **ex-voto** paintings. For the most part, they are folk paintings depicting a grace or miracle received. This large collection is definitely worth a stop for anyone interested in authentic locally inspired folk art.

MASCALUCIA

South of Nicolosi is the lovely agricultural town of **Mascalucia**. The town is dominated by the **Passionist Monastery** with its modern church, **Santuario dell'Addolorata**. The monastery is home to a religious community of Catholic Passionist priests and is set in a lush farmland area within view of Mount Etna. From July 15 to September 15, the **Casa di Accoglienza** (the Reception House) accepts guests who wish to spend a few days in the tranquility and beauty of the monastery, from which they can tour the area or simply get away from it all by enjoying rest and quiet reflection.

To make arrangements, call Padre Giuseppe Finazzo. Tel: 39 (095) 727-4309.

Mascalucia also has the interesting **Agriturismo Azienda Trinità**, owned by Salvatore Bonajuto, which offers rustic cottages, lunch, or dinner. The complex has an organic citrus grove, a vineyard, and what Signor Bonajuto calls a **Giardino Lavico** (Lava Garden), with a botanical collection of beautiful and varied native plants such as succulents, some very dramatic, and naturalized plants such as the prickly pear. Mr. Bonajuto also sells wine, honey, olive oil, and organic citrus fruits.

Agriturismo Azienda Trinità, Via Trinità 34. Tel: 39 (095) 727-2156 or e-mail info@aziendatrinita.it.

CALTAGIRONE

Caltagirone, with its rich clay deposits, has been a center for the production of ceramics since ancient times. Local earthenware products later fell under the influence of Greek shapes, but it was the Arabs' arrival in the ninth century that brought about the most important changes. The Arabs introduced Eastern designs and glazing techniques that rendered objects impermeable to water. Their exquisite geometric patterning and stylized decoration, using blue, green, and yellow as the predominant colors, were modeled on plants and animals. It is thought that the Arabs were also responsible for the town's name, perhaps derived from the Moorish word for "castle" or "fortress of vases."

The town's architecture is enriched with highly decorative ceramic elements, making it unique. The beautifully decorated **Ponte di San Francesco**, a bridge elegantly embellished with polychrome tiles that include the city's coat of arms, provides an impressive entrance to the town. The massive, still ominous-looking building that served as the Bourbon prison can be seen from the bridge. Today it is put to much better use as the **Museo Civico** (Town Museum), which has historical and archeological collections and as well as an art gallery—Tel: 39 (0933) 41315.

The wall surrounding the **Villa Comunale** (public garden), built in the mid-nineteenth century, is full of ceramic sculptures, figures, and fountains. The balustrade along Via Roma is accented with vases and planters. The park, modeled on English gardens, is beautifully landscaped with well-kept flower beds at every turn. The imposing glass-domed bandstand is the centerpiece of this lovely park.

The spectacular **Scala di Santa Maria del Monte** is a staircase in which each of the 142 steps has a ceramic riser in different patterns and designs. From the summit of the stairs there is a spectacular view of the town. Each year, for the feast of San Giacomo on July 24, this staircase comes to life as a tapestry of colored lights called **Luminaria**; thousands of lights placed in colored paper sleeves illuminate the steps in the design that has won the annual competition. Past designs can be seen in the **Museo Regionale della Ceramica**, a museum of ceramics that houses an impressive and well-documented collection, with pieces dating from prehistory to our time. The Museum of Caltagirone and the Museum of

Faenza are the two most important museums of ceramics in Italy. Open 9 a.m. to 6:30 p.m., Via Roma 10. Tel: 39 (0933) 41812. The façade of the **Chiesa di San Pietro** in the old quarter of town is an elegant neo-Gothic structure faced with ceramic tiles and accents in blue, green, and yellow. The town is home to the **Istituto d'Arte della Ceramica Luigi Sturzo**, a major institute for the study of ceramic art. This art form was created in antiquity and enjoys an unbroken tradition; there are dozens of studios that are free and open to the public. The town is compact and easy to tour on foot. Take advantage by walking and visiting the artists' studios to admire and talk with the artists. Since Caltagirone is a mountain town, all the views of the surrounding area offer unforgettable panoramas that include the majestic Mount Etna.

GRAMMICHELE

South of Catania is **Grammichele**, a lovely town designed as a series of concentric hexagons that extend outward from the elegant town square. The town was planned and built after the destruction brought about by the earthquake of 1693. The original plan is preserved in the nineteenth-century **Palazzo Comunale** (town hall), which also houses the **Museo Civico** (Town Museum) with its rich collection from the sixth-century **Necropolis of Terravecchia**. The handsome eighteenth-century Chiesa Madre, which is dedicated to Saint Michael, stands next to the Town Hall.

VIZZINI

The old town, with its narrow streets and even narrower alleyways, recalls the traditional urban plans of typical Sicilian towns. Vizzini was the birthplace of Giovanni Verga, the nineteenth-century writer, and provides the setting for some of his stories.

One of Verga's short stories was made into the libretto for *Cavalleria Rusticana*, the well-known opera by Pietro Mascagni, which has remained in the repertoire of most opera companies since its premiere in 1890. In July 2005, another of his stories was used as the subject of the contemporary opera *La Caccia al Lupo*, *The Hunt for the Wolf*, by the Sicilian composer Tommaso Lorenzo Toscano, which had its premiere, appropriately, in Vizzini.

CHAPTER 10

MESSINA

Messina is the gateway to Sicily. It is reached by a short ferry ride that crosses the two-mile strait separating it from the Italian mainland. Plans to build the world's largest suspension bridge to connect Messina with Reggio Calabria have been mired in controversy from the inception of the project. Originally scheduled to be completed by 2012, as of 2007, the bridge project has been cancelled. Messina is well located for easy access to highways connecting to other parts of Sicily.

Although it dates to 700 BC, a "new" city along the coast set against the surrounding Peloritani hills can be seen from the ferry. The modern city of Messina developed around the harbor and expanded in a regular grid with wide avenues, making it an easy city to navigate. Although it has its roots in antiquity, it was rebuilt as a modern city at the beginning of the twentieth century after a devastating earthquake on December 28, 1908, leveled the old city. The tsunami that followed and was seen and reported by eyewitnesses decimated the population, claiming between 80,000 and 100,000 lives. Because of its strategic location, it became a Nazi stronghold and was bombed during World War II, but once again, it rose and was rebuilt.

Messina has a university that lends vitality to the city. The **Museo Regionale** is a major art museum that preserves the artistic heritage of the city of Messina by exhibiting many of the paintings, sculptures, and architectural details that were saved after the earthquake of 1908. The museum is justly proud of its five fifteenth-century panels of the *Polyptych of Saint Gregory,* by great painter and famous native son **Antonello da Messina**, and the seventeenth-century masterpieces *The Raising of Lazarus* and *The Nativity* by Michelangelo Merisi, known as **Caravaggio**. While the works of Antonello da Messina represent the artistic and cultural golden age of Messina, Caravaggio's stay in the city, though brief, exerted an important stylistic influence on future artists.

    Viale della Libertà. Tel: 39 (090) 361-292. Open 9 a.m. to 2 p.m. daily and from 3 p.m. to 5:30 p.m. on Tuesday, Thursday, and Saturday.

    Of the eleventh-century duomo (cathedral), all that remains is the lower portion of the façade with its bands of colored marble and the three imposing Gothic portals. The **campanile** (bell tower), which stands next to the duomo, has the largest mechanical clock in the world. It comes to life at noon every day, with moving figures symbolizing important events in the history of Messina, while the south side of the tower displays astronomical phenomena. Facing the duomo is the sixteenth-century **Fontana di Orione** (Orion's Fountain), named for the mythical giant who supposedly founded Messina and one of the few beautiful monuments to have survived the earthquakes and World War II.

    To enjoy beautiful views of the sea, a passeggiata or stroll along the **Marina** is a welcome and refreshing experience.

Milazzo

The city of **Milazzo** is dramatically situated at the end of a promontory that juts out three and a half miles into the **Mar Tirreno** (Tyrrhenian Sea) on Sicily's northern coast. Surrounded by sandy beaches, it is the departure point for the Aeolian Islands. Milazzo's thirteenth-century **castello** (castle) still dominates the modern city below. The city has a long history but is best known for the important and decisive battle of July 1860, when Garibaldi and his "mille" (army of 1,000 redshirts) freed Sicily from the Bourbons, paving the way for the unification of Italy.

Capo Milazzo, situated at the end of the promontory, can be reached by the western road at sea level, leading to **Baia del Tono** (Tuna Bay), site of an old "Tonnara" (tuna fishing station), or by the eastern road over the hills, leading to **Il Faro** (the lighthouse), which is set in an area of lush vegetation at the end of the peninsula.

Isole Eolie

The archipelago of the **Isole Eolie**, or Aeolian Islands, just north of Milazzo is made up of seven volcanic islands. Named by UNESCO as a World Heritage Site, the islands are very different from one another, and each one maintains its individual uniqueness. The largest three are Lipari, Vulcano, and Salina. To the east are Filicundi and Alicundi, and to the northwest, Panarea and Stromboli. The volcanoes of Stromboli and Vulcano are still active. Seeing the Aeolians from the air creates a sense of wonderment as to how these remote places with their steep slopes and sheer cliffs rising out of the sea could have been populated. Yet, the first inhabitants lived on these islands as far back as the Neolithic period.

The beauty, sheer variety of the rugged landscape, and the clear and intense color of the water and sky make this a memorable destination. The Aeolians live by agriculture, fishing, and tourism. **Lipari**, the largest island, and **Salina** grow the grapes that are sun dried on the vines to produce the incomparable **Malvasia** wine. Almonds and olives are also grown, as are capers, which are among the best in Sicily. Lipari exports its pumice stone all over the world.

In the magnificent 1986 film *Kaos* (*Chaos*) directed by Paolo and Vittorio Taviani, there is an unforgettable scene of children, all dressed in white, jumping down the white powdery pumice hill and running into the deep blue sea. Of course, Roberto Rossellini had already made the island of Stromboli famous in the 1950s as the setting of the film by the same name. More recently, *Il Postino* (*The Mailman*) was filmed entirely in Salina.

Another product of Lipari, which was particularly important in ancient times, is obsidian, a black, lustrous volcanic glass. When broken, it is far superior to flint as a cutting tool or weapon and was used and traded by Neolithic populations. The islands can be reached by ferries or hydrofoils from Milazzo, but also from Messina, Palermo, or Naples. Lipari is the largest and most populated of the seven islands. The sixteenth-century **Castello Spagnolo** (Spanish Castle), with its massive walls, sits above the harbor on a natural stone platform. The **Museo Archeologico Regionale Eoliano**, which occupies part of the castle, is considered to have some of the finest collections in Sicily. It exhibits what has been unearthed in the islands from local prehistoric cultures dating back to the Upper Neolithic, the Bronze Age, the Early Iron Age, and the relatively recent Greco-Roman period. It also has an outstanding collection of theatrical masks from ancient Greece, the largest such collection in the world.

Open daily from 9 a.m. to 2 p.m. and from 4 p.m. to 7 p.m. Tel: 39 (090) 988-0174.

The road that circles the island of Lipari connects the main villages and provides the visitor with vistas and photo opportunities at every turn. South of Lipari, from **Quattrocchi**, is a magnificent series of coves along the coastline. The nearby island of Vulcano offers a glimpse of its steaming cone. On the west coast, the **Terme di San Calogero**, the thermal baths that have been used for their therapeutic effect on the body since ancient times, still attract people who come for treatments. To the north are the vineyards, which prosper in the fertile volcanic soil and lush vegetation. From **Puntazze** on the northern tip of the island, there is a view of the island of Alicudi on the west all the way to Stromboli on the northeast—a view nothing short of spectacular. Rounding the island on the northern side and heading south, there are two very different but equally beautiful beaches. First is the white beach of **Spiaggia della Papesca**, where the sand mixed with pumice dust turns the water a magnificent translucent blue, quite a contrast to the black sand on the beach of **Cannetto**, which is on the return road to Lipari.

VULCANO

Vulcano is quite different from Lipari in both appearance and smell. Lipari's lush vegetation gives way to lime, yellow, and rust-colored rocks that have been tinted by their mineral deposits. The smell of sulfur, which those going to the **fanghi** (mud baths) consider part of the therapy, immediately assaults the senses. The mud baths, which have been used for ages, are reputed to be highly effective for treating skin disorders and painful conditions such as arthritis and rheumatism. A trek to the main crater takes about an hour and requires good hiking shoes. Approaching the top, the smell of sulfur grows stronger and the landscape resembles a moonscape. From the crater, the panorama—with the sea, the islands, the surrounding cliffs, and the smoking, hissing, and popping sounds coming from the bowels of the earth—is spectacular. Realizing that this is a real volcano, not an image from a television show, makes this experience even more exhilarating.

SALINA

To the north of Lipari stand the twin peaks of Salina, which is another world compared to Vulcano. Rich with vegetation, the mountain's greenery is a refreshing sight. Here, on the climb up to **Monte dei Porri** or **Fossa Delle Felci**, now a nature reserve, the wooded areas get denser with evergreens and maples. Hard as it is to imagine, this is still Sicily. But at the top of the rocky peaks, on top of the world as it were, the magnificent views of the archipelago come into view again. Again, seen from this vantage point, we can only wonder exactly how these islands were ever invaded and colonized.

The equally beautiful, but less crowded, beaches of Salina are also very enticing. Boats arrive at **Santa Maria di Salina** on the eastern side of the island, and buses connect it to the villages of **Malfa** on the northern coast, **Pollara**, a hill town that spills from the side of a spent crater, **Leni**, and **Rinella**, the last a lovely fishing village on the southern coast. In this relatively unspoiled place, the ecology of the nature reserve that protects the vegetation of the twin cones attracts migratory birds and is a nesting ground for falcons, which flock there from faraway Madagascar.

One of the main products of the island is the distinctive and delicious Malvasia sweet wine, which is produced from sun-dried grapes. Although Malvasia wine can also be bought in the other islands, it is produced only in Salina, a perfect place to enjoy the amber sweetness of this local delicacy.

PANAREA

The little harbor of **Panarea**, the smallest of the islands and the earliest to have been formed, is the summer stopping-off point of elegant yachts. This lovely island, which has become a heaven with its manicured villas and vacation homes spilling over with flowers, presents a contrast to the ruggedness of the other islands. A highlight of Panarea is the **Villaggio Preistorico**, the prehistoric Bronze Age village whose remains can be seen close to the beautiful sandy beach of **Punta Milazzese** on the southern tip of the island.

STROMBOLI

Northeast of Panarea is **Stromboli**, the volcano that rises magically out of the sea. This is an active volcano that does not rest. It has mild but dramatic eruptions just about every hour, sending smoke appearing at night like plumes of fire to the sky, creating unforgettable natural fireworks. Licensed guides are available for hire for those wishing to climb to the crater. The amazing sight of red glowing lava trickling down the **Sciara del Fuoco** to the sea, seen from the summit of the highest cone or from the sea itself, is a truly awesome spectacle.

FILICUDI AND ALICUDI

The seemingly desolate islands of **Filicudi** and **Alicudi** are very much appreciated today because they represent nature, magnificently isolated and unspoiled, at its best. Visitors who seek peace, quiet, and solitude will find these remote and primitive islands food for the spirit. They can be circumnavigated by boat, but the hardy can also hike on them.

TINDARI

Back to Milazzo, going west along the coast is the lovely city of **Tindari**, which inspired poet Salvatore Quasimodo, the Sicilian Nobel Prize winner, to write *Vento a Tindari* (*Wind at Tindari*). The city also came to the public's attention with the publication of *La Gita a Tindari* (*The Trip to Tindari*) by the contemporary mystery writer Andrea Camilleri, who peppers his mystery novels with Sicilian words and phrases, many of which have become part of standard Italian. Founded by the Greeks, it has a wonderfully situated Greek theater, where, during the summer in the loveliest of natural settings facing the sea and overlooking the gulf, musical and classical drama performances are still given. The remains of Roman villas, baths, workshops, and stores dating back to the first-century BCE can also be visited in the **Archeological Park**, which is open daily from 9:00 a.m. until two hours before sunset. The clear layout and the possibility of actually walking through the streets of the city enables visitors to imagine what life there might have been like in ancient times. Extensive excavations have unearthed portions of the impressive walls that encircled the ancient city of Tyndaris; there, one of the Roman houses, with its marble mosaic floors, remains, and a partially extant majestic arched portal, which was the entrance to what was thought to be the gymnasium, makes the experience even more concrete. The **Santuario della Madonna di Tindari**, beautifully situated overlooking the sea bordering the Archeological Park and next to the **piazza**, is a pilgrimage destination for the devout who wish to visit the famous Byzantine **Madonna Nera di Tindari** (Black Madonna of Tindari), whose feast occurs on September 8.

The spectacular emerald lakes of the **Laguna di Oliveri** (Oliveri Lagoon) below Tindari are a natural preserve for a great diversity of migratory birds. The sandy beaches around them are among the best and most beautiful on the northern coast.

CAPO D'ORLANDO

Continuing westward on the northern coast is **Capo d'Orlando**. It lies at the foot of the **Nebrodi Mountains**, which separate the Madonie Mountains on the west from the Peloritani Mountains in the east and juts out just before the coast begins to run to the southwest. This is a rich citrus-growing area and a popular tourist spot with wonderful beaches. Above the town are the remains of a fourteenth-century castle and the fifteenth-century church of **Maria Santissima**. Of course, from the top of the cliff, the views of the beautiful harbor just below, of the Aeolian Islands in the Thyrranean Sea and of the Peloritani Mountains to the east, are breathtaking.

PARCO REGIONALE DEI MONTI NEBRODI

The **Parco Regionale dei Monti Nebrodi**, a large natural preserve with dense green vegetation of hardy evergreens and wooded forests in the higher altitudes, is a Sicilian wonder, especially when snow covered in winter. From Capo d'Orlando, following the coast on State Road 113, is **Sant'Agata di Militello**, a town that developed thanks to its location on a well-traveled road and to the fertility of the land which surrounds it. This is an area where agriculture and sheep grazing are very important to the economy; the sheep's-milk cheeses are excellent. The **Museo Etnoantropologico dei Nebrodi** is an interesting place to visit to learn about the country life, occupations, products, and folklore of this region. Via Cosenza 149. Tel: 39 (0941) 722308.

SAN FRATELLO

The town of **San Fratello**, just eleven miles south of Sant'Agata di Militello, has an interesting linguistic history. Settled in the eleventh century by people from Lombardy, it still retains its French/Lombard dialect, which goes back to the Norman period. The people of San Fratello, speakers of Sicilian, Italian, and the town's unique sub-dialect, are trilingual. The town is situated in the Nebrodi Mountains and is surrounded by gentle green hills where occasional horses enliven the pastoral landscape. When the Arabs occupied Sicily, they brought their horses onto the island. Over the centuries, as the Arabian horses mixed with the native variety, a new breed evolved, recognized now as the Sanfratellese breed. The Sanfratellese horses that breed in the wild can still be seen in the surrounding mountains, but especially in the **Parco Regionale dei Monti Nebrodi**.

For those who are interested, an exhaustive historical analysis of the Sanfratellan dialect was published by the American-Sicilian expert of the languages of Sicily, Dr. Joseph Privitera, under the title *Language as Historical Determinant: The Normans in Sicily*, American International Book Development Council, Washington, DC, 1995.

CHAPTER 11

PALERMO

CEFALÙ

Cefalù, commemorated in the beloved film *Cinema Paradiso*, is a city that is enchantingly situated on the northern coast between Messina and Palermo. It has rightfully become a major tourist stop. Seen from the sea or from the coastline, the panorama dominated by the two spires of the duomo with the rugged cliffs of **La Rocca** as a backdrop is a beauty to behold. The city is charming and the beach is wonderful. But its duomo is the pearl of the city.

Getting around on foot is a delightful experience, as there's no traffic allowed in the **centro storico** (historic center). Starting in **Piazza Garibaldi**, a stroll on **Corso Ruggero** leads to the duomo in the very center of Cefalù. This twelfth-century Norman church, with its elegant façade and portal flanked by two towers, has the oldest Byzantine mosaics in Sicily. The central and dominant figure of Christ in the apse makes use of the curvature of the dome in such a way that the gold-backed figures of **Cristo Pantocratore** (Christ, ruler of the universe) seems three-dimensional, as if he is embracing the world. The figures of Christ above Mary and the Archangels on the upper tier and the Apostles on the other two are also compelling. The mosaics are magnificent, but it is the central image of Christ that remains memorable.

The **Museo Mandralisca** houses the eclectic collection of the nineteenth-century scholar, art collector, and benefactor Baron Enrico Piraino di Mandralisca. Its pride is the masterpiece by Antonello da Messina, *Ritratto d'Ignoto (Portrait of an Unknown Man)*, which was painted on wood in 1465. The mysterious subject of this painting was taken by the contemporary Sicilian writer **Vincenzo Consolo** as the inspiration for his novel, *Il Sorriso dell'Ignoto Marinaio (The Smile of the Unknown Sailor)*, written in the 1970s. The rest of the collection consists of a huge collection of shells, ancient coins, ceramics from Lipari, and other curiosities. From the museum, following the sign **Accesso alla Rocca** on Corso Ruggero, a relatively short walk leads to one of the most spectacular views in Sicily.

MADONIE MOUNTAINS

South of Cefalù atop a mountain on the slopes of the Montagne delle Madonie is the lovely small town of **Polizzi Generosa**, where there is hiking in summer in the nature preserve and skiing in winter in nearby **Piano Battaglia**. The snows of the Madonie Mountains have earned them the name the Alps of Sicily. To the east is **Gangi** and nearby is **Gangivecchio**, home to the **Tenuta Gangivecchio**, a first-class country-style restaurant and inn that serves the best in Sicilian food. Housed in the Tornabene Estate, a former Benedictine abbey, the restaurant was the brainchild of Wanda and Giovanna Tornabene. Mother and daughter became internationally famous after publication of their book, *La Cucina Siciliana di Gangivecchio: Gangivecchio's Sicilian Kitchen*. High in the Madonie Mountains, Tenuta Gangivecchio has won high praise since it opened in 1978, and it is worth a special side trip. Reservations can be made by calling 39 (0921) 44804.

PALERMO

Palermo is situated in a magnificent setting that fans out beyond the natural harbor and is encircled by mountains with **Monte Pellegrino** standing watch over the city. The beautiful garland of citrus groves that once graced the **Conca d'Oro** no longer fill the valley with golden lemons, yet Palermo's geographical setting is still a wondrous spectacle of natural and man-made beauty. Palermo was settled in the eighth century as a port by the Phoenicians, who named it Ziz. The Greeks later called the city Panormos, meaning "all port." Although the earliest religion was Orthodoxy, many of the churches were turned into mosques after the Moor invasion in 831. The Norman conquest of Palermo took place in 1071, by which time Palermo was already a melting pot of the various civilizations that had flourished there. For the next several decades, it rivaled London in wealth.

Medieval Palermo came into prominence under Arab rule as one of the most beautiful cities of its time. It continued to ascend in power and influence, becoming a great cultural center under the emperor Frederick II, who was known as Stupor Mundi, or Wonder of the World. Frederick II was multilingual, a patron of the arts, and a student of the sciences. It was in this court that the Sicilian literary tradition that continues to this day had its flowering with the Sicilian School of Poetry and the invention of the sonnet form. His birth was dramatic. His 40-year-old mother, Constance of Hauteville, a Sicilian princess and later Queen of Sicily, was the daughter of King Roger II. She married Holy Roman Emperor Henry VI of Germany, and delivered her baby on December 26, 1194, in public so that there would be no question that she was the mother. Frederick II continued to govern in the liberal and enlightened tradition of this mother and grandfather to keep Palermo one of the great cities of its time. Constance is the subject of *Travels with a Medieval Queen* by Mary Taylor Simeti, the contemporary American writer who has made her home in Sicily. Queen Constance is regally buried with her father, husband, and son in the Cathedral of Palermo.

Today the vigor of the city's past is seen in its distinctive architecture, which tells its history. The twelfth-century duomo was begun in the late Norman period; changes and additions were made in the fourteenth and fifteenth centuries, and the cupola was completed in the late eighteenth century. The late Roman-esque façade, flanked by two beautiful towers, includes a magnificent portico with three arches leading to the entrance. Inside are the tombs of the Norman kings and the Hohenstaufen emperors, among them Frederick II and his mother. The duomo is an exceptional integration of ideas, periods, and styles throughout the centuries. The final result is a harmonious whole that has remained dear to the hearts of the Palermitani.

The **Palazzo dei Normanni or Palazzo Reale** (Norman Royal Palace), the seat of the **Assemblea Regionale Siciliana** (Sicilian Parliament) since 1947, is one of Palermo's most noteworthy historic buildings. The jewel of the building is the richly decorated **Cappella Palatina**, commissioned in 1132 and richly decorated with mosaics and fine art. It combines Norman, Arab, Byzantine, and Christian motifs. The mosaic floor and lower walls faced with marble are topped with a spectacular twelfth-century wooden caisson ceiling, the work of Arab and Sicilian craftsmen. Above the altar in the vault of the apse is an image of Christ done in classic Byzantine style. In the cupola is another figure of Christo Pantocratore, surrounded by angels and archangels; prophets, saints, and evangelists are portrayed below the dome. The figurative Byzantine mosaics and limitlessly inventive Arabic patterns are reflected on every surface, even on the risers of the steps to the altar. The designs, with their brilliant colors and dazzling goldleaf, afford the visitor an unparalleled aesthetic and spiritual experience.

Open Saturday from 9 a.m. to 11:45 a.m., Sunday from 9 a.m. to 9:45 a.m. and 12 p.m. to 12:45 p.m., and afternoons from 3 p.m. to 4:45 p.m.

The twelfth-century church of **San Giovanni degli Eremiti** (Saint John of the Hermits), orginally a mosque, is a typical example of the work of Arabic and Sicilian masons and craftsmen. Austere and simple in shape, the building is decorated on its summit with a small red spherical dome that matches the other four and gives the building its traditional Arabic style. The interior is very simple and unadorned. Nearby, the lovely thirteenth-century Norman cloister and its beautiful garden enclosed by elegant double arches is a restful place for thought and meditation. Via dei Benedettini 18. Open Monday to Saturday 9 a.m. to 1 p.m. and 3 p.m. to 7 p.m.; Sunday 9 a.m. to 1 p.m. Following along Corso Vittorio Emanuele toward La Cala is **Piazza Vigliena**, better known as **I Quattro Canti**, or the four corners. This is the center of the city. The four corners, long the center of city life, refers to the beautiful octagonal town square with its elegant Baroque curved façades located at the intersection of Palermo's two main streets, Via Maqueda and Corso Vittorio Emanuele. This crossroads divides the city into four quartieri, or neighborhoods: the northwestern **Capo** section, the northeastern **Vucciria**, the southeastern **Kalsa**, and the southwestern **Albegheria**. The sixteenth-century **Fontana Pretoria** (Pretoria Fountain), in Piazza del Municipio, was dubbed **Piazza della Vergogna** (Square of Shame), because of the dozens of nude marble statues lining it. In the first tier are figures representing the seasons, in the second are statues of the Spanish kings, and on the third level are the statues of the patron saints of the four quartieri: Agata, Olivia, Ninfa, and Cristina.

Piazza Bellini is graced with two magnificent structures, the only Norman churches in Palermo: the **Chiesa della Martorana** and the **Chiesa San Cataldo**. The former church is also known as Santa Maria dell'Ammiraglio because it was built by the commander of the fleet of Ruggero II (Roger II), Admiral Giorgio di Antiochia (the Greek admiral, George of Antioch), called Ruggero's "Emir of Emirs." Under Ruggero II, who died in 1154, the kingdom of Sicily became a modern state.

The **Chiesa della Martorana** is considered a highpoint of Norman design and architecture, although today the symmetrical Norman lines are covered over by a Baroque façade. Still, it is considered the loveliest Greek church remaining in Sicily. The twelfth-century bell tower was destroyed by an earthquake in 1726 but was restored in the nineteenth century. Together with those of the Cappella Palatina, the interior mosaics are among the oldest and finest in Sicily. Ruggero II brought the best craftsmen from Constantinople to create the images. The beautiful mosaic of **Ruggero Incoronato da Cristo** (Roger II being crowned by Christ) on the right wall represents the king's authority as deriving directly from God, not the pope, an important political statement in twelfth-century Sicily. The **Madonna del Rosario** (Madonna of the Rosary) on the left wall and another mosaic of **Giorgio di Antiochia** (George of Antioch) worshipping the Madonna are other examples of superb Byzantine craftsmanship.

Piazza Bellini 3. Open Monday to Saturday 9:30 a.m. to 1 p.m. and 3:30 p.m. to 6:30 p.m.

Next to the Church of the Martorana is the twelfth-century **Chiesa di San Cataldo**. Designed in strict geometric form, it clearly reflects Arabic design and craftsmanship with its contrasting rose-colored domes and elegantly pointed windows and doors. The main altar and pavement in the unadorned interior preserve the original mosaics.

Piazza Bellini 3. Open Tuesday to Friday 9 a.m. to 5 p.m. on Saturday; 9 a.m. to 1 p.m. on Sunday.

Palermo's ancient and medieval quarter is among the largest of any Italian city; only Rome and perhaps Naples surpass it in size. The **Kalsa** district is one of the most characteristic, if least affluent, parts of the city. Still marked by the ravages of World War II bombings and, until the late 1990s, in the grip of the Mafia, this area is now coming back to life and is being restored and gentrified.

The **Oratorio di San Lorenzo** has an interior richly decorated with stucco decoration, the masterpiece of Giacomo Serpotta, who worked on them between 1698 and 1710. His spirited and beautiful **puttini** (little cherubs) are a delight, as are the graceful figures depicting events in the lives of San Lorenzo and San Francesco, which adorn the oratorio.

Via dell'Immacolatella, just South of Corso Vittorio Emanuele. Open Monday to Saturday 9 a.m. to 12 p.m.

The beautiful church of **San Francesco d'Assisi**, near the Oratorio of San Lorenzo, was built over two decades starting in 1255 as a shrine to St. Francis of Assisi. Its showy Gothic portal is from the original thirteenth-century structure, but its restrained interior recalls the Franciscan churches built in the Middle Ages. It also has allegorical figures by Giacomo Serpotta and the arch sculpted by Francesco Laurana and Pietro de Bonitate in 1468. The lovely rose window is one of the finest in Sicily.

Just to the east is **Piazza Marina**, one of the largest squares in old Palermo. The well-maintained park was originally created in the nineteenth century by Giovan Battista Basile and planted with extraordinary ficus trees, which have become the centerpiece of the piazza. On the eastern corner is **Palazzo Chiaramonte**, headquarters of the infamous and dreaded Inquisition in the seventeenth century, and now part of the University of Palermo. A short walk north leads to the **Museo Internazionale delle Marionette**, which exhibits not only the justly famous traditional Sicilian pupi, but a history of folk art through the display of puppets, marionettes, backdrops and stage sets from other countries. In October, the museum presents classic productions of the Sicilian **Opera dei Pupi** as well as productions from other countries.

Via Butera 1. Open Monday to Friday 9 a.m. to 1 p.m. and 4 p.m. to 7 p.m.; Saturday 9 a.m. to 1 p.m.

Walking South on via Butera and turning right onto Via Alloro is the **Palazzo Abatellis** (Abatellis Palace), which is the home of the **Galleria Regionale della Sicilia** (Sicilian Regional Gallery). It boasts sculptures by fifteenth-century sculptor **Francesco Laurana**, such as the exquisite and timeless marble bust of Eleonora d'Aragona, and masterworks by painter **Antonello da Messina**, such as his famed *Annunciation* and *San Girolamo*, as well as the mature work of sixteenth-century sculptor **Antonello Gagini**.

Next to the Galleria Nazionale is **La Gancia**, a church built in the fifteenth century and dedicated to Santa Maria degli Angeli. Its treasure is the wonderful sixteenth-century full-relief sculpture (*tondo*) of **L'Annunciazione** (the Annunciation) by Antonello Gagini and the Baroque stucco decorations by Giacomo Serpotta, as well as an organ dating back to the late 1500s, the oldest in Palermo.

Continuing south and turning right on Via Lincoln is the **Villa Giulia** and the **Orto Botanico**. Villa Giulia is a beautiful eighteenth-century Italian-style garden designed by Nicolò Palma as the first public park in the city of Palermo. A lovely fountain dominates its center, and busts of famous Palermitani grace the walkways.

Open daily 8 a.m. to 8 p.m.

The **Orto Botanico** (botanical garden), which houses a herbarium, is also home to an enormous variety of plants, from both Sicily and all over the world. They thrive in the fertile Sicilian soil of the twenty-five-acre garden.

Heading back north, across the street from the church of San Francesco d'Assisi, is the famed restaurant **Antica Focacceria**. It offers traditional Sicilian food such as **arancini** (deep-fried filled rice balls), **panelle** (chick pea fritters), **cazzilli** (potato croquettes), and many other favorites.

Crossing Via Vittorio Emanuele east of Via Roma leads to the most colorful market in Palermo, the **Vucciria**, where street food is enjoyed by Palermitani and tourists alike. Recommended are the **arancini** (each version is different) or **pani** and **panelle** (buns filled with a chick pea fritter). Those seeking authentic fare should try **pani ca meusa** (a soft bun filled with hot cooked spleen), either "**schiettu**" or "**maritatu**" (single or married), meaning plain or with a slice of fresh ricotta. This delicious concoction is definitely for the more adventurous and is incredibly rich, so plan to share it with a friend. A welcome refreshment is a piece of **noce di cocco** (fresh coconut) chilled under running water or some **fichi d'India** (prickly pears). Let the vendor slice through the spiny skin so that the luscious sweet fruit can be eaten with your hands. Be sure to try one.

If Vucciria is too noisy and folksy for your taste, go diagonally across town to the **Albergheria** district and the **Mercato Ballarò**, one of the liveliest markets in the city, where everything from food to jeans is sold. While there, plan a visit to the early seventeenth-century **Chiesa del Carmine** to admire the unusually colorful cupola encrusted with polychrome majolica ceramic tiles and held up by monumental figures flanked by Corinthian columns. It is a must.

For a bit of the Old World straight out of *The Leopard* (the 1957 novel by Giuseppe Tomasi di Lampedusa posthumously published), stop at "**Le Palme**," which is how those in the know referred to the **Grand Hotel et des Palmes** in the nineteenth century. This is located on Via Roma, where you can rest and have a caffè in the charmed atmosphere of the most famous hotel in Palermo.

From Le Palme, walk over to the **Oratorio del Rosario di San Domenico** and to the **Oratorio del Rosario di Santa Zita**, also known as **San Cita**. The oratori were the social clubs of the aristocrats of Palermo. The Giacomo Serpotta chapel of the San Domenico has delightful cello-playing cherubs, together with allegorical figures, seashells, and other marvels. Not to be missed is the magnificent *Madonna del Rosario* by Anthony Van Dyck (1599–1641) on the altar and *L'Incoronazione della Vergine* (*The Coronation of the Virgin*) by Italian Baroque painter Pietro Novelli (1603–1647) in the vault. The Santa Zita, or San Cita, Oratorio has splendid Giacomo Serpotta stucchi representing the intervention of the Virgin in the Battle of Lepanto, as well as master sculptures by Antonello Gagini.

San Domenico: Open 9 a.m. to 1 p.m. and 2 p.m. to 5:30 p.m.; Saturday 9 a.m. to 1 p.m.

Santa Zita: Open 8 a.m. to 12 p.m. and Saturday 9 a.m. to 1 p.m.

Crossing Via Roma, you'll find the **Museo Nazionale Archeologico** (National Archeological Museum), one of the major museums in Sicily. Enjoy the lily pond in the inner courtyard. Among the important ancient treasures are the **metopes**, stone-carved panels depicting scenes from Greek mythology, taken from one of the temples at Selinunte, together with other sculptures from the same temples. There is a wonderful sixth- and fifth-century BCE Etruscan collection, a large and equally important and magnificent collection of Greek vases, Greek sculptures from the fifth and fourth century BCE, and ancient Roman sculptures, elegant ancient bronzes, and a fine numismatic collection. Open Monday to Friday 9 a.m. to 1 p.m. and 3 p.m. to 7 p.m.; Saturday 9 a.m. to 1 p.m.

Take Via Roma north and turn left on Via Cavour across Via Marqueda to the newly restored **Teatro Massimo** on Piazza Verdi. It is the largest theater in Sicily and one of the most prestigious in Italy. Designed by the architect Giovan Battista Filippo Basile, who competed in a competition to build it, it was fraught with construction delays and was completed only after Basile's death in 1891 by his son Ernesto. The magnificent neoclassic façade stands atop an imposing staircase. The interior, which is reputed to have near perfect acoustics, is elegantly decorated and contains five tiers of boxes. The recent reopening of this theater after endless delays in its restoration was seen as another sign that the Palermitani, headed by their no-nonsense mayor, Leoluca Orlando, had reclaimed their city.

The nineteenth-century **Teatro Politeama Garibaldi** on Piazza Ruggero Settimo is a handsome circular neoclassic building with a majestic arch that recalls classic monumental architecture. It is adorned on the façade with a beautiful low-relief sculpture and topped by a dramatic bronze group of six equestrian statues whose outlines enliven the sky. The top floor houses the **Galleria d'Arte Moderna**, which exhibits a broad collection of modern and contemporary art.

The Teatro Massimo and the Politeama are located in the modern part of Palermo. They are connected by the elegant Via Ruggero Settimo, which continues as Viale della Libertà and ends at **La Favorita**, the beautiful public park at the foot of **Monte Pellegrino**, which is about a mile and a quarter from the city of Palermo. The park was originally created as a hunting/fishing preserve and a botanical garden when the Bourbon king Ferdinand III was exiled to Palermo from Naples. This magnificent green oasis continues to be enjoyed by the people who live in or visit Palermo for the woodlands, but also for its variety of well-equipped modern sports facilities and ample parking.

The **Palazzina Cinese** (Chinese Palace) at the edge of La Favorita became the summer palace of Ferdinand I of the Two Sicilies (the kingdom of Naples and Sicily) and his consort Maria Carolina, who lived in forced exile in Palermo at the end of the eighteenth century during the French occupation of most of southern Italy. The many design elements and Chinoiserie decorations make the Palazzina exotic and unique; it remains an unusual bit of eighteenth-century whimsy.

In the halls adjoining the Palazzina Cinese is the **Museo Etnografico Siciliano Pitrè**, housing the collection of Giuseppe Pitrè, an Italian folklorist who died in 1916. Pitrè compiled a twenty-five-volume collection of Sicilian oral culture, which offers a fascinating look at Sicilian customs, folklore, and typical and traditional activities such as farming, hunting, and creative handicrafts. On display are ceramics, embroideries, carpet weaving, costumes, children's toys, and even musical instruments. The collection also includes the typical *carretti siciliani* (Sicilian carts), now seen only in museums, and a traditional working *teatru ri pupi* (puppet theater). The objects put together by Pitrè and his foresight in doing so when it was still possible to collect them makes this one of the most interesting collections of its kind in Sicily.

The once glorious twelfth-century **Castello della Zisa** was originally reflected in a pond and surrounded by the lush vegetation of a park. Originally a residence for the Norman kings, it was purchased and restored by the **Regione Siciliana** and merits a visit. It is an elegant building with an interesting collection on the second floor, which houses the **Museum of Arab Art and Culture**.

Piazza Guglielmo il Buono. Open Monday to Saturday 9 a.m. to 1 p.m. and 3 p.m. to 7 p.m., and Sunday 9 a.m. to 12 p.m.

Midway between La Zisa and La Cuba, the twelfth-century summer place built by William III is the **Convento dei Cappuccini** (Capuchin Convent), rebuilt in 1623 above the remains of the original medieval church. A visit to the **catacombe** is a fascinating experience. The natural temperature and humidity of the catacombs allow the cadavers to dehydrate so that they are preserved and mummified. Thousands of cadavers, many fully clothed in garments of the period, have been preserved throughout the centuries and are hung or laid out on shelves. There are both clergy and laity, including women, some eerily dressed in their wedding gowns, probably victims of childbirth. The most recent body to have been mummified is that of a small child, placed there in 1920 when she died at age two. The perfectly preserved body, with its wispy hair tied in a ribbon and eyelashes still in place, is a strange sight indeed, even seemingly unreal in its eternal sleep. Giuseppe Tomasi di Lampedusa, author of *The Leopard,* was buried in the cemetery of the Cappuccini upon his death in 1957.

Monastero dei Cappuccini, Piazza Cappuccini 1. Open daily 9 a.m. to 12 p.m. and 3 p.m. to 5 p.m.; during summer months, open until 7 p.m.

La Cuba is a twelfth-century Norman palace and like La Zisa was built in a park. La Cuba, encircled by a pond, was used as a pavilion for whiling away summer afternoons. It was so famous in its time that Giovanni Boccaccio set one of his novellas from *The Decameron* in this pleasure palace. The sixth story of the fifth day is one in which a lovely young woman is kidnapped from Ischia and given to King Frederick of Sicily, who keeps her in La Cuba. The austere but graceful building is now a military building, which can be visited.

Corso Calatafimi 1:00. Open Monday to Saturday 9 a.m. to 7 p.m., Sunday 9 a.m to 1 p.m.

The **Parco Letterario Tomasi di Lampedusa** is the headquarters for learning more about the life and places dear to Giuseppe Tomasi di Lampedusa, great writer, linguist, and man of learning. There are exhibitions, guided tours, gastronomic programs, "sentimental" journeys, etc.

Vicolo Della Neve all'Alloro 2-5 (near Piazza Marina). Tel: 39 (091)616-0796. Friends have recommended the affordable and well-located Grande Albergo Sole Corso Vittorio Emanuele 291. 90133; Palermo Tel: 39 (091) 604-1111.

MONTE PELLEGRINO

Monte Pellegrino stands high and keeps watch over Palermo. With cliffs rising on all sides of the mountain, except the south, it is the crown of Palermo. The drive to the peak offers some of the most spectacular panoramic views of the city of Palermo, the Conca d'Oro, the coast, and the intensely blue Mediterranean. The faithful make pilgrimages to the **Santuario di Santa Rosalia**, which is the shrine of the Patron Saint of Palermo. Santa Rosalia was a hermit who took refuge in a cave in Monte Pellegrino, where she died in 1166. On her feast day of July 15 there is a procession in Palermo, and on September 4, the procession goes to the **santuario** (sanctuary) on Monte Pellegrino.

Continuing north, in an inlet between Monte Pellegrino and Monte Gallo, is the **Lido di Palermo**, the beach of **Mondello**, a beautiful sandy beach offering sunning, swimming, and dining, as well as the lively nightlife of Mondello.

USTICA

The island of **Ustica** is located thirty-six miles off the northern coast of Palermo. It is also known as **La Perla Nera del Mediterraneo** (Black Pearl of the Mediterranean) because of the black volcanic rock. The island is actually the tip of an underwater volcano. Established as the first Italian **marine reserve**, its crystalline and unpolluted blue-green water, the abundance of corals, sponges, sea plants, and fish, many in extraordinary shapes and colors, make it a heavenly area for underwater photography, swimming, snorkeling, scuba diving, underwater exploration, and fishing. Circling the island by boat reveals magnificent underwater caves such as the **Grotta Azzurra**, which are entered through a beautiful natural arch; **Grotta delle Barche**; **Grotta dell'Oro**; and countless others can be explored all along the rocky coastline. The **Museo di Archeologia Sottomarina** (Museum of Underwater Archaeology) offers fantastic deep-sea archeological tours, which explore sites of underwater treasures on the seabed. During the fascist regime, Ustica was used to exile political dissenters. Antonio Gramsci, one of the founders of the Italian Communist Party, who was sent there in December 1926, came to appreciate the isolation of the place. He made the best of the situation by exploring the island during his daily walks and wrote to his wife about the intense blue sea and sky and the magnificent rainbows. Today, Ustica is easily accessible, and its land, coast, and sea exploration is a source of knowledge and great pleasure.

MONREALE

Monreale is a town just south of Palermo known for its duomo, a bedazzling work of Norman, Arab, and Byzantine artistic styles, framed by traditional Romanesque architecture. The duomo's elegantly austere façade does not prepare the visitor for the amazing interior, studded with mosaics and figures depicted in mosaics, many on a background of gold mosaic tiles. Sicilians say, *"Cu veni a Palermu e nun va a Murriali vieni sceccu e torna maiali"* (He who comes to Palermo and doesn't go to Monreale arrives as a donkey and returns as a pig). Seeing this most grandiose work of human creativity, ingenuity, and craftsmanship can be life-changing.

A first glance at the main altar reveals the enormous Christ the Pantocrator, twelve meters (thirty-four feet) across by seven meters (twenty-two feet) tall, in the vault of the apse. His eyes follow you as his blessing arms embrace the congregation. Below the Christ sits **Mary Enthroned**, flanked by angels and saints, and below her are figures in clerical garb, solemn like all the others, isolated against the gold background. Just behind the altar, a repeat pattern cuts a horizontal band from which vertical strips of different mosaic patterns encircle the entire space. The elaborate capitals of the magnificent white marble columns and the arches they support form a counterpoint to the spectacular mosaics. Monreale is a place to take delight in every surface and every change of color, to revel in the richness of the patterns and biblical compositions, and to marvel at the perfect integration of all these elements. The duomo's **chiostro** (cloister) is the only part of the original monastery to have survived intact to the present day. The walks are buttressed by some two hundred double columns that hold up the graceful, pointed arches. They are marvelously diverse in design, some covered with mosaics and others decorated with beautiful bas-reliefs. The Arab fountain in the corner is like a small cloister of its own, with its own four-sided colonnade. With its magical gardens, the cloister is a showcase of Sicilian, Arabic, and Byzantine craftsmanship.

BAGHERIA

Nine miles south of Palermo is the town of **Bagheria**. A suburb of Palermo, where the eighteenth- and nineteenth-century nobles competed to build summer villas on a grand scale, it was brought to the world's attention by native son Giuseppe Tornatore, who filmed *Cinema Paradiso* there. Famed contemporary writer Dacia Maraini wrote about her childhood in her memoir *Bagheria*. The sumptuous **Villa Valguarnera** was her childhood home. Left to the Jesuit order by one of her aunts, it was sold because of the high cost to maintain it and is now once again in private hands.

The grand **Villa Cattolica**, built in 1736, juxtaposes its Baroque architecture with its collection of contemporary art housed in the **Galleria Comunale d'Arte Moderna e Contemporanea**. This collection was enriched by a large donation of works by Bagheria native **Renato Guttuso**, a famous painter to whom the gallery is dedicated. After his death in 1987, his friend, the equally famous sculptor **Giacomo Monzù**, designed a memorial for him in the park of the villa where he is buried. One of the curiosities of Villa

Cattolica is the **Stanza dello Scirocco**, an artificial cave used as a kind of naturally air-conditioned refuge on days when the hot and humid scirocco winds blow in from Africa.
Villa Consolare 9. Open Tuesday to Sunday 10 a.m. to 6 p.m.

Construction on **Villa Palagonia**, designed for Francesco Gravina, Prince of Palagonia, was begun in 1737 and continued over a decade. Also called the Villa of Monsters, because it was decorated by Gravina's eccentric grandson, Ferdinando Gravina Alliata, it originally housed some two hundred statues, ranging from odd to bizarre. Many people have seen the sculptures, but it was Johan Heinrich Bartels, quoted by Dominique Fernandez in his book *Grand Tour in Sicilia*, who said, "Fortunately they are made of such a soft and fast deteriorating stone that we needn't worry about passing them on to future generations as a monument to bad 18th century taste." So far that wish has been fulfilled, as only sixty of the two hundred statues survive, although those sixty continue to attract the interest and curiosity of the villa's many visitors.
Piazza Garibaldi. Open daily April to October 9 a.m. to 1 p.m. and daily November to March 9 a.m. to 1 p.m. and 3:30 p.m. to 5:30 p.m.

SEGESTA

Driving from Palermo to **Segesta** affords the traveler a view from afar of a magnificent Doric temple. It was built in about 430–420 BCE and never completely finished. Set southwest of Palermo on the slopes of **Monte Barbaro** and overlooking a vast panorama, the temple is splendidly isolated, surrounded by arid land and the characteristic low vegetation of the region. This ancient miracle survives intact after twenty-four centuries, making it one of the most important surviving Hellenistic temples in the world. It is possible to walk to the adjacent pine woods to take photographs or simply admire the temple's elegant proportions and the grace of its thirty-six columns framed by the lacy greenery. Equally splendid views can be enjoyed from the Teatro Greco (Greek Theater), which stands atop Monte Barbaro and faces north, offering views of the surrounding hills all the way to the Gulf of Castellammare. The classic plays performed in the Teatro Greco during the summer are a special treat in this wonderful setting.

Before leaving the province of Palermo, a word about the Mafia, which has been one of the many oppressors of the people of Sicily, is in order. Aided for years by the climate of fear, corruption, and by the rule of *omertà* (silence), it took the outrage of the entire country following the assassinations of Carlo Alberto Dalla Chiesa and his young wife in 1982 and Giovanni Falcone and Paolo Borsellino in 1992 to finally break the Mafia's stranglehold on Sicily.

Chief of Police Carlo Alberto Dalla Chiesa and magistrates Giovanni Falcone and Paolo Borsellino had been making enormous headway in the arrest, prosecution, and conviction of Mafia criminals. These fearless, committed public officials proposed and enacted legislation to confiscate illegally obtained money, goods, and property and made it a criminal offense merely to be a member of the Mafia. This legislation, together with the collaboration of the local people, broke the wall of silence that had protected this criminal element, making it possible for these outlaws to be arrested, charged, and brought to justice. The dedicated and energetic mayor of Palermo, Leoluca Orlando, carried on the reform and rebirth of Palermo through massive civic education, adherence to the rule of law, and the enactment of effective legislation. Through these efforts and in partnership with its citizens, Palermo was reclaimed. The criminals and those in government who were corrupted by them know that they can no longer hide behind the protection of omertà.

CHAPTER 12

TRAPANI

The province of Trapani takes great pride in having been at the forefront of important ecological and conservative initiatives. From the establishment of the Riserva Naturale dello Zingaro, the protection of the Saline (salt works), and the ever growing Pescaturismo, the region has led the country in responsible preservation of its natural gifts.

SAN VITO LO CAPO

At the northern end of a promontory which juts out at the northwestern tip of the Gulf of Catellammare is the lovely town of San Vito Lo Capo, a seaside resort located on a beautiful stretch of coast blanketed by a welcoming fine sandy beach. Situated about 7 miles from the northern entrance of the Riserva Naturale dello Zingaro, which is the great pride of Sicilian conservation, the rugged coastline is a wonder of coves, inlets, and shimmering blue sea with vestiges of unspoiled land and vegetation rich with native Mediterranean flora and fauna, making it a true national treasure. The landscape, with its silver olives, imposing carobs, brilliant yellow broom, when in bloom, and dwarf palms is really wondrous. The Riserva protects the ecology of the area, preserving the habitat for a large array of native species of both plants and animals and making it a treasure trove for those who travel to its shores to hike, study, explore, and observe and to delight in the spectacular views and panoramas of this magnificent natural wonder.

ERICE

Southwest of San Vito Lo Capo, in the lovely town of Erice, which is strategically located on **Monte San Giuliano** above the city of Trapani, you feel transported in time. The town's scale, the appearance of the streets, the cream-colored stone houses with their unique windows opening onto a ledge next to the door, the alleyways, often turning into stone staircases, and the cobblestone streets paved in different patterns all give Erice a quiet grace and balance.

It is possible to peek into the many flower-filled private alleyways and courtyards, where people sit behind their gates as they work and converse while keeping an eye on children at play. The patterns of the streets are each more inventive in design than the next, and the light reflected from the white stone is dazzling. The location affords spectacular views, and on a clear day the Tunisian coast of Africa as well as Mount Etna on the other side of Sicily can be seen. The sight of turrets, wooded areas, vineyards, cliffs, islands, and the splendid Mediterranean create a marvelous patchwork of natural and man-made beauty.

The plan of the city is a well-delineated triangle. Beginning at its base is the fourteenth-century **Chiesa Matrice**, which is dedicated to **La Madonna Assunta** (the Assumption). It has a beautiful Gothic portal and imposing bell tower, and the structure, entirely decorated with castle-like crenellations, is the home of a lovely *Madonna col Bambino* (*Madonna with Child*), a beautiful statue created in 1469 by Domenico Gagini, and a marble altarpiece created in 1513 by Giuliano Mancino.

Piazza Matrice is open daily from 9 a.m. to 1 p.m. and 3:30 p.m. to 7 p.m.

Corso Vittorio Emanuele, the *strada principale* (or main street), which is pleasantly lined with shops and tempting pasticcerie, rises uphill to the **municipio** (town hall) housing the **Museo Civico Antonio Cordici.** The collection, with many artifacts taken from the necropolis of Erice, includes a little head of Aphrodite, dating back to the fifth-century BCE. Noteworthy is the bas-relief of *L'Annunciazione* (*The Annunciation*) by Antonello Gagini, created 2,000 years later. Piazza Umberto 1, just off of Corso Vittorio Emanuele. Open Monday to Friday 9 a.m. to 1:30 p.m., Monday and Thursday 2:30 p.m. to 5:30 p.m., and Sunday 9 a.m. to 2 p.m.

The **Giardino del Ballo,** named after the Norman governor Baiulo, is a beautiful nineteenth-century English-style public garden, perched high on a citadel of the old city and brimming over with flowers in well-tended beds. Go there to visit the gardens and experience the truly spectacular view of the Trapani plains, the Egadi Islands, and other distant vistas.

Adjoining the gardens is the twelfth-century **Castello di Venere** (Venus Castle), built where the ancient temple of the Venere Erycina once stood at the summit of **Monte San Giuliano.** Standing there affords the most breathtaking and memorable views of all. Looking down, the **Palazzina Pepoli,** originally built as a hunting lodge in 1880 and now the symbol of Erice, can be seen perched dramatically on its ledge.

The September **Festivale di Musica Medioevale e Rinascimentale** (Festival of Medieval and Renaissance Music) draws an international audience, as does the well-known **Centro Internazionale di Cultura Scientifica Ettore Majorana** (Ettore Majorana International Science Center), which hosts international scientific conferences of great importance and has literally put this enchanting town on the map.

The delicious **dolci ericini,** which in the past were traditionally made in the convents, are now available at the famous **Pasticceria Grammatico** in via Vittorio Emanuele. The owner of the pasticceria, Maria Grammatico, learned the age-old techniques of making the delicious sweets during the time when she lived in the **Instituto Don Carlo** during World War II. Her moving story was made famous in Mary Taylor Simeti's book *Bitter Almonds*. The pasticceria is a welcome stop as you visit this magnificent town, which must be seen on foot to savor its every corner.

Trapani

The Greek name for Trapani was Drepanon, or "sickle," named for the shape of its harbor. The **saline** (salt pans), fishing (particularly tuna fishing), fish salting industries, coral carving, and goldsmithing give Trapani its economic base. Important to this day are the protection and conservation of the traditions tied to these typical industries. The salt ponds dotted by graceful windmills characterize the city. The province, of which Trapani is the capital, has been in the forefront of environmental conservation by keeping the sea unpolluted and by protecting the salt marshes even though salt is still extracted. Trapani has shown leadership in setting up the important **Riserva Naturale dello Stagnone** (Stagnone Nature Reserve). Since its inauguration, **pescaturismo** (fish tourism) has been very successful as a unique venture that allows tourists the opportunity to enjoy, learn about, and participate in fishing and exploring the sea, the gulf, and the nearby islands by going out with experienced local fishermen. Fish is king in Trapani. The most typical dish is **cuscus** (couscous) served with fish, which demonstrates the importance of seafood to the economy and to the cuisine, while recalling the Arab ancestry of this area. Trapani is still an important port, and it is from there that tourists can reach the Egadi Islands and the island of Pantelleria.

Piazza Vittorio Veneto with its **Palazzo d'Alì**, the town hall, is the center of the town. The nearby **Villa Margherita** is a wonderful green oasis in which to stop for a restful breath of fresh air. If you are there in July, don't miss one of the open-air opera, ballet, or musical theater events of the **Luglio Musicale Trapanese**, with productions given in the park at 9 p.m. The Ente Luglio Musicale Trapanese on Viale Regina Margherita, Villa Margherita (Tel/Fax 39 (0923) 22934) also sponsors the Giuseppe Di Stefano international music competition, named for the famous Sicilian tenor.

Piazza Vittorio Veneto leads to **Rua Nova**, also called by its modern name, **Via Garibaldi**. Laid out in the thirteenth century, it is Trapani's main street and is lined with beautiful churches, statues, and the eighteenth-century palazzi of the local nobility. The second main thoroughfare of the town, **Corso Vittorio Emanuele**, is a pedestrian area also called **Rua Grande** and dates from the thirteenth century. Lined with elegant Baroque *palazzi*, it is the spot favored by Trapanesi for the evening *passeggiata* (stroll). The seventeenth-century **Cattedrale di San Lorenzo**, built on the site of an earlier fourteenth-century building, has a beautiful eighteenth-century Baroque façade.

Although work on the façade of the **Chiesa del Purgatorio**, which is near Piazza Garibaldi, was begun at the end of the seventeenth century, its façade was redone in the eighteenth century. It is divided into two sections and ornamented with twelve statues of the Apostles. It also houses the famous sculptures of the **Misteri**, twenty groups of life-sized seventeenth- and eighteenth-century sculpted wooden figures depicting Christ's passion, that are carried in an annual procession on Good Friday. This is one of the longest, oldest, and most famous processions in all of Italy.

Open daily from 8:30 a.m. to 12:30 p.m. and 4 p.m. to 8 p.m.

A walk east leads to the **Palazzo della Giudecca**, a dignified sixteenth-century building with a lovely portal. It stands as a testament to the once-thriving Jewish quarter and community that for centuries had been an integral part of the city until the people were expelled by a foreign power from a distant land. Guideccas were Jewish settlements in many parts of Italy and Sicily that dated from Roman times. The Jews of Sicily were expelled by a decree from Spain in 1492, ordering Jews who were not willing to convert to Christianity banished from Spain and all its occupied territories, which included Sicily. Many of the Jewish families settled in Ferrara and Ancona in the Italic peninsula, long before Italy existed as a nation, and they remain there today, although they still trace their roots to Sicily.

The story of one such family is told by Dr. Lucia Servadio Bedarida, who was born in 1900 and was still vibrant at 105 years of age. Dr. Bedarida, a physician by profession, came to the United States after she and her physician husband founded the Italian Hospital of Tangiers after they were forced to move there from their native Italy just before World War II. She came to live in the United States in the 1980s with her family and wrote an autobiographical essay that appears in the 2002 book, *The Most Ancient of Minorities: The Jews of Italy*, edited by Stanislao G. Pugliese.

From the Palazzo della Giudecca a ride north on Via XXX Gennaio and east on Via G.B. Fardella past Piazza Martiri d'Ungheria onto Via Conte A. Pepoli leads to the L'Annunziata and to the Museo Regionale Agostino Pepoli. The **Santuario dell'Annunziata** is the most important church in Trapani. It retains the original fourteenth-century façade with its lovely rose window, the early fifteenth-century Gothic portal, and the seventeenth-century Baroque campanile, or bell tower. The interior pays homage to the importance of the sea with the sixteenth-century **Cappella dei Pescatori** and the **Cappella dei Marinai**, the chapels dedicated to fishermen and sailors. On the altar is the **Madonna di Trapani**, attributed to Nino Pisano. Equally noteworthy is the **Cappella della Madonna**, situated behind the high altar that boasts a marble arch decorated with the beautiful reliefs created by brothers **Antonino and Giacomo Gagini** between 1531 and 1537.

Open daily 8 a.m. to 4 p.m. Tel: 39 (0923) 432-111.

The **Museo Regionale Agostino Pepoli** is housed in the cloister of L'Annunziata, a former fourteenth-century Carmelite monastery. Count Pepoli began putting together the collection at the beginning of the twentieth century, and today it includes a wonderfully varied collection of archeological artifacts, paintings, sculptures, and lovely coral carvings for which Trapani has been traditionally known. Chief among its treasures is the moving painting of the stigmatization of **San Francesco** (St. Francis) by great sixteenth-century Venetian painter Tiziano Vecellio, known as Titian; *Profilo d'un Vecchio*, (*Profile of an Old Man*) by Sicilian Baroque painter Pietro Novelli; a beautiful marble sculpture of **San Giacomo** (St. James) by Sicilian sculptor Antonello Gagini, whose life spanned the fifteenth and sixteenth centuries; and a magnificent **Natività** (Nativity scene) executed in local coral. This last piece together with others in the collection demonstrate the superb workmanship of Trapanese coral artists and craftsmen. Via Conte Agostino Pepoli 200. Open Monday to Saturday 9 a.m. to 1:30 p.m. and Sunday 9 a.m. to 12:30 p.m. Tel: 39 (0923) 553-269.

South of the city, along the coast between Trapani and Marsala, are the numerous **saline** (salt basins or salt pools). These basins, which began to be built in Phoenician times, are shallow muddy depressions in the salt marshes that stay flooded during the tidal cycle. The extraction of salt is an important local industry that dates back to antiquity. The combination of the water's undiluted salinity, little rainfall, and predictable tides has created the ideal conditions for this industry, and the town's commitment to keeping the sea pollution free ensures the future of this traditional production. The white piles of salt in rhythmic repetition, the reflecting pools, and the windmills make this one of the most unusual and unique landscapes in all of Sicily. The lagoons, which stretch to Mozia, are a natural reserve for many species of migratory birds. Three miles to the south of Trapani is the **Museo delle Saline**, which demonstrates within its building complex and with its beautiful windmills how salt is extracted.

Contrada Nubia, open daily from 9 a.m. to 12 p.m. and from 3 p.m. to 6 p.m.

ISOLE EGADI

The **Isole Egadi** (Egadi Islands) are just southwest of Trapani and can be reached by boat or hydrofoil from the city. The archipelago includes the islands of Favignana, Levanzo, and Marettimo and the reefs of Formica and Maraone.

The largest of the islands in the group is **Favignana**. Its limestone quarries, which once supplied the tufa building stone for

Sicily and even North Africa, are now inactive, but they can be seen by tourists who enjoy hiking in this rugged terrain. The houses of the town, called **dammusi**, are traditional cubic constructions that attest to the Arab ancestry of the islands. In the town, also named Favignana, the houses are grouped in a picturesque cluster on the north shore.

The **mattanza**, or tuna fishing, takes place in the waters off the coast of Favignana. Each year in May the transparent blue water turns into a red sea as the tuna are trapped and then slaughtered. The mattanza still attracts visitors for the annual ritual, and fishing is still very important as an industry and as recreation, particularly since the advent of *pescaturismo*, an initiative in which experienced fishermen take tourists out to sea to have them experience and learn about the island's most important industry. Water sports, including swimming, underwater photography, and scuba diving in the magnificent waters, are a chief attraction.

Tourist information:

Pescaturismo Margherita Charters:

www.pescaturismomargherita.com

Molo Pescherecci 91010, Favignana (TP). Tel.: 333 3813477

Pro Loco in Piazza Madrice (Tel: 39 (0923) 921647) arranges guided tours of the tuna fishery and other excursions.

The island of **Levanzo** has a beautiful town built along a slope on the southern coast. The pastel-colored **dammusi**, as the typical houses are called, crowd around the port like a village in an exotic storybook. The road seems to ascend vertically up the hill behind the cluster of houses before it turns into a more conventional horizontal direction. The hills are covered with shrubbery that intermingles with wild herbs and succulents that carpet the slopes with color and fragrance. The ubiquitous caper plant, with its beautiful white and purple flowers coming from the overgrown buds (which produce the prized capers), peek out from every crevice. The treasure of the island is the **Grotta del Genovese**, which has remarkable cave paintings, remnants of prehistoric human habitation from the Upper Paleolithic era, representing people and animals. Natale Castiglione is the owner and guide who provides tours. He can be reached at 39 (0923) 924-032.

The island of **Marettimo** rises into the summit of **Monte Falcone**. The village of Marettimo is on the east coast, and the island, like the others, has beautiful caves that can be visited. Divers enjoy the crystalline waters, and swimmers and snorkelers delight in the clarity of the aquamarine water and in the richness of the marine life it supports; hikers come for the beautiful scenery, the unspoiled natural growth, and the fragrance of its greenery. This is a restful environment to remember and cherish.

The Island of **Pantelleria**, which is twenty-five miles south and slightly west of Sicily, is actually closer to Tunisia than it is to the island of Sicily. The characteristically low, Arab-inspired cubic dammusi typical of the Egadi Islands keep their inhabitants cool in summer and warm in winter. Exposed to winds blowing north from Africa, the houses are kept low, as are the vines and capers growing in terraced slopes, to provide shelter from the winds. The coastline is made up of jagged cliffs and rocks, which are loved by swimmers, divers, and underwater photographers who come to delight in the clear water, richness and diversity of marine life, and coral, sponges, and occasional ancient wreck sitting on the Mediterranean floor.

Although shrubs, pines, and capers dominate the wild vegetation, Pantelleria, owing to its volcanic soil, hot African winds, and blazing hot sun, produces the hardy zibibbo grapes. Some of these grapes are left to dry on the vine to produce the famous **Moscato Passito di Pantelleria**, an extraordinarily rich dessert wine considered one of the best in Sicily. Pantelleria is also home to curious prehistoric monuments called **sesi**, domed burial mounds in rough stone, some quite large and with several entrances. The largest that has survived is the **Sesi del Re** (King's Tomb). Over time the sesi have provided a natural quarry of stones for the construction of the local dammusi. Another of the beautiful natural wonders of the island is the **Arco dell'Elefante** (Elephant's Arch), a large rock formation that spills into the sea, forming the natural arch that stands as an entrance beckoning into the sea from the lovely cove. The island is well connected to Sicily and the mainland by air or sea.

MOZIA

Back to the mainland going south from Trapani, just before arriving in Marsala, is the **Laguna dello Stagnone**, the largest lagoon in Sicily, with the shallow salt pools and island of **Mozia** visible off the coast. This is the closest island to Sicily, so close that it is connected with an ancient causeway that is still visible in low tide. Covered by shallow water, until fairly recent times it was crossed by the carretti siciliani (sicilian carts) to bring the grape harvest to Marsala. The island was purchased by Joseph Whitaker, whose family was the major producer of Marsala wine. One of the so-called English Sicilians, Whitaker's family came to Sicily in the early nineteenth century. Whitaker began archeological excavations at the beginning of the twentieth century and placed the treasures that were found in the handsome Whitaker Villa, which became the town museum. The highlight of the collection is the magnificent **Giovane con la Tunica** (Youth in a Tunic). Dominique Fernanadez in his book Grand Tour in Sicily calls the figure of the beautiful youth with its clinging tunic "a miracle of elegance and mystery." (*Grand Tour in Sicilia*, p. 93.)

Azienda Autonoma Provinciale per l'Incremento Turistico di Trapani, Via San Francesco d'Assisi, 27. 91100 Trapani. Tel: 39 (0923) 29430. E-mail: apttp@mail.cinet.it.

MARSALA

Marsala, the next city to the south, occupies what the Arabs who invaded the city in the ninth century called Marsa-Allah, or Harbor of God, hence its name. The largest producer of wine in

Sicily, Marsala is known worldwide for its delightful dessert wine. For guided tours of the winery and wine tastings, visit the **Cantine Florio**. Advance reservations are necessary and can be made by calling 39 (0923) 781-111.

Bastions with four gates link the **Piazza della Loggia**, the town's central piazza, enclosing the city within a perfect square; this is unusual for Italians, who generally prefer a less formal balance. The seventeenth-century duomo (cathedral), dedicated to Saint Thomas of Canterbury, has a wonderful set of eight sixteenth-century Flemish tapestries of the capture of Jerusalem, which are on exhibit at the **Museo degli Arazzi Fiamminghi** behind the duomo.

Marsala is very important to the history of Italy as the landing place of **Giuseppe Garibaldi** and **I Mille**—that is, Garibaldi and the "thousand" red shirts who landed in Marsala on May 11, 1860, and, assisted by the population, freed Sicily from Bourbon rule. The date is remembered in the name of the street, Via XI Maggio (Eleventh of May Street), where the **Museo Civico** is located. The museum is devoted to Giuseppe Garibaldi and the unification of Italy, as well as to the folklore and to the archeological history of the region.

The Museo Archeologico, situated along the **Lungomare Boeo**, has a prehistoric collection of artifacts that includes Roman mosaics from **Capo Boeo** and the museum's greatest treasure, a 115-foot third-century BCE Punic ship, the remains of which were discovered in 1969 by English nautical archaeologist Honor Frost. She and her team salvaged and reconstructed the ship, which is the only remaining example in the world of a Carthaginian warship. Important knowledge about ancient shipbuilding was gained through this project, particularly that Phoenician construction included prefabricated sections identified by letters for speedy assembly. They also discovered the use of iron nails, which, amazingly, in two thousand years have not rusted (*Aramco World Magazine*, Nov/Dec 1986).

Open 9 a.m. to 2 p.m. Also Wednesday, Saturday, and Sunday from 4 p.m. to 7 p.m. Tel: (0923) 952-535.

MAZARA DEL VALLO

To the southeast of Marsala is **Mazara del Vallo**, a bustling port at the mouth of the Mazaro River, which even in antiquity was an important trading post. Mazara del Vallo is a vibrant city with a diverse and productive population. It is an important wine-producing area and a major fishing station with one of the best-equipped fishing ports in Sicily. The vitality of the city is best seen in early morning when the fishing boats arrive, sales are negotiated, crates are neatly stacked, and refrigerated trucks are loaded. The city takes pride in its multicultural and multiethnic population. Over eight thousand immigrants from Eastern Europe, Tunisia, and Morocco live with their families in Mazara del Vallo and work in the fishing industry. Indeed, one of the most interesting areas of the city is the Tunisian quarter, centered on **Piazza Bagno**; the colorful streets and alleyways with their shops and typical cafés are an exotic experience.

SELINUNTE

The **Parco Archeologico di Selinunte** embraces a vast territory covered with some of the most glorious creations of man's ingenuity, both past and present. The **Acropolis**, which is the city of Selinunte proper, is located in the middle of the park on high land between the Medione River in the west and the **Gorgo di Cottone** in the east. The name is thought to derive either from the nearby Selinon River or from the Greek *selinon*, a form of wild parsley tasting like celery—the same parsley that mingles with fennel, marguerites, and yellow blooming oxalis carpeting the landscape with low vegetation and scenting the air.

Selinunte was settled between 650 and 630 BCC by the island Greeks of Megara Iblea near Siracusa; the new colony quickly grew in importance but was destroyed by Segesta, its rival to the north, with the help of the Cartheginians. The Romans continued the attacks at the end of the first Punic War. Disastrous earthquakes in medieval times finished the destruction, completely obliterating the site until it was rediscovered in the nineteenth century, when excavations began.

Part of the miracle of Selinunte is that the temples have not only survived but have remained protected from the encroachment of contemporary civilization. The splendid Doric temples are a testament to the builders' skill and esthetic, but the achievement of reconstructing them in modern times from ancient fragments is also quite extraordinary. The beauty of these colossal structures, even the parts where the reconstruction has been incomplete, seems as perfectly realized as the armless *Venus de Milo*.

The temples have been assigned letters of the alphabet, since it is not known to which deities the temples were originally dedicated. Seeing the ancient rubble of the temples makes the twentieth-century restoration of the fourteen columns to **Temple C** all the more impressive. Although the rather complete restoration of **Temple E** in the 1950s raised controversy, the majestic result is awesome because the visitor can easily conjure up the splendor of this ill-fated ancient colony.

East of the Acropolis is **Temple G**, with its one, huge fifty-two-foot-tall column. Re-erected in 1832, it is important because it is one of the most monumental temples in all of antiquity, and its restoration has added immeasurably to modern scientific knowledge of classical civilizations.

CHAPTER **13**

AGRIGENTO

SCIACCA

Sciacca in the province of Agrigento is a picturesque seaside town in the shadow of majestic **Monte San Calogero**. It is built on the shores of the Mediterranean but also extends up the side of the mountain. The houses seem to rise directly out of the sea behind the colorful boats anchored in its busy harbor. Known since ancient times for its therapeutic waters, it is a popular spa and summer resort. The natural terraces divide the city into three sections: north of Via Licata is the medieval section of Terravecchia, between Via Licata and Piazza Scandaliato are the most important buildings, and below the piazza is the harbor. The municipio (town hall) faces **Piazza Scandaliato**, a magnificent terrace superbly located overlooking the sea and a favorite evening meeting place for the townpeople of Sciacca. This is a walking town, so take the steps that lead to the harbor directly from the piazza.

The twelfth-century Norman duomo, which stands east of the town hall, was rebuilt in the seventeenth century with a Baroque façade richly decorated with marble statues, some of which are among the masterworks of Antonello and Domenico Gagini.

The nearby **Casa Museo Scaglione** is an eighteenth-century former private residence, now a museum. It exhibits the collection of Francesco Scaglione, which includes prints, small bronzes, archeological artifacts, a numismatic collection, ceramics, and

153

paintings, primarily by Sicilian artists. The floors have the original locally created majolica tiles for which Sciacca is still famous. Piazza Don Minzoni, 4. Tel: 0925/83089. Open Tuesday to Sunday 8:30 a.m. to 1 p.m. and 3 p.m. to 7 p.m.

Near the magnificent promenade in the eastern part of town is the modern **Grand Hotel delle Terme** (Via della Terme, 92010, Sciacca. Tel. 39 [092] 523-33). There are spectacular views from the promenade and the hotel. The imposing Renaissance **Palazzo Steripinto**, with its diamond-point surface decoration and beautiful twin light mullioned windows, stands as an outstanding example of sixteenth-century Spanish Sicilian architecture.

The hot springs attract visitors who come to treat respiratory and rheumatic diseases in beautiful surroundings enlivened by the wealth of ceramic shops; many of them specialize in the traditional majolica tiles of Sciacca, which are prized and attract the attention of vacationers and foreign tourists. Visit the **Terme Selinuntine**, a beautiful spa complex facing the sea and surrounded by a lovely park (www.termesciacca.it. Tel: 39 [0925] 961-111).

Castello Bentivegna, called the **Castello Incantato** (Enchanted Castle), is the work of folk artist Filippo Bentivegna, who returned to his native town after having spent many years in the United States. He has since dedicated himself to the creation of over three thousand faces carved out of lava stone, which are set in a property he purchased just outside of town and where he creates his sculptures.

Open Tuesday to Saturday 10 a.m. to 12 p.m. and 4 p.m. to 6 p.m.

CASTELBELLOTTA

Visible from Sciacca, though twelve miles inland, is the mountain village of **Caltabellotta**. Because of its three-thousand-foot rocky summit of Monte Castello dominating its gray-roofed houses,

Matteo Collura, author of **Sicilia Sconosciuta** (*The Unknown Sicily*), calls it the most beautiful village he has ever visited anywhere, finding it a place of peace and enchantment. Its place in history was assured as the site for the signing of the thirteenth-century peace treaty that ended the **Vespri Siciliani** (Sicilian Vespers), the rebellion against French rule made famous by Giuseppe Verdi in his opera by the same name. Giovanni Boccaccio also commemorates the event in the *Decameron*.

This lovely medieval town thrived throughout the ages because of a trio of factors: plenty of water, fertile soil, and the town's naturally unassailable location. It has not succumbed to twentieth-century expansion and maintains its traditional look, taking great pride in its picture-book beauty and grace. The recently restored Norman **Chiesa Madre** still boasts its beautiful original portal. **L'Eremo di San Pellegrino**, a monastery set on the western side of the mountain, stands watch over the town, giving it a focal point. Matteo Collura calls Caltabellotta a place for the spirit and a refuge for the imagination.

From the heights of Caltabellotta, a return to the coast offers a treat of another kind.

AGRIGENTO

The ancient city of **Agrigento**, named Akragas by its Greek founders, beautifully situated on a high plain within sight of the glistening Mediterranean, opens up to what can only be described as the magical sight of the fifth-century **Valle dei Templi** (Valley of the Temples). Because of its mild climate, the almond trees bloom in winter, making the valley in early February spectacularly beautiful and delightfully fragrant at the same time. Built on two hills, the city has a fantastic view of the magnificent Greek temples and the blue Mediterranean. Agrigento was the birthplace of fifth-century philosopher Empedocles, twentieth-century Nobel Laureate writer and dramatist Luigi Pirandello, and late-twentieth-century writer Leonardo Sciascia.

The temples are the city's main attraction, but a few other sites are worth visiting, such as the twelfth-century **Cattedrale and Museo Diocesano** on Piazza Minzoni in the northwestern part of Agrigento. The Cattedrale was built high on a site chosen by the ancient Greeks. Because it sits atop a majestic staircase that sets off the elegant façade's portal and massive fifteenth-century bell tower, it has a graceful vertical thrust that belies its mass.

The **Teatro Pirandello**, which is part of the municipio, stands across the way in Piazza Pirandello and comes to life with performances of Pirandello plays during the first week of July or August for the **Settimana Pirandelliana** (Week of Pirandello performances).
Piazza Pirandello. Tel: 39 (0922) 20391.

San Lorenzo, also known as **Chiesa del Purgatorio**, is a splendid Baroque church with an elegant façade; its grand portal between two spiral columns frames a beautiful Baroque door. The church is richly decorated inside and out with allegorical figures representing the **Virtù Cristiane** (Christian virtues), which were created in the early 1700s by brothers Giuseppe and Giacomo Serpotta. The spirited Baroque artwork by the Serpottas is certainly worth a stop. Another reason to visit it is to see the extraordinary fifth-century BCE underground drinking water and drainage system, which was thousands of years ahead of its time at the time of its construction.
Piazza del Purgatorio just off Via Atenea is open daily.

Convento di Santo Spirito and the church, historically known as the Badia Grande, is still one of the best-known churches in the city. The eleventh-century network of church buildings and cloisters, including a Chapter House, was founded by a member of the Chiaramonte family, whose name also describes the architectural style, which features elegantly decorated Gothic façades. In the convent, a beautiful Gothic arch is flanked by twin windows, also set in elegant stone arches with ornamental designs repeating those of the main one. Don't miss seeing the cloister, and before you leave, try the delicious almond sweets and the dessert couscous made by the nuns.

Salita Santo Spirito, above Via Atenea. Open daily 9 a.m. to 1 p.m.

The thirteenth-century Romanesque Church of **San Nicola**, with its simple but austere façade dominated by a beautiful portal, stands in what was the old city on the way to the Valley of the Temples. The front of San Nicola has a spectacular view of the Valley of the Temples, which extends in a wide panorama below the church. The church was constructed from the ruins of the temples, which provided a kind of ready-made quarry for centuries of local construction. Inside the single-nave church is a magnificent Roman sarcophagus of Phaedra. The fifteenth-century wooden crucifix over the altar, **Il Signore della Nave** (The Lord of the Ship), was the inspiration for the Pirandello story by the same name in which he describes the church and the feast that takes place in September.

The **Museo Archeologico Regionale** (Regional Archeological Museum), which incorporates the old cloister of San Nicola with the recently built part, is one of the great museums of Sicily. The collection, which is exhibited in chronological order, abounds in masterpieces, chief among them the colossal twenty-five-foot standing Telemon, or male caryatid, which was reconstructed from its original segments and is beautifully exhibited in its original standing position in Room VI, where the heads of three others are set in niches. Room III displays a magnificent collection of Greek vases in red ware and black ware; among the red-figure pieces is the Chalice Krater, dating back to the fourth century BCE. Room X, which can be seen with special permission, houses a collection of Greek, Roman, Byzantine, and Norman coins minted in gold, silver, and bronze. Room X features the justly famous marble figure of the Ephebus of Agrigento, which dates back to 470 BCE. This is truly a magnificent and beautifully displayed collection.

The view of the Valley of the Temples from above is without question a memorable sight. The antiquities are interspersed among the vegetation, which sometimes appears brightly and other times delicately hued. The rows of trees look like bushes from the distance, and this entire scene creates a magnificent contrast with the brilliantly blue sea.

The archeological area of Agrigento was designated a UNESCO World Heritage Site in 1997 because of the antiquity of the structures, the site's historical importance at the time of its greatest glory, and the remarkable state of survival to the present day. A first glimpse of the temples at night is quite dramatic as the floodlit ancient structures come to life in an extraordinary panoramic view of the valley. But it is in the dazzling Sicilian light that the beauty and elegance of the string of Doric temples can be enjoyed. Each temple was built facing east, as was customary in the Greek tradition, to bathe the front in the rising sun. This magnificent panorama, with its temples from the distant past, is very moving, whether seen for the first or the hundredth time.

The park is divided into the enclosed western zone and the open eastern zone. The temples were built of the local yellow limestone, which, archaeologists believe, might have been covered with a plaster of white marble dust. The stones, some rebuilt, some still on the ground, are softened by the silvery olive and lovely almond trees. This is a special site at all times of the year, but it is particularly beautiful when the almond trees are in full bloom before winter's end in February.

Approaching the temples from the **Strada Panoramica**, the first is the fifth-century **Tempio di Giunone** (Temple of Juno; *Hera* to the Greeks). It stands on a hill isolated from the rest and dominates the surroundings from its elevation. Similar in size to the Temple of Concord, all the columns on its southern side have been preserved, as have some on the eastern side. A view of the entire valley can be enjoyed from this temple.

Continuing west on Via Sacra is the fifth-century BCE **Tempio della Concordia** (Temple of Concord), which is one of the best preserved Doric temples in the world. The fact that it was converted into a Christian basilica at a later time accounts for its excellent state of preservation. Although the pediment and metopes are lost, this magnificent temple was restored to its original classical form in the eighteenth century.

The next temple is the sixth-century BCE **Tempio di Ercole** (Temple of Hercules), which is the oldest temple in Agrigento. Much of it is still in ruin, but the eight standing columns were re-erected in the early twentieth century.

A path to the right leads to the entrance of the **catacombe**, or the catacombs, which are open to the public and interesting to visit.

Just past and to the left of the **Piazzale dei Templi** (Square of the Temples), which was the ancient **Agorà** and still functions as a public space and a market place, is the **Tomba di Terone** (Tomb of Theron), a Roman tribute to one of the rulers of Agrigento.

On the western side of the Piazzale stands the **Tempio di Zeus Olimpico** (Temple of Olympian Zeus). Although left unfinished, this temple was or would have been the largest Doric temple ever built. The pediment of this grand temple was held up by columns and Telomones, or giant caryatids, giving height, elegance, and lightness to what was in fact a massive construction. This, of course, was the genius of ancient Greek architects. A sandstone copy of a Telemon rests on the ground, immense and heavy, not in the way it was meant to be seen but interesting nevertheless, especially when compared to one of the original ones standing in the Museo Archeologico.

Just northwest of the Temple of Zeus are the **Sacelli e l'Altare della Divinità** (Sanctuary of the Chthonic Divinities). Nearby is a shrine dedicated to Demeter and Persephone with a round altar. The wonderful book by Mary Taylor Simeti, *On Persephone's Island*, gives life to this important deity.

Southwest of the altar is the **Tempio di Castore e Polluce** (Temple of Castor and Pollux), named for the twin sons of Zeus. It was erected in the early nineteenth century from found pieces not original to the structure, but these four columns have become so familiar that they have achieved their own grace and have become the symbol of Agrigento.

South of the row of temples between the Temple of Concord and the Temple of Hercules stands the **Tempio di Asclepio** (Temple of Asclepius). Dedicated to the god of healing, it is located in the midst of an almond grove west of the river **Akragas**, which retains the ancient name for Agrigento.

For a super-deluxe treat, stay at the **Hotel Villa Athena** within view of the Tempio della Concordia, or have a lovely dinner in the torch-lit terrace while enjoying the magic of the temple. Visitors might also consider lunch in this excellent and wonderfully located restaurant: Via Passeggiata Archeologica 33. Reservations a must. Tel: 39 (0922) 596-288.

Open daily 8:30 a.m. to 7 p.m. Tickets at the East and West entrances to the Valley of the Temples. Tel: 39 (0922) 497-341.

The **Casa Natale di Luigi Pirandello**, the birthplace of the author of **Novelle per un Anno** (*Short Stories for a Year*), **Enrico IV** (*Henry the IV*), and **Sei Personaggi in Cerca d'Autore** (*Six Characters in Search of an Author*), is a museum with objects and belongings pertaining to Pirandello's life. The urn containing his ashes is embedded in a rock on the grounds of his house under Pirandello's favorite pine tree.

The **Biblioteca Luigi Pirandello** (Pirandello Library) has a large selection of books by Sicilian authors.

The museum/house is located in Contrada Kaos near Agrigento. Open Monday to Saturday 9 a.m. to 1 p.m. and 2 p.m. to 7 p.m. Tel: 39 (0922) 511-826.

The library is located in Via Regione Siciliana 120, Agrigento.

Parco Letterario Luigi Pirandello, Il Cerchio, Via Ugo La Malfa a monte 1, Agrigento. Tel: (0922) 402-862, www.parcopirandello.it.

PORTO EMPEDOCLE

Southwest of Agrigento is **Porto Empedocle**, the embarkment point for ferries to the **Isole Pelagie** (Pelagie Islands), comprising the three islands of Lampedusa and Linosa, which are limestone islands, and Lampione, which in reality is the tip of an inactive volcano. There are also flights from Palermo. The Pelagie archipelago is actually closer to Africa than it is to Sicily, and the gentle winds from Africa, the delightfully chilly summer nights, crystalline waters, and rich marine life are making these rather distant islands a summer tourist attraction.

ISOLE PELAGIE – PELAGIE ISLANDS

Lampedusa takes its name from author Giuseppe Tomasi di Lampedusa's family, who owned it until the mid-nineteenth century. Although the island can be explored overland, the best way to experience it is to take a boat trip around the coast to see lovely grottos, dramatic cliffs, and secluded coves and inlets. Dammusi, the traditional houses that still dot the island, are simple cube constructions of Moorish origin. One of the beaches of Lampedusa, the **Baia dell'Isola dei Conigli**, a wide sandy bay, with a little island in the middle, is a natural reserve set up to protect the Caretta Caretta sea turtles who lay their eggs and then bury them in the white sand. When the little turtles are hatched, they make their mad dash to the sea before they can be attacked by predators.

Seals sun themselves on the more isolated shores, and falcons can be seen against the magnificent blue sky. Because of the deforestation that took place in the nineteenth century, there is little agriculture, but the rugged natural environment is still rich in flora and fauna. The chief attraction is the sea, with its rich variety of marine life, including coral and sponges, which are still harvested. But most of all, it is the magnificent clear water, with its emerald, turquoise, aquamarine, and cobalt hues, that attracts people to these unspoiled shores. The cuisine is Sicilian but is strongly influenced by the Tunisian fisherman population. The couscous made with the local fresh fish is outstanding.

Linosa, with its cliffs plunging into the deep blue sea, is a haven for divers, snorkelers, and scuba divers. The typical houses are pastel colored with the windows, doors, and the corners of the buildings outlined in red. The volcanic soil is fertile and provides pasture land for the cattle raised on the island. The three dark peaks of the island stand out against the sky. Cala Pozzolana, the only beach and port on the island, is surrounded by cliffs in an amazing spectrum of colors from bright yellow to dark red.

The island of Lampione houses a solitary lighthouse but is otherwise uninhabited. Its vertical cliffs rising out of the uncontaminated water offer an underwater haven for scuba divers and sportsmen interested in underwater explorations.

CHAPTER 14

CALTANISSETTA

CALTANISSETTA

Caltanissetta, built high on a hill with gentle slopes, is located in the very center of Sicily in a glorious location with magnificent sweeping views. In the nineteenth century, the wealth of the town came from the sulfur mines, which were major producers and exporters. Eventually, with greater competition and diminished demand, the area turned to agriculture.

Tourist information: Corso Vittorio Emanuele 109. Tel: (0934) 530-411.

Piazza Garibaldi is at the intersection of the town's two main streets, Corso Vittorio Emanuele and Corso Umberto I, and is the lively historic center of town. The **municipio**, or town hall, stands on the northeastern corner of the two streets with the sixteenth-century **Palazzo Moncada** next to it on Via Umberto I.

The **Cattedrale**, also known as the church of Santa Maria la Nuova, is a handsome late-Renaissance-style building enhanced with a nineteenth-century cupola. It is located on Piazza Garibaldi.

Across the piazza is **San Sebastiano**, an imposing Baroque church with a grand columned façade and an equally grand *campanile*, or bell tower. The middle of the piazza is defined by the **Fontana del Tritone**, a 1956 work by native artist Michele Tripisciano.

The church of **Sant'Agata**, up the street from the municipio, occupies a lovely location on the Corso Umberto. Built in the early seventeenth century, it has a graceful façade designed with dark red decorations that contrast with the marble and the dark volcanic tufa stone. The interior is beautifully decorated in stucco and multicolored marble. Behind the church is the **biblioteca comunale**, or public library.

A short walk away from Piazza Garibaldi, taking Via San Domenico to the left of the Cattedrale, is the sixteenth century **Chiesa di San Domenico**, with its eighteenth-century convex façade. Open 4:00 p.m. to 5:30 p.m. Tel: (0934) 25-104.

Caltanissetta has two museums, the **Museo Archeologico**, which incorporates exhibits from the Museo Civico and reflects the history of the area going back to ancient times through interesting artifacts discovered in the province, and the **Museo Mineralogico**, which is tied to the city's traditional mining of sulfur and other minerals. Housed in the Istituto Tecnico Industriale, the museum showcases the varicolored and crystalline composition of sulfur and other minerals that are extracted in the area and also exhibits minerals from other parts of the world. The equipment and tools used for the extraction and refining of sulfur in the nineteenth and early twentieth century is of special interest. Fortunes were made and lost in the sulfur mines. The family of Nobel laureate Luigi Pirandello went into ruin after the mine that had belonged to his wife and was being managed by his father was flooded. The wife's psychological frailty plagued the couple for the rest of their marriage.

Museo Archeologico: Via Napoleone Colajanni (near the railroad station). Open daily 9 a.m. to 1 p.m. and 3:30 p.m. to 7:30 p.m. Closed on the last Monday of the month. Tel: (0934) 504-240.

The best time to visit Caltanissetta is during Easter week. Festivities begin on Wednesday with the **Processione dei Misteri**, in which devotional sculptures of the Passion of Christ are taken in procession along the streets of the city accompanied by the clergy, the representatives of the confraternities or religious brotherhoods, and the devout, culminating on Good Friday in the procession of the Black Christ.

Racalmuto

Racamulto, the birthplace in 1921 of another great twentieth century writer, **Leonardo Sciascia**, was also the setting of many of his stories. His depiction of the sulfur mines and the exploitation of its labor force is from the perspective of a person who had lived there most of his life and knew his subject intimately. As a young man he taught elementary school in town, and that experience inspired him to write one of the masterpieces, *Le Parrocchie di Regalpetra* (*The Praises of Regalpetra*), a fictitious town patterned after his birthplace. In this writings, Sciascia represented the region's history, culture, ideas, and ideals, and gave life to powerful characters, yet he never shied away from Sicily's problems. A promoter of social justice, he was elected to national public office and served until his untimely death from cancer in 1989. The center of Racalmuto houses the seventeenth century Chiesa Madre Dell'Annunziata with its Gothic style façade and two bell towers, one with a clock and the other with a sun dial.

Parco Letterario Leonardo Sciascia. Fondazione Leonardo Sciascia, Viale della Vittoria 3, Racalmuto, Tel: 39 (0922) 941-933.

Gela

The province of Caltanissetta reaches to the Mediterranean with Gela on the coast. The Greeks founded Gela shortly after Siracusa in the seventh-century BCE. The classic writer Aeschylus, who lived both in Greece and in Sicily, died in Gela, where he was living at the time. Legend has it that an eagle dropped a turtle to break its shell and it hit the poet on the head, killing him. The contemporary city was made famous during World War II when American troops disembarked in Gela during their invasion of Sicily. The discovery of oil in the 1950s has led to the industrialization of the city with petrochemical plants.

Gela has an important museum, the **Museo Archeologico Regionale**, with a chronologically arranged collection of artifacts from local archeological sites and a wonderful collection of Greek vases from necropolises in the area, as well as coins and works in terra-cotta. The painted terra-cotta vases from Gela were sought after in antiquity. Located at the eastern end of the city in Corso Vittorio Emanuele. Open 9 a.m. to 1 p.m. and 3 p.m. to 6:30 p.m. Tel: 39 (0933) 912-626.

Near the museum is the ancient **Acropolis**, which is divided into a temple zone and what was the inhabited section to the north. One column remains from one of the two ancient temples. On the other side of town, more of Gela's classic past can be seen. Northwest of the city are the fortifications of **Capo Soprano**, a site that was protected for ages by high sand dunes and was only discovered in the mid-twentieth century. Remains of the original walls, now protected by Plexiglass because of their fragility, are visible.

Open from 9 a.m. to one hour before sundown. Tel: 39 (0933) 930-975.

North along the golden sandy beaches of the coast is the beautiful **Castello di Falconara**, which seems to grow straight out of the rock. The castle stands majestically on its magnificent promontory facing the sea. The name of the castle, which is now privately owned, comes from its former use, which was to train falcons.

CHAPTER 15

ENNA

Enna is located in the very center of Sicily, but distinguishes itself as the provincial capital city with the highest elevation in all of Italy. Built on a high plateau ending in a peak inhabited all the way to the top (an altitude of over three thousand feet), it naturally attracts visitors for the enchanting views of the surrounding fertile land and the distant vistas. Enna is the only province that does not reach the sea, but it compensates as the belvedere, or panoramic balcony, of Sicily, with arresting views of the Madonie Mountains and even of Mount Etna, which can be seen on the east coast of the island. The altitude naturally affects the weather, sometimes causing Enna to be enveloped in fog but also delightfully reducing the summer temperature. Beautiful Norman castles, lovely hill towns, and its main glory, the magnificent Villa Casale in Piazza Armerina, are its pride and joy.

The fourteenth-century duomo retains its original apses and transept, although when the church was rebuilt after a devastating fire, it was given its stately sixteenth-century entrance with a lovely bas relief from the life of **San Martino**. The main façade, however, with its perfectly centered eighteenth-century campanile, is set on a magnificent and very dramatic sculptural staircase with a set of semicircular stairs projecting out in front. The cattedrale stands imposingly like a stage set framed by the intense blue sky.

Adjoining the duomo is the **Museo Alessi**, which exhibits clerical vestments, candelabra, the precious gold and diamond

studded Madonna's Crown, an excellent numismatic collection, and the art gallery, all of which are part of the **tesoro**, or treasury of the cathedral.
Museo Alessi is open Tuesday to Sunday 9 a.m. to 1 p.m. Tel: 39 (0935) 24-072.

The **Palazzo Varisano**, facing the duomo, houses the **Museo Archeologico**, which has a collection of prehistoric, Greek, and Roman archeological findings and artifacts that were unearthed in the province of Enna.
Piazza Mazzini. Open 9 a.m. to 1:30 p.m. and 3:30 p.m. to 6:30 p.m. Tel: 39 (0935) 528-100.

Via Roma is the town's main street and a pedestrian haven for the evening passeggiata. With its beautiful palazzi and churches, the entire city has a tidy appearance and exhibits pride of place.
The thirteenth-century **Torre di Federico**, with its unusual octagonal plan, graces the **giardini pubblici** (public gardens) of the city and offers spectacular views from its belvedere. The tower was part of a larger fortification complex called the **Castello Vecchio**, of which only the tower is left.
Via Roma intersects Via Pergusa, and continuing from there on the same street is the seventeenth-century church of **San Marco**. San Marco was built over an old synagogue from the time when this was the Jewish quarter, before the expulsion of the Sicilian Jews in 1492 at the hands of the Spanish Inquisition. Many Sicilian Jews settled in Northern Italy after leaving Sicily.
The **Castello di Lombardia**, originally built over previous Arab fortifications, stands on one of the highest points of the city. The castle once had twenty towers, of which only six remain. The tallest is **Torre Pisana**, which affords a 360-degree view of the entire island of Sicily. The first courtyard near the entrance is used for outdoor summer performances.
The town is divided into fifteen confraternities. They dress in their individual costumes beginning on Palm Sunday and participate in processions through the streets to the duomo. On Good Friday the participants hold torches as they carry venerated

statues and reliquaries in procession through the city. On Easter Sunday the Resurrected Christ meets the Virgin Mary in Piazza Duomo. These religious processions are displays of heartfelt devotion, not tourist attractions, so proper decorum is required from the public.

CALASCIBETTA

The nearby hill town of **Calascibetta**, which can be seen looking north from Enna, is at an altitude of 2,250 feet. The town is cradled in the concave side of the hill, and the buildings seem to merge with the rock formations in a wonderful fusion of natural and man-made form. The eleventh-century medieval structure of the town still asserts itself in the manner in which the streets follow the contour of the land. Towns like this are called **Nidi d'Aquila**, or Eagles' Nests, for the memorable views they offer. From the piazzale (square) of the eleventh-century **Torre Normanna**, which is on the side of the **Chiesa di San Pietro**, there is a breathtaking view of the city of Enna to the right and the Lago di Pergusa below. The Lago di Pergusa is the mythological site of the kidnapping of Persephone, daughter of Zeus and Demeter.

TROINA

Northeast of Enna, high in the Nebrodi Mountains, is the town of **Troina**. An old Arab town of narrow and steeply inclined streets, it became a Norman stronghold in the twelfth century. From the belvedere there are spectacular views of the mountains. The town is home to **L'Oasi di Troina**, an extraordinary complex for the diagnosis, care, education, and rehabilitation of Sicilian children and adolescents with disabilities who, prior to its founding, could not be treated in Sicily. L'Oasi is a nonprofit, self-sustaining complex that for several decades has been a model for community-centered care and for study and research into neurological disabilities. L'Oasi now treats Alzheimer patients as well as young people so that neither group lives in isolation. Staffed with medical professionals, scientists, teachers, caretakers, assistants, and volunteers, it focuses on prevention, research, therapy, and rehabilitation, aiming to get as many of the residents as possible reintegrated into society.

South of the city are the sulfur mines, which have been so important to the economy and history of this area. The site of one of the most important ones has been developed as the **Parco Minerario Floristella**, or the Floristella Sulphur Field. On the site behind the **Palazzina Pennisi**, which was built in 1750 by the mine owners for their home and office, is the entire complex. It shows the workings of the mine, which was active until the latter part of the twentieth century. Pirandello wrote about a *caruso*, or child laborer, in **Ciaula Scopre La Luna** (*Ciaula Discovers the Moon*). Sciascia also wrote eloquently about carusi, boy laborers, and their *picconiere*, the pickman who extracted the sulfur and who bought the use of a child from desperately poor parents to haul the mineral to the surface.

Those who want to relive history and follow the thread of sulfur mines as literary subjects can stay or lunch at the **Azienda Agriturismo Grottacalda**, which is housed in what were the old miners' houses, and visit the **Chiesetta di Santa Barbara**, where local miners had their wedding ceremonies in the heyday of the mine.

The park is located on Strada Provinciale 4 in Valguarnera. For information, write to Ente Parco Minerario Floristella, Casella Postale 60, 94019 Valguarnera, or call (0935) 958-105.

AZIENDA AGRITURISTICA Grottacalda. Grottacalda Piazza Armerina: Tel. (0935) 958 533; cell: (360) 969 720.

Piazza Armerina

Piazza Armerina, with the nearby Roman Villa Casale, is the jewel of the province. The city was originally called simply Piazza. It is thirty miles southeast of Enna and rises on three hills of the

Monti Erei at an altitude of over two thousand feet. The city is surrounded by a very fertile region of greenery, wooded areas, beautiful trees, and mountains. The imposing duomo, with its great cupola, dominates the panorama. Built over an earlier church, it incorporates the original fifteenth-century campanile. The façade is enlivened by pilasters and four spiral columns that flank the entrance. The duomo stands in the medieval quarter of the city, which is characterized by its quaint narrow streets.

Via Cavour. Open daily from 8:30 a.m. to 12 p.m. and from 3:30 p.m. to 7 p.m. Tel: (0935) 85 605.

On the right of the duomo stands the beautiful eighteenth-century **Palazzo Trigona**. Continuing on Via Floresta is the massive and handsomely geometric fourteenth-century **Castello Aragonese**, which began life as a castle, became a prison, and is now again a castle, privately owned.

The historical section centers on Piazza Garibaldi. On the north side of the piazza stands the elegant eighteenth-century **Palazzo di Città**, the seventeenth-century Baroque **Chiesa di San Rocco**, and the nineteenth-century **Teatro Garibaldi**, a handsome neoclassical building crowned by a sculptural group on the façade.

Piazza Garibaldi. Tel: (0935) 684-136.

A perfect time to visit Piazza Armerina is the month of August, when on the thirteenth and fourteenth the **Palio dei Normanni** takes place. This is a feast commemorating Conte Ruggero II's triumphal entrance into the city after liberating Sicily from the Muslims. The Palio starts on August 13 with a procession of beautiful period costumes in Piazza Duomo and continues on the fourteenth with an equestrian competition among the members of the various guilds of the city.

Information at the Tourist Office in Via Cavour. Tel: (0935) 680-201.

Where to stay:

Ostello del Borgo is not, as the name might suggest, a youth hostel, but a lovely hotel housed in the former Benedictine convent of San Giovanni. The rooms are the former nuns' quarters

and are spacious and pleasantly furnished. It is also very close to
the center of town.

Largo San Giovanni 6. Tel: (0935) 687-019.

The Roman **Villa Casale** remains a marvel of the ancient
Roman world for its beautiful mosaics and was named a World
Heritage Site by UNESCO. This magnificent villa from Imperial
Rome is truly one of the extraordinary sights of Sicily. The villa
may have originally belonged to Marcus Aurelius at the end of the
third century, and was subsequently passed on to other Roman
emperors. It was occupied by the Arabs until a fire destroyed it in
the twelfth century. Then, in the second half of the twelfth century the villa was buried by a landslide and flood, which paradox-
ically helped to preserve the magnificent mosaics. Rediscovered
at the end of the nineteenth century, archeological excavations
began in 1927 and were taken up again in the 1950s.

Today, visitors view the mosaics from a covered walkway built
over the villa's floor. The quality, quantity, refinement, vitality,
and even humor of the mosaics are quite astounding. The grace
of the young Sicilian girls in what look like bikinis has charmed
the world and is one of the world's most reproduced works of art.
Built with unlimited funds for luxurious living, to receive guests
in style and for official entertaining, it had a grand entrance that
led into the **atrium**, an open court that then led into the magnificent courtyard with **peristyle**, or a row of columns, surrounding
the space and a decorative pool with statuary. Although hunting
scenes are a recurring theme, nowhere in the villa is it more spectacularly shown than in the **Corridor of the Great Hunt**, where
the enormous space is completely covered with hunting scenes
and depictions of an African safari, where exotic animals are being
captured for shipment to Rome. Crossing the Corridor of the Great
Hunt, which at 16 by 196 feet and carpeted with magnificent
mosaics is a wonder to behold, leads to the **basilica**, or throne
room, with private apartments on both sides and the clover-leaf
shaped **triclinium**, or great dining hall, on the right. The villa
also included a **terme**, or thermal spa complex, consisting of a

caldarium, or hot baths and sauna, and a **tepidarium** for cooling off before entering the **frigidarium**, with two cold pools. Massage rooms and a gymnasium completed the wing, which was situated behind the atrium. A heating system functioned by circulating hot steam under the floors and between the walls.

Open daily 8 a.m. to 6:30 p.m.

Aidone

Southeast of Enna is the city of **Aidone**. The **Museo Archeologico Regionale** makes for an interesting visit before reaching **Morgantina**, site of the remains of an important trading center in Greek and Roman times. A reconstruction drawing by Princeton University archaeologists who excavated the site in 1955 shows the **agorà**, or marketplace, in the middle of a large enclosure housing a gymnasium and a theater that could seat as many as a thousand people carved directly out of the hill. Part of a paved street just beyond the city walls has miraculously survived. While the Princeton archeological group was excavating in Morgantina, a young local man made friends with one of them, who urged his Sicilian friend to call him if he ever came to America. When the young man later immigrated to the United States, he remembered his friend from Princeton and called him. The man the young Sicilian had befriended was Thomas Hoving, who, in the intervening years, had been named director of the Metropolitan Museum of Art in New York City. The Sicilian, Filippo Suffia, who was initially hired as a guard, quickly learned English, and eventually rose to an important position in security for the museum. For a time, many of the security guards at the Met were Sicilians, including one Mario Giarratana from the author's hometown of Ragusa.

CHAPTER 16

REGIONE SICILIANA— REGIONAL OFFICES

Assessorato del Turismo, delle Cominicazioni, e dei Trasporti
Regional Council for Turism, Communications, and Transport

Organizzazione Turistica
Regional Tourist Organization

Assessore: On. Francesco Cascio
Dirigente Generale Dipartimento Turismo, Sport, e Spettacolo:
Dott. Agostino
Porretto
Via Emanuele Notabartolo 9, 90141 Palermo
Tel: 39 (091) 696-8201
turismo@regione.sicilia.it
www.regione.sicilia.it/turismo

UFFICI REGIONALI—REGIONAL OFFICES

AGRIGENTO (AG)
Presidente: Dott. Vincenzo Fontana
Direttore: Dott. G.B. Petruzzella
Viale Della Vittoria 255, 92100 Agrigento
Tel: (0922) 401-352
aapitag@libero.it

CALTANISSETTA (CL)
Commissario Straordinario: Prof. Filippo Collura
Direttore Reggente: Avv.Giuseppe Impaglione
Corso Vittorio Emanuele 109, 93100 Caltanissetta
Tel: 39 (0934) 530-411
sedecentrale@aapit.cl.it
info@aapit.cl.it

ENNA (EN)
Presidente: Prof. Cataldo Salerno
Direttore F.F.: Dott. Michelangelo Trebastoni
Via Roma 411, 94100 Enna
Tel: 39 (0935) 528-229
apt-enna@apt-enna.com
www.apt-enna.com

CATANIA (CT)
Presidente: On. Raffaele Lombardo
Direttore: Dott. Angelo Cavallaro
Via Domenico Cimarosa 10, 95124 Catania
Tel: 39 (095) 730-6211
apt@apt.catania.it
www.apt.catania.it

MESSINA (ME)
Presidente: Salvatore Leonardi
Direttore: Giampiero Mannino
Via Calabria 301, 98122 Messina
Tel: 39 (090) 640-221
aptme@tiscalinet.it

PALERMO (PA)
Presidente: Dott. Salvatore Sammartano
Direttore: Arch. Vincenzo Sortino
Piazza Castelnuovo 35, 90141 Palermo
Tel: 39 (091) 605-8111

mail@palermotourism.com
www.palermotourism.com

SIRACUSA (SR)
Presidente: Sebastiano Butera
Direttore F.F.: Dott. Silvio Di Miceli
Via San Sebastiano 43, 96100 Siracusa
Tel: 39 (0931) 481-200
info@apt-siracusa.it
www.apt-siracusa.it

RAGUSA (RG)
Presidente: Dott. Girolamo Carpentieri
Direttore: Dott. Francesco Ferrera
Via Capitano Bocchieri 33, 97100 Ragusa
Tel: 39 (0932) 622-288
info@ragusaturismo.com
www.ragusaturismo.com

TRAPANI (TP)
Presidente: Giulia Adamo
Direttore: Dott. Giuseppe Butera
Via San Francesco d'Assisi 27, 91100 Trapani
Tel: 39 (0923) 545-511
apttp@apt.trapani.it
www.apt.trapani.it

Annual Events and Festivals

Acireale CT

| February | Carnival | Spectacular floats & parade |

Agrigento AG

| February | International Folk | Almonds in Bloom Festival |
| July–August | Pirandello Week | Theatrical performances |

Aidone-Morgantina EN

| July–August | Greek Theater | Classic theater performances |

Bronte CT

| September | Pistachio Festival | Picking, tours, tastings |

Caltagirone CT

| July 24 & 25 | San Giacomo | Luminaria on the staircase |

Caltanissetta CL

| Holy Week | Real Maestranza | Parade, Good Friday, Mystery procession |

Catania CT

| April 3 | Sant'Agata | Processions & fireworks |

Enna EN

| Holy Week | Confraternite | Parade & processions |

Erice TP

| July | Music | Medieval & Renaissance music |

Messina ME

August 13 & 14	Cavalcata	Parade of the Giants
August 15	Assumption	Grande Vara—Triumphal Parade

Modica RG

Easter Sunday	Maronna Vasa-Vasa	Mary Kisses Risen Christ

Monreale PA

Nov.–Dec.	Monreale Cathedral	Sacred Music Week

Noto SR

Third week May	Infiorata	"Paintings" from flower petals

Palermo PA

July 10–15	Santa Rosalia	Procession & triumphal cart
September	Int. Tennis Championships	Palermo Tennis Club
October	Coppa Degli Assi	Show jumping competition

Pegusa EN

April–Oct.	Car & Motorcycle Races Championships	Piazza Armerina
July	The Norman's Palio	Medieval tournament

Ragusa RG

June–July	Ibla Festival	Int. Classical Music Competition
August 29	San Giovanni	Feast, procession & fireworks

San Fratello ME

September	Horse Tournament	Best Sanfratellan horses

Segesta TP

July–August	Greek Theater	Classical drama

Sciacca AG

February	Carnival	Float parade & burning cart

Siracusa SR

May–June	Greek Theater	Classical drama

Taormina ME

June–August	Greek Theater	Taormina Arte

Tindari ME
July–August   Greek Theater   Drama, music, & dance

Trapani TP
Holy Week   I Misteri   Solemn procession

Organized Tours of Sicily

For assistance in planning a personal or a group tour of Sicily, I recommend the following:

Anna Maria Sorrentino
President
Shop Wine and Dine
P.O. Box 415
Short Hills, NJ 07078
U.S.A.
E-mail: annamaria@shopwineanddine.com
Phone: 973-467-4418
Mobile: 973-271-5117
Fax: 973-379-7241

Exciting tours to Sicily's premier wine regions.

Scheduled departures, custom tours for individual travelers, meetings, incentives, trade missions, corporate travel, and special occasions.

www.shopwineanddine.com

Hotels and Restaurants

It is said that you can't get a bad meal in Italy. Sicily, with its fertile land, flavorful fruits and vegetables, abundant fresh fish, delicious cheeses, and rich cuisine confirms the popular wisdom. You will eat well whether in a trattoria, a stand in the Vucciria Market in Palermo, or in a four-star restaurant. Hotel restaurants also offer decent food and varied menus as you travel around the island.

Ragusa (RG)

CHIARAMONTE GULFI

Villa Nobile ★★
Corso Umberto I, 168, Chiaramonte Gulfi (RG) 97012
Tel: 39 (0932) 928-537
fabcoc.recept@tiscaline.it
www.ibla.net/villanobile
Single 35–40 euro, double 45–56 euro, private garden, groups welcome, pets allowed, garage.

Where Else to Eat

Majore
Via Martiri Ungheresi 12, Chiaramonte Gulfi (RG) 97012
Tel: 39 (0932) 928-019
www.majore.it
Moderate prices. Famous in the entire province for its excellent pork dishes. Specializes in a great variety of traditional pork dishes. Definitely a treat.

185

ISPICA

Hotel Ispica ★★
Contrada Garzalla, Ispica (RG) 97014
Tel: 39 (0932) 951-652
3stelle@tin.it
www.hotelispica.it
Single 40–45 euro, double 70–80 euro, TV, air-conditioning, bar, restaurant, groups welcome, conference facilities, garage, TV room.

MODICA

Bristol ★★
Via Risorgimento 8B, Modica (RG) 97015
Tel: 39 (0932) 762-890
hotelbristolmodica@virgilio.it
www.hotelbristol.it
Single 43–47 euro, double 70–88 euro, TV, air-conditioning, elevator, bar, restaurant, private park, parking, wheelchair accessible, groups welcome, client transportation.

Torre Palazzelle ★
Contrada Torre Palazzelle, Modica (RG) 97015
Tel: 39 (0932) 901-200
info@torrepalazzelle.it
www.torrepalazzelle.it
Single 40 euro, double 65 euro, breakfast, TV, air-conditioning, bar, restaurant, vegetarian menu, private park, wheelchair accessible, reading room, TV room, conference facilities, pets allowed, soccer.

Where Else to Eat

Fattoria Delle Torri
Vico Napolitano 14, Modica (RG) 97015
Tel: 39 (0932) 751 286
peppebarone1960@libero.it
You'll go through fragrant lemon trees to enter the restaurant located in an eighteenth-century palazzo. For wine lovers, there is an extensive enoteca with over 450 wines. For passionate gourmets, traditional regional specialties, including the rich and delicious chocolate of Modica, are served. Closed Mondays. This very fine restaurant is a member of the Viaggio Enogastronomico, a group of excellent restaurants that pair the gourmet food of Sicily with vast Sicilian wine lists. Visit www.lesostediulisse.it for the complete list of participating restaurants.

Trattoria Delle Torri
Via Nativo 30-32, Modica (RG) 97015
Tel: 39 (0932) 751-286
Expensive. Delicious traditional Sicilian food prepared with great care.
Reservations a must. Closed Mondays.

Trattoria La Rusticana
Viale Medaglie d'Oro 34, Modica (RG) 97015
Tel: 39 (0932) 942-950
Moderate prices. Excellent Sicilian cooking. Closed Sundays. No credit
cards.

CAFFÈ AND PASTICCERIE

Antica Dolceria Bonajuto
Corso Umberto I 115, Modica (RG) 97015
Tel: 39 (0932) 941-225
Serves delicious chocolate made according to the original Aztec recipe
without milk, butter, or cream; cocoa and sugar are heated until the
cocoa melts while the sugar retains some crunch. Specialty: chocolate
with pepper.

AGRITURISMO FARMS

Fattoria Della Contea
Via S. Alessandra 1, Modica (RG) 97015
fattoriadellacontea@tiscali.it
Small, family-run agriturismo farm serving their own food, vegetables,
and wines.

Villa Teresa
Via Crocevia Cava d'Ispica, Modica (RG) 97015
Tel: 39 (0932) 771-690
An eighteenth-century farm with rooms surrounded by lovely gardens.

POZZALLO

Continental ★★★
Contrada Daniele-S.P. Modica/Pozzallo, Pozzallo (RG) 97016
Tel: 39 (0932) 958-858
hotelcontinental@tiscalinet.it
www.pozzallo.it/hotelcontinental
Single 40–60 euro, double 70-90 euro, TV, bar, restaurant, wheelchair
accessible, groups welcome, client transportation, conference facilities.

Where Else to Eat

Pasticceria Fratelli Sciuto
Via Mazzini 31, Pozzallo (RG) 97016
Tel: 39 (0932) 953-022
Enjoy traditional pastries and snacks, but also try their magnificent marzipan fruits.

RAGUSA

Eremo della Giubiliana ★★★★
Contrada Giubiliana, Ragusa (RG) 97100 (near Marina di Ragusa)
Tel: 39 (0932) 669-119
Luxurious accommodations and service in a rural setting; private airfield connects with the islands off the coast of Sicily.

Mediterraneo Palace ★★★★
Via Roma 189, Ragusa (RG) 97100
Tel: 39 (0932) 621-944
info@mediterraneopalace.it
www.mediterraneopalace.it
Single 68–92 euro, double 90–118 euro, TV, air-conditioning, elevator, bar, restaurant, wheelchair accessible groups welcome, client transportation, conference facilities, pets allowed, conference facilities, garage.

Montreal ★★★
Via San Giuseppe 8, Ragusa (RG) 97100
Tel: 39 (0932) 621-133
montreal@sicily-hotels.net
www.hotelmontreal.sicily-hotels.net
Single 50–55 euro, double 75-90 euro, TV, air-conditioning, elevator, bar, restaurant, wheelchair accessible, groups welcome, client transportation, conference facilities, pets allowed, garage, conference facilities.

Rafael ★★★
Corso Italia 40, Ragusa (RG) 97100
Tel: 39 (0932) 654-080
Single 26–52 euro, double 42–83 euro, TV, air-conditioning, elevator, bar, restaurant, wheelchair accessible, groups welcome, client transportation, and garage.

Jonio ★★
Via Risorgimento 49, Ragusa (RG) 97100
Tel: 39 (0932) 624-322
Corso Italia 40, Ragusa (RG) 97100
Tel: 39 (0932) 654-080

Single 33 euro, double 50 euro, TV, air-conditioning, elevator, bar, restaurant, parking, groups welcome, pets allowed, conference facilities, garage.

Where Else to Eat

Alla Corte di Bacco
S.S. 115 Km 314 Contrada Castiglione, Ragusa (RG) 97100
Tel: 39 (0932) 256-340
Serves the best seafood in town, particularly the varied and delicious homemade antipasti.

Fumia
Via Dei Cappuccini 23, Ragusa (RG) 97100
Tel: 39 (0932) 621-463
Moderate prices. Popular local eatery with good traditional dishes. Closed Mondays.

Villa Fortugno
Srada Provinciale to Marina di Ragusa, (RG) 97100
Tel: 39 (0932) 667-134
Expensive. Lovely country house. Serves the traditional food of the Ragusa region. Elegant party facilities available for groups.

AGRITURISMO FARM

Azienda Agrituristica Degli Altopiani Adamo-Battaglia
C.da Mangiapane S.P. 14 Km. 6,55, Ragusa (RG) 97100
Tel: 39 (0932) 619-279
Excellent typical cuisine of Ragusa; serves freshly made ricotta and scaccie.

CAFÉS, PASTRY SHOPS, GOURMET SHOPS

The main street, Via Roma, is lined with cafés, where they serve snacks, pastries, cannoli, and delectable gelato. Walk down the steps of the piazza in front of the Cathedral of San Giovanni and enjoy coffee and desserts at the famous Bar Italia.

Pasticceria di Pasquale
Corso Vittorio Veneto 104, Ragusa (RG) 97100
Tel: 39 (0932) 624-701
The best local pasticceria, known for their almond confections that they ship all over the world as well as their fabulous cakes and tarts. Eat in or take out.

Caffè Pasticceria Ambassador
Via Archimede 6, Ragusa (RG) 97100
Tel: 39 (0932) 6240-701

This pasticceria is an *enoteca*, so you can enjoy savory snacks, good wine, and traditional sweets.

Casa del Formaggio Sant'Anna
Corso Italia 387, 97100, Ragusa (RG) 97100
Tel: 39 (0932) 227-485

Offers a huge assortment of gourmet food, including Caciocavallo Ragusano, honey from Monti Iblei, and sun-dried tomatoes. Will vacuum-pack cheeses for traveling or shipping.

RAGUSA IBLA

Il Barocco ★★★
Via Santa Maria La Nuova 1, Ragusa Ibla (RG) 97100
Tel: 39 (0932) 663-105
ilbarocco@hotmail.com
www.ilbarocco.it
Single 45–65 euro, double 80–110 euro.

Palazzo Degli Archi ★★★
Corso Don Minzoni 6, Ragusa Ibla (RG) 97100
Tel: 39 (0932) 685-602
Single 45–90 euro, double 90–130 euro.

Where Else to Eat

Il Barocco
Via Orfanotrofio 29, Ragusa Ibla (RG) 97100
Tel: 39 (0932) 652-397
www.ilbarocco.it
Excellent local cuisine and a popular restaurant in town.

Il Duomo
Via Capitano Bocchieri 3, Ragusa Ibla (RG) 97100
Tel: 39 (0932) 651-265
www.ristoranteduomo.it
duomo@inwind.it

The restaurant is located in the beautiful Baroque Palazzo La Rocca in the historic center of Ragusa Ibla. Chef Ciccio Sultano offers an excellent innovative cuisine based on local tradition with a wide Sicilian, national, and international wine collection. It's considered one of the best new restaurants in Sicily. Closed Sunday nights and Mondays.

Member of the Viaggio Enogastronomico, a group of excellent restaurants that pair the gourmet food of Sicily with vast Sicilian wine lists. Visit www.lesostediulisse.it for the complete list of participating restaurants.

Locanda Don Serafino
Via Orfanotrofio 39, Ragusa Ibla (RG) 97100
Tel: 39 (0932) 248 778
www.locandadonserafino.it
info@locandadonserafino.it
Located on the ground floor of an eighteenth-century palazzo, Locanda Don Serafino offers the most delicious and traditional dishes of Ragusa and Sicily, presented in refined and elegant surroundings. It also has a wine cellar with over seven hundred choices. Closed Tuesdays. Member of the Viaggio Enogastronomico. Visit www.lesostediulisse.it for the complete list of participating restaurants.

U Saracinu
Via Convento 97, Ragusa Ibla (RG) 97100
Tel: 39 (0932) 246-976
Moderate prices. With view of the beautiful Cathedral of San Giorgio, it serves excellent local dishes. This is a popular restaurant of the Ragusani.

PIZZERIE AND TAVOLE CALDE

Rosticeria
Piazza Duomo 12, Ragusa Ibla (RG) 97100
Excellent typical dishes of Ragusa at modest prices. Outdoor seating right on the piazza.

Gelati Divini
Piazza Duomo 20, Ragusa Ibla (RG) 97100
Tel: 39 (0932) 228-989
Divini could mean either made with wine or divine. The wine-flavored gelati or the more conventional variety is truly divine!

VITTORIA

Grand Hotel ★★★
Vico II Carlo Pisacane 53b, Vittoria (RG) 97019
Tel: 39 (0932) 863-888
grandhotelvittoria@tin.it
Single 35–50 euro, double 45–70 euro, TV, air-conditioning, bar, wheelchair accessible, conference facilities.

Europa ★★
Vico II Carlo Pisacane 53b, Vittoria (RG) 97019
Tel: (0932) 863-888
info@albergohoteleuropa.com
www.albergohoteleuropa.com
Single 15–25 euro, double 30–45 euro, parking, groups welcome, client transportation.

Sicilia ★★
Via Cernaia 62, Vittoria (RG) 97019
Tel: 39 (0932) 981-087
hotelsicilia@tiscalinet.it
www.hotelsiciliacjb.net
Single 13–30 euro, double 25–50 euro, TV, bar, parking, groups welcome, client transportation, pets allowed.

Where Else to Eat

Sakalleo
Località Scoglitti Piazza Cavour 12, Scoglitti (RG) 97019
Tel: 39 (0932) 871-688
Excellent fish menu. Specialties: marinated shrimp and anchovies.

SIRACUSA (SR)

NOTO

Oasi Don Bosco ★★★
Contrada Arco Farina Pianette, Noto (SR) 96017
Tel: 39 (0931) 946-275
www.fattoriadonbosco.it
Single 36–72 euro, double 72–113 euro, breakfast, TV, air-conditioning, elevator, bar, restaurant, parking, wheelchair accessible.

Villa Giulia ★★★
Contrada San Lorenzo, Noto (SR) 96017
Tel: 39 (0931) 591-688
info@hotelvillafavorita.it
www.hotelvillafavorita.it
Single 46–74 euro, double 85–121 euro, breakfast, TV, air-conditioning, room service, bar, restaurant, parking, wheelchair accessible, reading room, private beach, tennis, swimming pool.

Where Else to Eat

Ristorante Neas
Via San Rocco Pirri 30, Noto (SR) 96017
Tel: 39 (0931) 573-538
Expensive. Excellent menu. Specializes in fish, particularly grilled fish. Closed Mondays.

Trattoria del Carmine
Via Ducezio 9, Noto (SR) 96017
Tel: 39 (0931) 838-705
Moderate prices. Delicious traditional cooking in a charming Baroque town.

Caffè Sicilia
Corso Vittorio Emanuele 125, Noto (SR) 96017
Tel: 39 (0931) 835-013
Well-known traditional pastry shop with delectable Sicilian desserts, fresh fruit gelati, and orange marmalade made from organic oranges.

ORTIGIA

Posta ★★★
Via Trieste 33, Ortigia (SR) 96100
Tel: 39 (0931) 218-19
hotelposta@excite.com
www.hotelpostasiracusa.com
Single 55–70 euro, double 75–100 euro, breakfast, TV, air-conditioning, elevator, bar, wheelchair accessible, client transportation.

Where Else to Eat

Don Camillo
Via Maestranza 96, Ortigia (SR) 96100
Tel: 39 (0931) 671-33
ristorantedoncamillo@tin.it
www.ristorantedoncamillosiracusa.it
Located in one of the most beautiful streets of historic Ortigia, Don Camillo specializes in regional seafood and other traditional dishes and boasts the best wine cellar in Ortigia with over seven hundred wines, including the best ones from Sicily. Chef/owner Giovanni Guarneri has made the award-winning Don Camillo into a world-renowned restaurant. Member of the Viaggio Enogastronomico. Closed Sundays.

La Foglia
Via Copodieci 29, Ortigia (SR) 96100
Tel: 39 (0931) 662-33
Delicious food at moderate prices. Near the Fountain of Aretusa, this elegant restaurant is decorated in the style of a private mansion with fine old china and glassware on embroidered tablecloths. Definitely a treat.

Zsa
Via Romana 73, Ortigia (SR) 96100
Tel: 39 (0931) 222-04
Moderate prices. Serves traditional Sicilian food and the specialties of Siracusa, such as pasta with anchovies, pine nut,s and raisins as well as grilled fish.

La Scaletta
Largo Porto Marina 1, Ortigia (SR) 96100
Tel: 39 (0931) 247-27
Moderate prices. Delicious "cucina casalinga," or traditional home cooking, served along with view of the blue sea. A lovely treat.

Ristorante Archimede
Via Gemellaro 8, Ortigia (SR) 96100
Tel: 39 (0931) 697-01
Moderate prices. A local favorite of the Siracusani for its traditional menu of fish and seafood with a wonderful choice of Sicilian antipasti. Closed Sundays during low season.

SIRACUSA

Grand Hotel ★★★★
Viale Giuseppe Mazzini 12, Siracusa (SR) 96100
Tel: 39 (0931) 464-600
info@grandhotelsr.it
www.grandhotelsr.it
Single 102–145 euro, double 142-217 euro, breakfast, room service, TV, air-conditioning, elevator, bar, restaurant, parking, wheelchair accessible, reading room, conference facilities, private beach.

Hotel Holiday Inn ★★★★
Viale Teracati 30, Siracusa (SR) 96100
Tel: 39 (0931) 440-440
holidayinn.siracusa@alliancealberghi.com
www.holiday-inn.com/siracusaitaly
Single 79–159 euro, double 93–183 euro, room service, TV, air-conditioning, elevator, bar, restaurant, parking, conference facilities.

Jolly Hotel ★★★★
Corso Gelone 45, Siracusa (SR) 96100
Tel: 39 (0931) 461-111
siracusa@jollyhotel.it
www.jollyhotel.it

Single 68–119 euro, double 88–155 euro, room service, TV, air-conditioning, elevator, bar, restaurant, parking, wheelchair accessible, conference facilities, pets allowed.

Bellavista ★★★
Via Diodoro Siculo 4, Siracusa (SR) 96100
Tel: 39 (0931) 411-355
www.hotel-bellavista.com

Single 55–65 euro, double 69–97 euro, room service, TV, air-conditioning, elevator, bar, restaurant, private park, parking, wheelchair accessible, reading room, solarium.

Fontane Bianche ★★★
Viale Mazzarò 1, Siracusa (SR) 96100
Tel: 39 (0931) 790-611
fontane.direzione@ventaglio.com
www.ventaglio.com

Single 50–70 euro, double 65–90 euro, breakfast, TV, air-conditioning, elevator, bar, restaurant, private park, wheelchair accessible, client transportation, conference facilities, dancing, private beach, tennis, swimming pool.

Hotel Del Santuario ★★★
Via Del Santuario 1, Siracusa (SR) 96100
Tel: 39 (0931) 465-656
hoteldelsantuario@virgilio.it
www.hoteldelsantuario.it

Single 60–70 euro, double 80–100 euro, TV, air-conditioning, room service, elevator, bar, restaurant, wheelchair accessible, conference facilities, pets allowed, garage.

Park Hotel Helios ★★★
Viale Filisto, Siracusa (SR) 96100
Tel: 39 (0931) 412-233
parkhotel.helios@tin.it
www.heliosgroup.com

Single 52–93 euro, double 67–156 euro, air-conditioning, room service, elevator, bar, restaurant, parking, wheelchair accessible, pets allowed, satellite TV, tennis, swimming pool, solarium conference facilities.

Archimede ★★
Via Francesco Crispi, Siracusa (SR) 96100
Tel: 39 (0931) 462-458
info@hotelarchimede.sr.it
www.hotelarchimede.sr.it

Single 35–50 euro, double 50–75 euro, breakfast, TV, air-conditioning, room service, elevator, bar, restaurant, wheelchair accessible, client transportation, garage, reading room, solarium.

Riviera ★★
Via Francesco Crispi, Siracusa (SR) 96100
Tel: 39 (0931) 462 458
hotelrivierasiracusa@tiscalinet.it
www.hotelrivierasiracusa.com

Single 51–61 euro, double 67–82 euro, breakfast, TV, air-conditioning, elevator, bar, restaurant, solarium.

Where Else to Eat

Capriccio
Contrada Canalicchio on the Srada Statale 124, Siracusa (SR) 96100
Tel: 39 (0931) 698-85

Modest prices. Located just one mile from the Greek Theater, this popular local pizzeria and restaurant is a great place to meet friends while enjoying its wide selection of Sicilian antipasti, the piano bar, and delicious pizza, which is served only at dinner.

Darsena-da Iannuzzo
Riva Garibaldi 6, Siracusa (SR) 96100
Tel: 39 (0931) 615-22

Moderate prices. The well-prepared fish is fresh and delicious.

Fratelli Bandieri
Via Trieste 42, Siracusa (SR) 96100
Tel: 39 (0931) 650-21

Modest prices. A well-known old restaurant that continues to serve a remarkable variety of traditional dishes. Closed Mondays.

Porticciolo
Via Trento, Siracusa (SR) 96100
Tel: 39 (0931) 619-14

Moderate prices. It serves delicious lobsters and specializes in *pesce alla griglia*, the traditional mixed-fish grill. Closed Mondays.

Ristorante Minerva
Piazza Duomo 20, Siracusa (SR) 96100
Tel: 39 (0931) 694-04
Moderate prices. Well located near the magnificent duomo, it serves a traditional menu of delicious local dishes. Open for lunch and dinner. Closed Mondays.

AGRITURISMO

Casa Dello Scirocco
Contrada da Piscitello, Carlentini (SR) 96100
Tel: 39 (095) 447-709
www.enexa.com/casascirocco
This is a beautiful homestead in an old country mansion. The excellent restaurant serves delicious traditional Sicilian specialties.

La Perciata
Via Spinagallo 77 along the Mare-Monti Road, Siracusa (SR) 96100
Tel: 39 (0931) 717-366
Enjoy country living in a beautiful homestead, offering a swimming pool, tennis courts, and horseback riding.

Limoneto
Provincial Rd 14, Siracusa (SR) 96100
(toward Canicattì along the Mare-Monti road)
Tel: 39 (0931) 717-352
Only 5½ miles from Siracusa, the farm stands in the midst of lemon, olive, and fruit groves.

CATANIA (CT)

ACI CASTELLO

Grand Hotel Baia Verde ★★★★
Via Angelo Musco 8, Aci Castello (CT) 95020
Tel: 39 (095) 491-522
direttore@baiaverde.it
www.baiaverde.it
Single from 180 euro, double from 250 euro, breakfast, air-conditioning, elevator, bar, restaurant, private park, private beach, swimming pool, babysitting service.

Where Else to Eat

Barbarossa
Strada Provinciale SS114, Aci Castello (CT) 95020
Tel: 39 (095) 295-539
Delicious specialties; wonderful fish with a great wine list. 60 euro and
up.

ACIREALE

Aloha d'Oro ★★★★
Viale Alcide de Gasperi, 10, Acireale (CT) 95024
Tel: 39 (095) 768-7001
info@hotel-aloha.it
www.hotel-aloha.it
Single 60–100 euro, double 80–140 euro, TV, air-conditioning, bar, restaurant, private garden, groups welcome, client transportation, pets
accepted, convention facilities, babysitting, dancing tennis, swimming,
water skiing.

Orizzonte Acireale ★★★★
Via Cristoforo Colombo 2, Acireale (CT) 95024
Tel: 39 (095) 886-6006
www.hotelorizzonte.it
Single 80–160 euro, double 108–216 euro, TV, air-conditioning, elevator,
bar, restaurant, vegetarian menu, private garden, parking, wheelchair
accessible, groups welcome, client transportation, convention facilities,
pets admitted, babysitting, garage, swimming.

Hotel delle Terme ★★★
Via Alcide De Gasperi 20, Acireale (CT) 95024
Tel: 39 (095) 604-480
info@hoteldelleterme.net
www.hoteldelleterme.net
Single 30–60 euro, double 60–120 euro, breakfast, TV, air-conditioning,
bar, restaurant, vegetarian menu, groups welcome, client transportation,
convention facilities.

ACI TREZZA

Eden Riviera ★★★
Via Litteri 57, Aci Trezza (CT) 95026
Tel: 39 (095) 277-760
eden@hoteledenriviera.it
www.hoteledenriviera.it

Single 40–80 euro, double 50–100 euro, breakfast, TV, air-conditioning, bar, restaurant, private garden, groups welcome, client transportation, pets accepted, babysitting, swimming pool, parking.

I Malavoglia ★★★
Via Provinciale 5, Aci Trezza (CT) 95026
Tel: 39 (095) 711-7850
direzione@albergoimalavoglia.it
www.albergoimalavoglia.it
Single 45–60 euro, double 70–90 euro, breakfast, TV, air-conditioning, elevator, bar, restaurant, private garden, groups welcome, pets accepted, garage, swimming, tennis, parking.

Where Else to Eat

Holiday Club
Via Dei Malavoglia 10, Aci Trezza (CT) 95026
Tel: 39 (095) 277-575
Excellent food in a lovely setting with spectacular views. 60 euro for house wine.

BRONTE

La Cascina ★★
Contrada Piana Cuntarati, Bronte (CT) 95034
Tel: 39 (095) 772-1991
Single 25–41 euro, double 38–56 euro, TV, bar, restaurant, parking, wheelchair accessible, groups welcome, pets allowed, babysitting service.

Where Else to Eat

Conti
Corso Umberto I 275, Bronte (CT) 95034
Tel: 39 (095) 691-165
Treat yourself, at least once, with the most delicious pistachio pastries you will ever have. Eat in or take out.

CALTAGIRONE

Gran Hotel Villa San Mauro ★★★★
Via Porto Salvo 10, Caltagirone (CT) 95041
Tel: 39 (0933) 26-500
sanmauro@framon-hotels.com
www.framon-hotels.com
Single 92.50–131 euro, double 131–187 euro, TV, air-conditioning, elevator, bar, restaurant, vegetarian menu, private garden, parking,

wheelchair accessible, groups welcome, pets allowed, babysitting service, convention facilities.

Monteverde ★★
Via delle Industrie 11, Caltagirone (CT) 95041
Tel: 39 (0933) 536-82
Single 37–45 euro, double 52–62 euro, TV, air-conditioning, bar, restaurant, private garden, parking, pets allowed, wheelchair accessible, groups welcome, convention facilities.

AGRITURISMO FARM

La Casa Degli Angeli
Contrada Angeli S.P. 39 al Km 9, Caltagirone (CT) 95041
Tel: 39 (0933) 253-17
A picturesque working farm with an olive grove, a vegetable garden, and fields of citrus trees. Offers guided tours, cooking lessons, and rentals of mountain bikes.

CATANIA

Grand Hotel Excelsior ★★★★★
Piazza Giovanni Verga 39, Catania (CT) 95131
Tel: 39 (095) 747-6111
excelsior-catania@thi.it
www.thi.it
Single 105–195 euro, double 165–345 euro, super deluxe, great location, breakfast, TV, air-conditioning, elevator, bar, restaurant, private garden, parking, wheelchair accessible, groups welcome, pets allowed, babysitting, convention facilities.

Jolly Hotel Bellini ★★★★
Piazza Trento13, Catania (CT) 95129
Tel: 39 (095) 316-933
catania@jollyhotels.it
www.jollyhotels.it
Single 64–128 euro, double 165–345 euro, reliably excellent, TV, air-conditioning, elevator, restaurant, bar, parking, groups welcome, pets allowed, convention facilities.

Etnea 316 ★★★
Via Etnea 316, Catania (CT) 95129
Tel: 39 (095) 250-3076
hoteletnea316@aruba.it
www.hoteletnea316.com

Single 40–75 euro, double 70–125 euro, breakfast, TV, air-conditioning, wheelchair accessible, groups welcome, garage.

Hotel del Duomo ★★★
Via Etnea 28, Catania (CT) 95131
Tel: 39 (095) 250-3177
info@hoteldelduomo.it
www.hoteldelduomo.it
Reliably excellent. Single 60–90 euro, double 100–150 euro, breakfast, TV, air-conditioning, restaurant, bar, wheelchair accessible, garage.

La Vecchia Palma ★★★
Via Etnea 668, Catania (CT) 95128
Tel: 39 (095) 432-025
info@lavecchiapalma.com
www.lavecchiapalma.com
Double 46–90 euro, breakfast, TV, air-conditioning, restaurant, private garden, parking, wheelchair accessible, groups welcome, garage.

Novecento ★★★
Via Monsignor Ventimiglia 35-39, Catania (CT) 95127
Tel: 39 (095) 310-488
info@hotelnovecentocatania.it
www.hotelnovecentocatania.it
Single 50–95 euro, double 65–130 euro, breakfast, TV, air-conditioning, elevator, bar, parking, wheelchair accessible, garage.

Poggio Ducale ★★★
Via Paolo Gaifami 5-7, Catania (CT) 95126
Tel: 39 (095) 330-016
poggioducale@poggioducale.it
www.poggioducale.it
Single 47–91 euro, double 62–125 euro, breakfast, TV, air-conditioning, elevator, bar, restaurant, parking, wheelchair accessible, groups welcome, convention facilities.

Miramare ★
Viale Kennedy 42, Catania (CT) 951261
Tel: 39 (095) 346-963
laplaja.club@flashnet.it
Single 34–67 euro, double 58–114 euro, breakfast, TV, air-conditioning, elevator, restaurant, private garden, parking, wheelchair accessible, groups welcome, client transportation, convention facilities, babysitting, pets accepted, garage, private beach, swimming pool.

BED & BREAKFASTS

Asero Bed & Breakfast
Via Umberto 77, Catania (CT) 95100
Tel: 39 (0905) 312-670
Cell: 39 (347) 603-6477
www.aserobedandbreakfast.it
Located in the beautiful historic center of the city. 85 euro for double occupancy. Large, luminous rooms with private bath, heat, and air-conditioning.

Where Else to Eat

Cortile Bellini
Via Landolina 46, Catania (CT) 95131
Tel: 39 (095) 316-117
Moderate prices. Typical Sicilian cooking.

Ristorante La Siciliana
Viale Marco Polo 52/a, Catania (CT) 95126
Tel: 39 (095) 376-400
www.lasiciliana.it
Expensive. Considered one of the best in Catania.

Sicilia in Bocca Alla Marina
Via Dusmet 35, Catania (CT) 95100
Tel: 39 (095) 250-0208
Moderate prices. Fish specialties and a lovely welcoming atmosphere.

Osteria Antica Marina
Via Pardo 29, Catania (CT) 95131
Tel: 39 (095) 348-197
Moderate prices. Excellent fish. Closed Wednesdays.

TAVOLE CALDE, CAFFÈ, PASTICCERIE

Spinella
Via Etnea 300, Catania (CT) 95129
Well located opposite Villa Bellini, it's the best place for hot and cold snacks as well as wonderful desserts. Try their famous arancini with salmon.

Savia
Via Etnea 302, Catania (CT) 95129
Tel: 39 (095) 322-335
Great traditional arancini and the best Cassata Siciliana.

Menza
Viale Mario Rapisardi 143, Catania (CT) 95129
Tel: 39 (095) 350-606
Famous rotisserie with all the delicious local specialties.

Caffè Europa
Corso Italia 304, Catania (CT) 95129
Tel: 39 (095) 372-655
Elegant café with a huge selection of pastries with each more delicious than the next.

Nuovo Caffè Italia
Corso Italia 247, Catania (CT) 95127
Tel: 39 (095) 388-807
The best arancini in Catania.

AGRITURISMO FARM

Bagnara
Contrada Cardinale, Catania (CT)
Tel: 39 (095) 336-407
Enjoy country living in a farm with oranges, peaches, pears, and olive trees, as well as prickly pears to sample in season. Also offers horseback riding.

Fondo 23
Via San Giuseppe La Rena, Catania (CT)
Tel: 39 (095) 592-521
A beautiful farmhouse built with the lava stone in the Catania region and enlivened by oleanders and other beautiful flowering plants. Offers cycling and horseback riding.

EXCURSIONS TO MOUNT ETNA

CAI—Club Alpino Italiano
Piazza Scamacca 1, Catania (CT) 95131
Tel: 39 (095) 715-3515
Trips to Mount Etna.

Excursion to Mount Etna from the Catania Central Station
Stazione Centrale Piazza Papa Giovanni XXIII Catania (CT) 95129
Tel: 39 (095) 730-6255
Bus service to the Sapienza Refuge on Mount Etna from the Catania Central Station.

Gruppo Guide Alpine Etna Sud
Via Etnea 49, Nicolosi (CT) 95030
Tel: 39 (095) 791 4755
www.etnaguide.com
Professionally guided private and group excursions to Mount Etna.

Train Tour of Mount Etna (July–September)
Via Caronda 352 Catania (CT) 95128
Tel: 39 (095) 541-250
Take the train to the town of Randazzo, and from there take a bus tour of Mount Etna. Tour train leaves from Catania at 8 a.m. and returns at 7 p.m. Cost is 14 euro plus the price of lunch.

LINGUAGLOSSA

Happy Day ★★
Via Mareneve 9, Linguaglossa (CT) 95915
Tel: 39 (095) 643-484
Single 35–40 euro, double 65–70 euro, air-conditioning, bar, restaurant, private park, parking, wheelchair accessible, groups welcome, client transport, pets allowed.

MASCALUCIA

Casa Di Accoglienza
Padri Passionisti, Via Del Bosco 1 95030 Mascalucia (CT)
Tel: Padre Giuseppe Finazzo at 39 (095) 727-4309

NICOLOSI

Biancaneve ★★★
Via Etnea 163, Nicolosi (CT) 95030
Tel: 39 (095) 911-060
hotel@hotel.biancaneve.com
www.hotel.biancaneve.com
Single 52–104 euro, double 78–155 euro, breakfast, TV, elevator, bar, restaurant, private garden, parking, wheelchair accessible, groups welcome, client transport, pets allowed, conference facilities, children's playground, garage, dancing, tennis, swimming pool, soccer.

Where Else to Eat

Al Buongustaio
Via Etnea 105/f, Nicolosi (CT) 95030
Tel: 39 (095) 791 5760
Inexpensive. Delicious Sicilian fare with a selection of homemade antipasti.

Il Cantuccio
Via Torino 1, Nicolosi (CT) 95030
Tel: 39 (095) 910-667
Reasonably priced. Family-run restaurant with delectable pastas and excellent homemade antipasti.

Etna
Via Etnea 93, Nicolosi (CT) 95030
Tel: 39 (095) 911-937
Moderate prices. Serves a wide variety of delicious typical food of the region, including pizza, which is only served in the evening. Closed Mondays.

RANDAZZO

Scrivano ★★★
Via Bonaventura 2, Randazzo (CT) 95036
Tel: 39 (095) 921-126
Single 31–52 euro, double 52–78 euro, breakfast, bar, restaurant, vegetarian menu, garden, wheelchair accessible, parking.

Where Else to Eat

Trattoria Veneziano
Via Romano 8, Randazzo (CT) 95036
Tel: 39 (095) 799-1353
Moderate prices. A fine trattoria with delicious traditional local specialties.

MESSINA (ME)

ALICUDI, ISOLE EOLIE

Ericusa ★★
Isola Alicudi—Località Perciato, Alicudi 98050
Tel: 39 (090) 988-9902
Double 55–60 euro, bar, restaurant, separate TV room, groups welcome.

CAPO D' ORLANDO

Hotel Amato ★★★
Via Consolare Antica 150, Capo d'Orlando (ME) 98071
Tel: 39 (0941) 911-476

Single 36–56 euro, double 51–92 euro, breakfast, TV, air-conditioning, bar, restaurant, private garden, parking, groups welcome, conference facilities, tennis, swimming.

La Tartaruga ★★★
Lido San Gregorio 70, Capo d'Orlando (ME) 98071
Tel: 39 (0941) 955-012
Single 25–65 euro, double 45–105 euro, TV, air-conditioning, elevator, bar, restaurant, vegetarian menu, parking, wheelchair accessible, conference facilities, client transport, pets accepted, TV room, babysitting, dancing, swimming pool.

CAMPING

Santa Rosa
Località Tavola Grande, Via Trazzera Marina, Capo d'Orlando (ME) 98071
Tel: 39 (0941) 901-723

AGRITURISMO FARM

Milio
San Gregorio Km. 2, Capo d'Orlando (ME) 98071
Tel: 39 (0941) 955-008
A working farm with a grove of olive trees and orchards of fruit trees just a short walk to the sea. Hikes are organized from the farm to the Parco dei Nebrodi.

Where Else to Eat

CAPRI LEONE

Antica Filanda
S.P. 157 Contrada Raviola, Capri Leone (ME) 98070
Tel: 39 (094) 919-704
info@anticafilanda.it
www.anticafilanda.it
With view of the beautiful Aeolina Islands, the restaurant is located in one of the most picturesque areas of Sicily. The stars of the menu are the black pork and the lambs of the Nebrodi Mountains, which together with the fresh cheeses, wild greens, and home-baked breads make for some of the finest dining experiences in Sicily. Master chefs Nunzio Campisi and Pinuccia di Nardo crossed the ocean in 2006 to introduce their specialties at the Agata and Valentina Restaurant in New York as guest chefs for two weeks. Definitely a treat.

FILICUDI—ISOLE EOLIE

La Canna ★★★
Via Rosa 43, Isola Filicudi (ME) 98050
Tel: 39 (090) 988-9966
infgo@lacannahotel.it
www.lacannahotel.it

Double 60–120 euro, TV, air-conditioning, bar, restaurant, vegetarian menu, groups welcome, client transportation, reading room, TV room, pets allowed, swimming pool. Moderate prices. Wonderful traditional homemade food and great panoramic views.

GIARDINI NAXOS

Assinos Palace Hotel ★★★★
Via Consolare Valeria 33, Giardini Naxos (ME) 98030
Tel: 39 (0942) 544-049
info@assinospalacehotel.com

Single 70–98 euro, double 93–160 euro, TV, air-conditioning, elevator, bar, restaurant, vegetarian menu, private park, parking, wheelchair accessible, groups welcome, client transportation, TV room, garage, swimming pool.

Naxos Beach Hotel ★★★★
Via Recanati 26, Giardini Naxos (ME) 98030
Tel: 39 (0942) 6611
prenotazioni@hotelnaxosbeach.com
www.hotelnaxosbeach.com

Double 124–217 euro, air-conditioning, elevator, bar, restaurant, private park, parking,, wheelchair accessible, groups welcome, conference facilities, client transportation, satellite TV, dancing, gym, garage, children's playground, babysitting, dancing, private beach, tennis, bocce, soccer, ping-pong, volleyball, canoeing, sailing, windsurfing, minigolf, skin diving, pool.

Sporting Baja Hotel ★★★★
Via Naxos 6, Giardini Naxos (ME) 98030
Tel: 39 (0942) 517-33

Single 49–110 euro, double 57–165 euro, TV, air-conditioning, elevator, bar, restaurant, parking, conference facilities, reading room, TV room, babysitting, dancing, garage, swimming pool.

Baia Degli Dei ★★★
Via Recanati, Giardini Naxos (ME) 98030
Tel: 39 (0942) 540-94

Single 41–47 euro, double 51–75 euro, breakfast, TV, air-conditioning, elevator, bar, restaurant, wheelchair accessible, TV room, groups welcome, client transportation, pets allowed.

Hotel La Riva ★★★
Via Trysandros 52, Giardini Naxos (ME) 98030
Tel: 39 (0942) 513-29
lariva@too.it
www.hotellariva.com
Single 45–55 euro, double 60–70 euro, air-conditioning, elevator, bar, restaurant, parking, groups welcome, pets allowed, parking, TV room.

Panoramic ★★★
Via Schisò 22, Giardini Naxos (ME) 98030
Tel: 39 (0942) 534-66
Single 45–61 euro, double 68–100 euro, TV, air-conditioning, elevator, bar, restaurant, groups welcome, pets allowed.

Where Else to Eat

Caffè Cavallaro
Via Umberto 165, Giardini Naxos (ME) 98030
Tel: 39 (0942) 251-269
Magnificent selection of delicious pastries. A real treat at any time of day. Try the ricotta pastries for breakfast.

Bar Pasticceria Salamone
Via Vittorio Emanuele 236, Giardini Naxos (ME) 98030
Tel: 39 (0942) 513-98
Serves delectable fresh fruit ice creams to fill a brioche and to have as the Sicilians do for breakfast.

LIPARI ISOLE EOLIE

Augustus ★★★
Vico Ausonia 16, Isola Lipari (ME) 98055
Tel: 39 (090) 981-1232
info@villaaugustus.it
www.villaaugustus.it
Single 55–110 euro, double 85–170 euro, breakfast, TV, air-conditioning, bar, private garden, pets, reading room, TV room, groups welcome, client transport, pets allowed, conference facilities, solarium, fitness.

Carasco ★★★
Porta Delle Genti, Lipari (ME) 98055
Tel: 39 (090) 981-1605
carasco@tin.it
www.carasco.it

Single 40–120 euro, double 70–240 euro, breakfast, elevator, bar, restaurant, private garden, reading room, groups welcome, client transport, private beach, swimming pool.

Mocambo ★★★
Via Cesare Battisti192 Località Canneto, Lipari (ME) 98052
Tel: 39 (090) 981-1442
info@hotel-mocambo.it
www.hotel-mocambo.it

Single 28–120 euro, double 40–170 euro, TV, air-conditioning, bar, restaurant, private garden groups welcome, client transport, pets allowed, babysitting, solarium, cycling.

MESSINA

Grand Hotel Liberty ★★★★
Via Settembre 15, Messina (ME) 98123
Tel: 39 (090) 640-9436
liberty@framon-hotels.com
www.framon-hotels.com

Single 128–169 euro, double 181–242 euro, air-conditioning, elevator, bar, restaurant, parking, wheelchair accessible, groups welcome, pets allowed, babysitting, conference facilities.

Royal Palace Hotel ★★★★
Via Cannizzaro Is 224, Messina (ME) 98123
Tel: 39 (090) 6503
royalpalace@framon-hotels.com
www.framon-hotels.com

Single 56–112 euro, double 79–159 euro, TV, air-conditioning, elevator, bar, restaurant, parking, wheelchair accessible, groups welcome, pets allowed, babysitting, conference facilities, garage.

Grand Hotel Lido ★★★
Lido di Mortelle-Via Consolare Pompea, Messina (ME) 98164
Tel: 39 (090) 321-017
giardinodellepalme@giardinodellepalme.com
www.giardinodellepalme.com

Single 42–62 euro, double 74–94 euro, TV, air-conditioning, elevator, bar, restaurant, private park, parking, wheelchair accessible, groups welcome, TV room, conference facilities, private beach, swimming pool.

Locanda Donato ★

Località Ganzirri—Via Caratozzolo 8, Messina (ME) 98165
Tel: 39 (090) 393-150
Double 62–72 euro, bar, restaurant, vegetarian menu, private park,
wheelchair accessible, pets allowed.

Villa Morgana ★★★

Via Consolare Pompeo 237 Località Ganzirri, Messina (ME) 98168
Tel: 39 (090) 325-575
villamorgana@tin.it
www.paginegialle.it/morgano-04
Single 35–50 euro, double 60 euro, breakfast, TV, air-conditioning, elevator, bar, restaurant, private garden, parking, reading room, TV room.
Pets allowed, groups welcome, conference facilities, solarium.

Where Else to Eat

Donna Giovanna

Via Risorgimento 16, Messina (ME) 98134
Tel: 39 (090) 718-503
Moderate prices. A popular restaurant with excellent typical Sicilian fare.

No.1

Via Risorgimento 192, Messina (ME) 98123
Tel: 39 (090) 717-411
Very affordable. Excellent pizza. Open only in evenings and closed
Tuesdays.

Hostaria Da Bacco

Via Cernaia 15, Messina (ME) 98123
Tel: 39 (090) 771-420
Moderate prices. Wonderful fresh fish prepared in traditional ways.
Closed Sundays.

MILAZZO

Hotel Garibaldi ★★★

Lungomare Garibaldi 160, Milazzo (ME) 98057
Tel: 39 (090) 924-0189
hotelgaribaldi@virgilio.it
Single 25–130 euro, double 40–200 euro, breakfast, TV, air-conditioning,
elevator, bar, restaurant, wheelchair accessible.

Silvanetta Palace Hotel ★★★
Via Aquaviole 1, Milazzo (ME) 98057
Tel: 39 (090) 928-1633
silvanet@octonline.it

Single 63–86 euro, double 100–136 euro, breakfast, TV, air-conditioning, elevator, bar, restaurant, private garden, parking, reading room, TV room. Pets allowed, groups welcome, conference facilities, dancing, private beach, tennis, swimming pool.

La Bussola ★★
Via XX Luglio 29, Milazzo (ME) 98057
Tel: 39 (090) 922-1244
labussola@genio.it

Single 30–60 euro, double 60 euro, breakfast, TV, air-conditioning, elevator, bar, parking, pets allowed, groups welcome.

Where Else to Eat

Salamone a Mare
Srada Panoramica 36, Milazzo (ME) 98057
Tel: 39 (090) 928-1233
Expensive. Excellent fish specialties and traditional pasta dishes.

Piccolo Casale
Via R. D'Amico12, Milazzo (ME) 98057
Tel: 39 (090) 922 4479
info@piccolocasale.it
www.piccolocasale.it

Piccolo Casale is located in the former residence of one of Garibaldi's generals and in the very town that had a decisive victory for the unification of Italy. It pays tribute to the past by offering the traditional cuisine of this lovely region as interpreted by its talented chefs, Andrea Scibilia and Franco Calafeo, as well as their wives, Mariella and Giancarla. The extensive wine cellar enhances and enriches the dining experience. This fine restaurant is a member of the Viaggio Enogastronomico, a group of excellent restaurants which pair the gourmet food of Sicily with vast Sicilian wine lists. Visit www.lesostediulisse.it for the complete list of participating restaurants.

PANAREA ISOLE EOLIE

Albergo La Piazza ★★★
Via San Pietro, Isola Panarea (ME) 98050
Tel: 39 (090) 983-649
hotelpiazza@netnet.it
Single 70–136 euro, double 140–308 euro, breakfast, TV, air-conditioning, bar, private garden, parking, groups welcome, client transportation, reading room, TV room, babysitting, conference facilities, private beach, swimming pool, skin diving.

Hotel Hycesia ★★
Via San Pietro, Isola Panarea (ME) 98050
Tel: 39 (090) 983-041
hycesia@netnet.it
Double 80–190 euro, breakfast, TV, air–conditioning, bar, restaurant, private park, TV room, client transportation, skin diving.

O Palmo ★
Via San Pietro, Isola Panarea (ME) 98050
Tel: 39 (090) 983-155
Single 40–95 euro, double 80–190 euro, breakfast, TV, restaurant, groups welcome, TV room, pets allowed.

Where Else to Eat

Hycesia
Via San Pierto, Isola Panarea (ME) 98050
Tel: 39 (090) 983-041
Moderate prices. Excellent choices of fresh fish and delicious local specialties.

SAN FRATELLO

Monte Soro ★
Via S. Latteri 23, San Fratello (ME) 98075
Tel: 39 (0941) 794-120
Single 20–28 euro, double 30–41 euro, bar, restaurant, wheelchair accessible.

STROMBOLI—ISOLE EOLIE

La Sirenetta Park Hotel ★★★
Via Marina 33, Isola Stromboli (ME) 98050
Tel: 39 (090) 986-124
lasirenetta@netnet.it
www.netnet.it/hotel/lasirenetta/index.html

Single 85–130 euro, double 120–280 euro, TV, air-conditioning, bar, restaurant, vegetarian menu, private park, parking, wheelchair accessible, groups welcome, client transportation, reading room, TV room, babysitting, conference facilities, dancing, tennis, swimming pool, waterskiing, skin diving, sailing, windsurfing.

Miramare ★
Via Vito Nunziante3, Isola Stromboli (ME) 98050
Tel: 39 (090) 986-047
lasirenetta@netnet.it
www.netnet.it/miramarestromboli

Single 45–70 euro, double 72–120 euro, TV, bar, restaurant, groups welcome, client transportation.

Villaggio Stromboli ★★★
Via Regina Elena, Isola Stromboli (ME) 98050
Tel: 39 (090) 986-018
villaggiostromboli@netnet.it
www.netnet.it/hotel/villaggiostromboli

Single 55–94 euro, double 95–162 euro, breakfast, TV, air-conditioning, bar, restaurant, vegetarian menu, private garden, reading room, TV room, groups welcome, client transport, pets allowed, children's playground, babysitting, skin diving, sailing, wind surfing.

Where Else to Eat

Locanda Barbablù
Via Vittorio Emanuele 17-19, Isola Stromboli (ME) 98050
Tel: 39 (090) 986-118

Expensive. Located in the garden of the hotel by the same name, it offers a fusion of Sicilian and Neapolitan food prepared by the owner/chef.

Villa Petrusa
Via Soldato Panettieri 4, Isola Stromboli (ME) 98050
Tel: 39 (090) 988-9956

Moderate prices. Very good local specialties.

TAORMINA

Ariston Hotel ★★★★
Via Bagnoli Croce 168, Taormina (ME) 98039
Tel: 39 (0942) 6190; Fax: 39 (0942) 619-191
sicily@parkhotel.it
The hotel is built on several beautifully landscaped terraces. Its excellent restaurant offers a pleasant piano bar for patrons.
Single 63–111 euro, double 100–204 euro, breakfast, TV, air-conditioning, elevator, bar, restaurant, private garden, pets allowed, groups welcome, swimming pool.

Bel Soggiorno ★★★
Via Luigi Pirandello 60, Taormina (ME) 98039
Tel: 39 (0942) 233-42
info@belsoggiorno.com
www.belsoggiorno.com
Single 50–65 euro, double 90–115 euro, breakfast, TV, air-conditioning, bar, private garden, parking, pets allowed, groups welcome, reading room, TV room, children's playground, babysitting.

Grand Hotel Miramare ★★★★
Via Guardiola Vecchia 27, Taormina (ME) 98039
Tel: 39 (0942) 234-01
ghmiramare@tiscalinet.it
Single 116–126 euro, double 200–210 euro, TV, air-conditioning, elevator, bar, restaurant, vegetarian menu, private garden, parking, groups welcome, tennis, swimming pool.

San Domenico Palace Hotel ★★★★★
Piazza San Domenico 5, Taormina (ME) 98039
Tel: 39 (0942) 613-111
san-domenico@thi.it
www.sandomenico.thi.it
Ultimate luxury and service. Single 205–250 euro, double 340–520 euro, breakfast, TV, air-conditioning, elevator, bar, restaurant, vegetarian menu, private garden, parking, wheelchair accessible, reading room, TV room, groups welcome, children's playground, babysitting, conference facilities, private beach, swimming pool, fitness, solarium, gym.

Sirius ★★★
Via Guardiola Vecchia 34, Taormina (ME) 98039
Tel: 39 (0942) 234-77
info@siriushotel.it
www.siriushotel.it

Single 51–82 euro, double 67–140 euro, air-conditioning, room service, elevator, bar, restaurant, vegetarian menu, private garden, parking, groups welcome, babysitting, Internet connection, satellite TV, tennis, swimming pool.

Villa Paradiso ★★★★
Via Roma 2, Taormina (ME) 98039
Tel: 39 (0942) 625-800
hotelparadiso@too.it

Single 68–118 euro, double 122–187 euro, TV, air-conditioning, elevator, bar, restaurant, vegetarian menu, reading room, TV room, groups welcome, babysitting, pets allowed, private beach, windsurfing.

Hotel Natalina ★★
Via Porta Pasquale 2, Taormina (ME) 98039
Tel: 39 (0942) 249-28
natalinahotel@too.it

Single 45–70 euro, double 60–95 euro, TV, air-conditioning, elevator, bar, restaurant, vegetarian menu, wheelchair accessible, groups welcome, babysitting, pets allowed.

Hotel Victoria ★★
Via Porta Pasquale 2, Taormina (ME) 98039
Tel: 39 (0942) 249-28
info@albergovictoria.it

Single 41–6 euro, double 72–103 euro, breakfast, TV, elevator, bar, parking, groups welcome, babysitting, pets allowed, reading room, TV room.

Where Else to Eat

Al Duomo
Vico Ebrei 11 (Piazza Doumo) Taormina (ME) 98039
Tel: 39 (0942) 625 656
info@ristorantealduomo.it
www.ristorantealduomo.it

Located in what was the Jewish quarter in the medieval period, Al Duomo offers a rich and varied selection of traditional Sicilian dishes with a rich wine list to match. Dine inside or on the beautiful flower-filled terrace with view of the fifteenth-century cathedral. This fine restaurant is a member of the Viaggio Enogastronomico.

Casa Grugno
Via Santa Maria dei Greci, Taormina (ME) 98039
Tel: 39 (0942) 221-208
info@casagrugno.it
www.casagrugno.it
Casa Grugno is located in a unique sixteenth-century building in the
heart of medieval Taormina. Chef Andreas Zangerl prepares seasonal
Sicilian dishes enriched by Enrico Briguglio's wine suggestions. Ranked
by Gambero Rosso, Casa Grugno is highly recommended by wine expert
Anna Maria Sorrentino of Shop Wine and Dine. This fine restaurant is a
member of the Viaggio Enogastronomico.

La Giara
Vico la Floresta1, Taormina (ME) 98039
Tel: 39 (0942) 233-60
Wonderful food selection, quality, service, and presentation.

Trattoria Porta Messina
Largo Giove Serapide 4, Taormina (ME) 98039
Tel: 39 (0942) 232-05
Located at the beginning of Corso Umberto, it offers great food at fair
prices, a varied menu, and a nice atmosphere, as well as indoor and out-
door seating with a lovely terrace.

Il Baccanale
Piazzetta Filea 1, Taormina (ME) 98039
Tel: 39 (0942) 625-390
Offers varied menu with an array of food to choose from. Even when
dining with a large group, everyone will find something he or she likes
and will be extremely satisfied with the quality and taste of the food.

Zammara
Via Fratelli Bandiera 15 (Piazzetta Cleone) Taormina (ME) 98039
Tel: 39 (0942) 244-08
www.zammara.it
Moderate prices, elegant restaurant, and *enoteca* with superlative tradi-
tional food and wonderful atmosphere.

Rosticceria di Cateno Aucello
Via Cappuccini 8, Taormina (ME) 98039
Serves great food made right in front of you by Cateno himself, and a
large selection of exotic lasagne.

VULCANO—ISOLE EOLIE

Eolian Hotel ★★★
Porto Ponente, Isola Vulcano (ME) 98050
Tel: 39 (090) 985-2151
eolian@eolianhotel.com
www.eolianhotel.com

Single 77–103 euro, double 120–170 euro, breakfast, TV, air-conditioning, bar, restaurant, private garden, reading room, TV room, groups welcome, client transportation, pets allowed, conference facilities, tennis, swimming, wind surfing.

Faraglione ★★
Località Porto Levante, Isola Vulcano (ME) 98050
Tel: 39 (0941) 985-2054
hotelfaraglione@lineafutura.it
www.lineafutura.it/hotelfaraglione

Single 40–114 euro, double 40–114 euro, breakfast, bar, restaurant, groups welcome, pets allowed.

Orsa Maggiore ★★★
Località Porto Ponente, Isola Vulcano (ME) 98050
Tel: 39 (0941) 901-779
orsamaggiore@usa.net
www.paginegialle.it/hotelorsamaggiore-me

Single 48–95 euro, double 80–160 euro, breakfast, TV, air-conditioning, bar, restaurant, vegetarian menu, private garden, parking, groups welcome, client transportation, reading room, pets allowed, babysitting, swimming pool, cycling, fishing, skin diving, fitness, thermal treatment.

Where Else to Eat

Lanterna Blu
Via Lentia 58, Isola Vulcano (ME) 98050
Tel: 39 (0941) 985-2178
Moderate prices. A popular local restaurant well known for its wonderful traditional fish dishes.

Da Vincenzino
Via Porto Levanre 25, Isola Vulcano (ME) 98050
Tel: 39 (0941) 985-2178
Very affordable. Simple and delicious local specialties.

PALERMO (PA)

CEFALÙ

Costa Verde ★★★★
Località San Nicola, Cefalù (PA) 90015
Tel: 39 (0921) 931-133
info@hotel-costaverde.it
www.hotel-costaverde.it
Single 70–150 euro, double 120–230 euro, TV, air-conditioning, elevator, bar, restaurant, private park, wheelchair accessible, reading room, TV room, children's playground, babysitting, dancing, private beach, tennis, golf, sailing, windsurfing, pool.

Baia Del Capitano ★★★
Contrada Mazzaforno, Cefalù (PA) 90015
Tel: 39 (0921) 420-005
baiadelcapitano@baiadelcapitano.it
www.baiadelcapitano.it
Single 45–50 euro, high season 90–105 euro, double 62–72 euro, high season 145 euro, TV, air-conditioning, elevator, bar, restaurant, private park, reading room, TV room, children's playground, babysitting, dancing, private beach, tennis, golf, sailing, windsurfing, minigolf, pool.

Carlton Riviera ★★★
Località Capo Plaia, Cefalù (PA) 90015
Tel: 39 (0921) 420-200
Single 51–77 euro, high season 77–129 euro, double 64–103 euro, high season 103–180 euro, breakfast, TV, air-conditioning, elevator, bar, restaurant, private park, parking, wheelchair accessible, reading room, TV room, children's playground, babysitting, dancing, private beach, tennis, horseback riding, archery, skin diving, waterskiing, sailing, windsurfing, minigolf, pool.

Santa Lucia—Le Sabbie D'Oro ★★★
Località Santa Lucia, Cefalù (PA) 90015
Tel: 39 (0921) 421-565
info@lesabbiedoro.it
www.lesabbiedoro.it
Single 51–82 euro, double 71–123 euro, TV, air-conditioning, elevator, bar, restaurant, private park, reading room, TV room, children's playground, babysitting, private beach, pool, bocce.

La Giara ★★
Via Veterani 40, Cefalù (PA) 90015
Tel: 39 (0921) 421-562
la_giara@freemail.it
www.paginegialle.it/hotelgiara

Single 40–80 euro, high season 45–90 euro, double 48–96 euro, high season 58–116 euro, air-conditioning, elevator, bar, restaurant, vegetarian menu available, wheelchair accessible, groups welcome, pets allowed, solarium.

Where Else to Eat

Try any of the trattorie and tavole calde along the lungomare for delicious and modestly priced local specialties.

Hosteria Del Duomo
Via Del Seminario 5, Cefalù (PA) 90015
Tel: 39 (0921) 421-838

A splurge but well worth it. Open-air restaurant overlooking the cathedral. Serves the best of Sicilian food.

Da Nino Alla Brace
Lungomare 11, Cefalù (PA) 90015
Tel: 39 (0921) 422-582

Moderate prices. Serves typical dishes in a lovely garden. Pizza served at dinner only. Closed Tuesdays.

GANGIVECCHIO

Tenuta Gangivecchio ★★★★
Contrada Gangivecchio, Gangi (PA) 90024,
Paolo Tornabene—Owner
Tel: 39 (0921) 644-804

Excellent inn and restaurant. Superlative food, wine, and ambiance. One of the places that is a must to visit in Sicily.

MONDELLO

Bye Bye Blues
Via del Garofalo 23, Valdesi, Mondello (PA) 90151
Tel: 39 (091) 684-1415
info@byebyeblues.it
www.byebyeblues.it

Sicilian specialties cooked by the award-winning chef and wine-expert team Patrizia di Benedetto and husband Antonio Baracco. Definitely a special treat. Member of the Viaggio Enogastronomico.

MONREALE

Carrubbella Park Hotel ★★★
Via Umberto I 233, Monreale (PA) 90046
Tel: 39 (091) 640-2189
Single 46–51 euro, high season 51–56 euro, double 72–82 euro, high
season 82–88 euro, TV, air-conditioning, elevator, bar, restaurant, private
park, parking, groups welcome, pets allowed, TV room, babysitting.

Ai Pini ★
Località San Martino Delle Scale – Villaggio Montano – Via S.M.6, 62
Monreale (PA) 90046
Tel: 39 (091) 418-198
Double 28–51 euro, bar, restaurant, private park, TV room.

Where Else to Eat

Try the many *focaccerie*, where you will get the freshly baked savory
pies filled with delicious local vegetables, or go to a store of *generi
alimentari* for delicious made-to-order sandwiches as an inexpensive portable feast.

Pizzeria Peppino
Via Benedetto Civiletti 12, Monreale (PA) 90046
Tel: 39 (091) 640-7770
Inexpensive. Serves the best pizza in town.

Osteria Delle Lumache
Via San Costrense 50, Monreale (PA) 90046
Tel: 39 (091) 640-7770
Inexpensive. A simple eatery where you can enjoy delicious traditional
local food.

PALERMO

Grand Hotel Federico II ★★★★★
Via Principe Granatelli 60, Palermo (PA) 90139
Tel: 39 (091) 749-5052
Single 87–95 euro, high season 185–229 euro, double 118–141 euro,
high season 222–276 euro, breakfast, TV, air-conditioning, elevator,
bar, restaurant, vegetarian menu, wheelchair accessible, reading room,
TV room, groups welcome, client transportation, pets allowed, garage,
Internet access, babysitting, fitness, sauna.

Baglio Conca D'Oro ★★★★
Località Borgo Molara – Via Aquino 19c-d, Palermo (PA) 90126
Tel: 39 (091) 640-6286
hotelbaglio@libero.it
www.pregiohotel.com
Single 52–93 euro, high season 64–114 euro, double 74–134 euro, high
season 98–160 euro, breakfast, TV, air-conditioning, elevator, bar, restaurant, private park, parking, wheelchair accessible, reading room, groups
welcome, babysitting, conference facilities.

Excelsior Palace ★★★★
Via Marchese Ugo 3, Palermo (PA) 90141
Tel: 39 (091) 625-6176
hotel@excelsiorpalermo.com
www.excelsiorpalermo.com
Single 70–140 euro, double 110–220 euro, TV, air-conditioning, elevator,
bar, restaurant, parking, wheelchair accessible, reading room, TV room,
groups welcome, garage, babysitting, conference facilities.

Grand Hotel et des Palmes ★★★★
Via Roma 398, Palermo 90139
Tel: 39 (091) 602-8111
des-palmes@thi.it
Worth a stop even if you're not staying. Single 65–178 euro, high season
65–188 euro, double 94–195 euro, high season 94–205 euro, breakfast,
air-conditioning, elevator, bar, restaurant, vegetarian menu, parking,
wheelchair accessible, pets allowed, groups welcome, client transport,
reading room, TV room, conference facilities, babysitting.

Grande Albergo Sole ★★★★
Corso Vittorio Emanuele 291, Palermo (PA) 90133
Tel: 39 (091) 604-111
sole@ghshotels.it
www.ghshotels.it
Single 45–141 euro, double 62–20 euro, TV, air-conditioning, elevator,
bar, restaurant, vegetarian menu, parking, wheelchair accessible, groups
welcome, conference facilities, babysitting, solarium.

Hotel Politeama Palace ★★★★
Piazza Ruggero Settimo 15, Palermo (PA) 90139
Tel: 39 (091) 322-777
mail@hotelpoliteama.it
Single 80–130 euro, double 120–185 euro, breakfast, TV, air-conditioning,
elevator, bar, restaurant, parking, groups welcome, conference facilities,
babysitting, reading room, TV room.

Vecchio Borgo ★★★★
Via Quintino Sella 1-7, Palermo (PA) 90139
Tel: 39 (091) 611-1446
hotelvecchioborgo@classicalhotels.com
Single 100–134 euro, double 120–180 euro, breakfast, TV, air-conditioning, elevator, bar, restaurant, private park, parking, wheelchair accessible, groups welcome, pets allowed.

Cristal Palace Hotel ★★★
Via Roma 477, Palermo (PA) 90139
Tel: 39 (091) 611-2580
cristal@shr.it
Single 40–125 euro, double 80–260 euro, TV, air-conditioning, elevator, bar, restaurant, parking, wheelchair accessible, groups welcome, TV room, conference facilities.

San Paolo Palace Hotel ★★★
Via Messina Marine 91, Palermo (PA) 90123
Tel: 39 (091) 621-1112
hotel@sanpaolopalace.it
www.sanpaolopalace.it
Single 77–106 euro, double 99–130 euro, breakfast, TV, air-conditioning, elevator, bar, restaurant, vegetarian menu, parking, wheelchair accessible, groups welcome, babysitting, TV room, conference facilities, fitness, swimming pool.

Posta ★★
Via Antonio Gagini 77, Palermo (PA) 90133
Tel: 39 (091)587-338
Single 26–78 euro, double 42–98 euro, breakfast, TV, air-conditioning, elevator, bar, private park, parking, wheelchair accessible, groups welcome, pets allowed, client transportation, conference facilities, reading room, TV room, babysitting.

Libertà ★
Via Mariano Stabile 136, Palermo (PA) 90139
Tel: 39 (091) 321-911
Single 50–60 euro, double 70–90 euro, TV, elevator, bar, restaurant, parking, wheelchair accessible, groups welcome.

Where Else to Eat

The famous Vucciria Market offers the best fast food in traditional Sicilian styles as well as cheeses and fruit. You can sample all kinds of delicious food, appetite teasers, and snacks as you make your way in this great market.

Antica Focacceria San Francesco
Via Alessandro Paternostro 58, Palermo (PA) 90133
Tel: 39 (091) 320-264
Very affordable. The oldest focacceria in Palermo and still the best for traditional dishes. Worth a visit just to see the array of typical Sicilian dishes that are not found in conventional restaurants.

Acanto Blu
Via Guardione 19, Palermo (PA) 90139
Tel: 39 (091) 326-258
Moderate prices. Excellent selection. Make reservations. Dinner only.

Cucina Papoff
Via Isidoro La Lumia 32, Palermo (PA) 90139
Tel: 39 (091) 325-355
Moderate prices. Although named after the Bulgarian founder, it's quintessentially a Sicilian restaurant that serves the best traditional fare. Open on Mondays, when most other restaurants are closed.

Charleston
Piazzale Ungheria 30, Palermo (PA) 90141
Tel: 39 (091) 321-366
Expensive. Elegant restaurant with excellent traditional Sicilian food and good service. Make reservations and dress up for a very special evening. Closed Sundays.

Gigi Mangia
Via Principe di Belmonte 104/d, Palermo (PA) 90139
Tel: 39 (091) 587-651
Moderate prices. Offers various choices of delicious vegetarian dishes including wonderful traditional pasta dishes.

Osteria Da Ciccio
Via Firenze 6, Palermo (PA) 90133
Tel: 39 (091) 329-143
Moderate prices. Wonderful fish dishes and seasonal vegetables. Closed Sundays.

Osteria dei Vespri
Piazza Croce dei Vespri 6 Palermo (PA)
Tel: 39 (091) 617-1631
osterideivespri@libero.it
www.osteriadeivespri.it
Located in the heart of Palermo, where some of the scenes of *Il Gattopardo* (*The Leopard*) were filmed by Visconti. Closed Sundays. A member of the

Viaggio Enogastronomico, a group of excellent restaurants which pair the gourmet food of Sicily with a vast Sicilian wine list. Visit www.lesostediulisse.it for the complete list of participating restaurants.

Pizzeria Bellini
Piazza Bellini 6, Palermo (PA) 90133
Tel: 39 (091) 616-5691
Moderate prices. A wonderful pizzeria right in the center of the town with view of La Chiesa Della Martorana. Open until after midnight during summer.

Self Service
Piazza Politeama, Palermo (PA) 90121
Inexpensive. Good Sicilian fare to eat in or take out for a movable feast.

USTICA

Grotta Azzurra ★★★★
Località San Fellicchio, Isola Ustica (PA) 90010
Tel: 39 (091) 844-9048
grottaazzurra@framon-hotels.it
www.framon-hotels.com
Single 97–161 euro, double 138–231 euro, TV, air-conditioning, elevator, bar, restaurant, vegetarian menu, private park, parking, groups welcome, client transportation, pets allowed, TV room, swimming pool, skin diving, sailing.

Clelia ★★★
Località San Fellicchio, Isola Ustica (PA) 90010
Tel: 39 (091) 844-9048
hotelclelia@tin.it
www.hotelclelia.it
Single 32–41 euro, high season 57–72 euro, double 56–68 euro, high season 85–110 euro, breakfast, TV, air-conditioning, elevator, bar, restaurant, wheelchair accessible, groups welcome, client transportation, reading room, TV room.

Ariston ★★
Via Della Vittoria 5, Isola Ustica (PA) 90010
Tel: 39 (091) 844-9042
Single 39–50 euro, double 55–81 euro, restaurant, groups welcome.

Patrice ★★
Via Rifugio 23, Isola Ustica (PA) 90010
Tel: 39 (091) 844-9053

Single 29–31 euro, high season 31–33 euro, double 47–48 euro, high season 48–56 euro, bar, restaurant, vegetarian menu, private park, parking, wheelchair accessible, groups welcome, client transportation, reading room, conference facilities, pets allowed.

Diana ★
Via Rifugio 23, Isola Ustica (PA) 90010
Tel: 39 (091) 844-9053
Single 23–30 euro, double 41–56 euro, bar, restaurant, private park, parking, wheelchair accessible, groups welcome, client transportation, reading room, TV room, babysitting, children's playground, conference facilities, pets allowed.

VILLAFRATI

Mulinazzo
Frazione Bolognetta, Villafrati (PA) 90121
Tel: 39 (091) 872-4870
mulinazzo@cena.it
Great traditional Sicilian Food.

TRAPANI (TP)

ERICE

Elimo Hotel ★★★
Via Vittorio Emanuele 75, Erice (TP) 91016
Tel: 39 (0923) 869-377
elimoh@comeg.it
Single 98–129 euro, double 170–250 euro, breakfast, TV, air-conditioning, elevator, bar, restaurant, private park, parking, groups welcome, conference facilities.

Moderno ★★★
Via Vittorio Emanuele 63, Erice (TP) 91016
Tel: 39 (0923) 869-300
modernoh@tin.it
www.pippocatalano.it
Single 70–80 euro, double 95–115 euro, breakfast, TV, air-conditioning, elevator, bar, restaurant, vegetarian menu, reading room, TV room, groups welcome, pets allowed, garage.

Ermione ★★
Via Pineta Comunale 43, Erice (TP) 91016
Tel: 39 (0923) 869-587
info@ermionehotel.com
www.ermionehotel.com
Single 35–63 euro, double 63–100 euro, breakfast, TV, elevator, bar, restaurant, private park, parking, menu, groups welcome, pets allowed, conference facilities, babysitting.

Where Else to Eat

Ristorante Monte San Giuliano
Vicolo San Rocco 7, Erice (TP) 91016
Tel: 39 (0923) 869-595
Pricey but excellent for a taste of the traditional cooking of the Trapani region.

Al Ciclope
Viale Nasi 45, Erice (TP) 91016
Tel: 39 (0923) 869-183
A wide range of menu prices. Excellent regional cooking.

Taverna di Re Aceste
Via Conte Pepoli, Erice (TP) 91016
Tel: 39 (0923) 869-084
Moderate prices. Colorful tavern famous for its delicious couscous, the signature dish of the region.

AGRITURISMO FARM

Pizzolungo
Contrada San Cusumano, Erice (TP) 91016
Tel: 39 (0923) 563-710
Stay at the villa of this beautiful fruit farm. Wheelchair accessible, bicycles and canoes available for rent.

YOUTH HOSTEL

G. Amodeo—Ostello per la Gioventù
Srada Provinciale Trapani-Erice, Erice (TP) 91016
Tel: 39 (0923) 552-964
Open all year.

FAVIGNANA—ISOLE EGADI

Aegusa ★★★
Via Giuseppe Garibaldi 11, Isola Favignana (TP) 91023
Tel: 39 (0923) 922-430
info@aegusahotel.it
www.egadi.com/aegusa
Single 40–78 euro, double 70–135 euro, TV, air-conditioning, bar, restaurant, wheelchair accessible, groups welcome.

Egadi ★★★
Via Cristoforo Colombo 17, Isola Favignana (TP) 91023
Tel: 39 (0923) 921-232
alchinehotel@libero.it
www.egadi.com/albergoegadi
Single 45 euro, double 80 euro, breakfast, TV, air-conditioning, bar, restaurant, reading room, transportation.

Hotel Delle Cave ★
Contrada Torretta, Isola Favignana (TP) 91023
Tel: 39 (0923) 925-423
info@hoteldellecave.it
www.hoteldellecave.it
Single 45–98 euro, double 85–1765 euro, breakfast, TV, air-conditioning, bar, restaurant, vegetarian menu, wheelchair accessible, groups welcome, children's playground, babysitting, sailing, skin diving.

Where Else to Eat

Egadi
Via Cristoforo Colombo 17, Porto Favignana (TP) 91023
Tel: 39 (0923) 921-232
Expensive. Well known for its delicious fresh tuna and other fish. Closed Wednesdays during low season.

El Pescador
Piazza Europa 38, Porto Favignana (TP) 91023
Tel: 39 (0923) 921-035
Expensive. Family-run restaurant well known for its daily catch of local fish. Closed Wednesdays during low season.

Ristorante Il Nautilus
Via Amendola 6, Porto Favignana (TP) 91023
Tel: 39 (0923) 921-671

Serves a la carte as well as inexpensive, fixed-price menu. Tuna and spaghetti with fresh fish and capers are the specialties of the house. Closed Tuesdays during low season.

LEVANZO ISOLE EGADI

Pensione dei Fenici ★★
Via Calvario 18, Isola Levanzo (TP) 91023
Tel: 39 (0923) 924-083
Single 45–50 euro, double 50–60 euro, air-conditioning, bar, restaurant, groups welcome.

Paradiso ★
Lungomare, Isola Levanzo (TP) 91023
Tel: 39 (0923) 924-080
Single 28–35 euro, double 56–70 euro, air-conditioning, bar, restaurant, pets accepted.

MARSALA

Delfino Beach Hotel ★★★
Contrada Berbaro, Marsala (TP) 91025
Tel: 39 (0923) 751-076
delfinobeach@delfinobeach.com
www.delfinobeach.com
Single 42–67 euro, double 62–110 euro, TV, air-conditioning, elevator, bar, restaurant, private park, parking, wheelchair accessible, client transportation, children's playground, babysitting, conference facilities, private beach, tennis, skin diving, swimming pool.

Hotel President ★★★
Via Nino Bixio 1, Marsala (TP) 91025
Tel: 39 (0923) 999-333
presidenthotel2002@libero.it
www.presidentmarsala.it
Single 58–65 euro, double 95–105 euro, TV, air-conditioning, elevator, bar, restaurant, private park, parking, wheelchair accessible, groups welcome, client transportation, children's playground, conference facilities, garage, pets accepted, gym, swimming pool.

Villa Favorita ★★★
Via Favorita, 27 Marsala (TP) 91025
Tel: 39 (0923) 989-100
info@villafavorita.com
www.villafavorita.com

Single 45–75 euro, double 70–110 euro, breakfast, TV, air-conditioning, bar, restaurant, private park, parking, wheelchair accessible, groups welcome, client transportation, children's playground, babysitting, conference facilities, tennis, swimming pool, bocce, soccer.

Where Else to Eat

Trattoria Garibaldi
Piazza Addolorata 35, Marsala (TP) 91025
Tel: 39 (0923) 953-006
Reasonably priced. Good traditional food including wine.

AGRITURISMO FARM

Baglio Vajarassa
Via Vajarassa 176, Spagnola (TP) 91025
Tel: 39 (0923) 968-628
Beautiful restored farmhouse with exhibitions of the historic objects and tools used by the farmer in a traditional country house.

MAZARA DEL VALLO

Kenpinski Giardino di Costanza Grand Hotel & Spa ★★★★★
Via Salemi 7+100, Mazara del Vallo (TP) 91026
Tel: 39 (0923) 907-763
info@giardinodicostanza.it
www.giardinodicostanza.it
Single 280–350 euro, double 360–430 euro, TV, air-conditioning, elevator, bar, restaurant, vegetarian menu, private park, parking, wheelchair accessible, groups welcome, conference facilities, client transportation, children's playground, babysitting, reading room, TV room, Internet connection, open and covered swimming pools, sauna, solarium, cycling, fitness, billiards.

Greta Hotel ★★★
Via Bessarione 107, Mazara Del Vallo (TP) 91026
Tel: 39 (0923) 653-889
gretahotel@gretahotel.it
www.gretahotel.it
Single 55–90 euro, double 70–160 euro, TV, air-conditioning, elevator, bar, restaurant, parking, wheelchair accessible, groups welcome, client transportation, reading room, TV room, pets allowed.

Hopps Hotel ★★★
Via G Hopps 29, Mazara del Vallo (TP) 91026
Tel: 39 (0923) 946-133
hoppshotel@tiscali.it
Single 53–65 euro, double 76–90 euro, TV, air-conditioning, elevator, bar, restaurant, private park, parking, wheelchair accessible, groups welcome, pets allowed, babysitting, conference facilities, dancing.

Where Else to Eat

Ristorante Alla Kabah
Via Itria 10, Mazara Del Vallo (TP) 91026
Tel: 39 (0923) 906-126
Reasonably priced; good food including wine.

PANTELLERIA ISOLE EGADI

Hotel Mursia ★★★
Località Mursia, Isola Pantelleria (TP) 91017
Tel: 39 (0923) 911-217
mursiahotel@pantelleria.it
Single 32–57 euro, double 52–98 euro, TV, air-conditioning, bar, restaurant, private park, parking, wheelchair accessible, groups welcome, client transportation, pets allowed, babysitting, conference facilities, private beach, tennis, swimming pool, sailing, skin diving.

Port Hotel ★★★
Lungomare Borgo Italia 71, Isola Pantelleria (TP) 91017
Tel: 39 (0923) 911-299
porthotel@pantelleria.it
Single 30–55, double 50–90 euro, TV, air-conditioning, elevator, bar, restaurant, parking, wheelchair accessible, groups welcome, client transportation, pets allowed.

Miryam ★★
Lungomare Borgo Italia 71, Isola Pantelleria (TP) 91017
Tel: 39 (0923) 911-299
miryamhotel@tiscali.it
www.miryamhotel.it
Single 29–55 euro, double 55–90 euro, TV, air-conditioning, elevator, bar, restaurant, parking, wheelchair accessible, groups welcome, client transportation, pets allowed, skin diving.

Where Else to Eat

Zabib
Porto di Scauri, Isola Pantelleria (TP) 91017
Tel: 39 (0923) 916-617
Expensive. Excellent food. Open only for dinner.

La Nicchia
Contrada Scauri Bassa, Isola Pantelleria (TP) 91017
Tel: 39 (0923) 916-343
Moderate prices. Excellent menu. Don't miss their couscous specialty.

Gabbiano Azzurro
Riva al Mare, Isola Pantelleria (TP) 91017
Tel: 39 (0923) 911-909
Affordable. A delightful place where you'll eat well and spend reasonably. Closed Fridays.

SELINUNTE

Il Gattopardo
Villa Anna Bed-and-Breakfast
Strada Statale 115 # 136 Castelvetrano-Selinunte (TP) 91022
Tel: 39 (0924) 468-81
Cell: 39 (329) 494-1335
www.gattopardobb.it
Single 35–40 euro, double 60–80 euro, triple and quadruple accommodations available all with bath and hydro-massage showers, TV, air-conditioning, terrace with panoramic view of the Temples of Selinunte, which are three miles away.

Where Else to Eat

Lido Azzurro
Via Marco Polo 51, Marinella di Selinunte (TP) 91022
Tel: 39 (0924) 462-11
Moderate prices. Good selections of delicious fresh fish and excellent pasta dishes.

TRAPANI

Crystal ★★★★
Piazza Umberto 1, Trapani (TP) 91100
Tel: 39 (0923) 200-00
reservations.cry@framon-hotels.it
www.framon-hotels.com

Single 82–200 euro, double 115–308 euro, TV, air-conditioning, elevator, bar, restaurant, parking, wheelchair accessible, groups welcome, reading room, conference facilities, garage, Internet, pets allowed.

Nuovo Albergo Russo ★★★
Piazza Umberto 1, Trapani (TP) 91100
Tel: 39 (0923) 221-66
Single 40–42 euro, double 70–80 euro, TV, air-conditioning, elevator, bar, groups welcome, reading room, pets allowed.

Cavallino Bianco ★★
Lungomare Dante Alighieri, Trapani (TP) 91100
Tel: 39 (0923) 215-49
cavallino-bianco@libero.it
www.initalia.it
Single 31–46 euro, double 51–77 euro, TV, elevator, bar, restaurant, wheelchair accessible, groups welcome, pets allowed.

Moderno ★★
Lungomare Dante Alighieri, Trapani (TP) 91100
Tel: 39 (0923) 215-49
Single 24–30 euro, double 40–50 euro, bar, groups welcome, pets allowed.

AGRIGENTO (AG)

AGRIGENTO

Baglio Della Luna ★★★★
Valle Dei Templi, Agrigento (AG) 92100
Tel: 39 (0922) 511-061
bagliodl@oasi.it
www.bagliodellaluna.com
Single 168 euro, double 336 euro, TV, air-conditioning, bar, restaurant, private park, parking, wheelchair accessible, reading room, TV room.

Colleverde Park Hotel ★★★★
Valle dei Templi, Agrigento (AG) 92100
Tel: 39 (0922) 295-55
mail@colleverde-hotel.it
www.colleverde-hotel.it
Single 70–110 euro, double 100–165 euro, breakfast, TV, air-conditioning, elevator, bar, restaurant, vegetarian cuisine available, pets allowed, private park, parking, wheelchair accessible, reading room, TV room.

Akrabello ★★★

Località Villaggio Mosè – Contrada Angeli, Agrigento (AG) 92100
Tel: 39 (0922) 606-277
athenahotels@asinform.it

Single 50–100 euro, double 93–130 euro, breakfast, TV, air-conditioning, elevator, bar, restaurant, vegetarian cuisine available, private park, parking, wheelchair accessible, reading room, TV room, children's playground, babysitting, dancing, tennis, swimming pool, sauna.

EOS ★★★

Contrada Cumbo – Villaggio Pirandello 87, Agrigento (AG) 92100
Tel: 39 (0922) 597-170
info@villaeos.it
www.villaeos.it

Single 50–80 euro, double 80–120 euro, breakfast, TV, air-conditioning, bar, restaurant, vegetarian cuisine available, private park, parking, reading room, TV room, private beach, tennis, swimming pool.

Tre Torri ★★★

Località Villaggio Mosè - Contrada Angeli Viale Cannatello 7, Agrigento (AG) 92100
Tel: 39 (0922) 606-733
info@hoteltretorri.eu
www.hoteltretorri.eu

Single 40–80 euro, double 90–130 euro, breakfast, TV, air-conditioning, elevator, bar, restaurant, vegetarian cuisine available, private park, parking, wheelchair accessible, reading room, TV room, children's playground, private beach, outdoor and covered swimming pools, sauna, fitness center.

Villa Athena ★★★★

Via Passaggiata Archeologica 33, Agrigento (AG) 92100
Tel: 39 (0922) 256-10

Single 67–130 euro, double 104–260 euro, TV, air-conditioning, elevator, bar, restaurant, vegetarian cuisine available, private park, parking, wheelchair accessible, babysitting, groups welcome, client transport, convention facilities, swimming pool.

Where Else to Eat

Villa Athena

Via Passaggiata Archeologica 33, Agrigento (AG) 92100
Tel: 39 (0922) 256-10

A big splurge. Excellent restaurant with spectacular views of the Valley of the Temples. This is definitely a very special treat. Have lunch or dinner even if you don't stay at the hotel. Make reservations.

Le Caprice
Srada Panoramica 51, Agrigento (AG) 92100
Tel: 39 (0922) 264-69
Another big splurge. Outstanding Sicilian food and unforgettable views
of the Mediterranean Sea. A real treat.

La Corte Degli Sfizzi
Via Atenea 4 Cortile Contanini, Agrigento (AG) 92100
Tel: 39 (0922) 595-520
Modestly priced. Restaurant and pizzeria with fixed-price menu. Serves
pizza at lunchtime.

Trattoria Il Simposio
Piano Lo Presti 19, Agrigento (AG) 92100
Tel: 39 (0922) 256-10
Inexpensive. Good food with a piano bar on weekends.

CALTABELLOTTA

Trattoria La Ferla
Via Roma 29 Caltabellotta (AG) 92010
Tel: 39 (0925) 951-444
Moderate prices. A wonderful traditional Sicilian restaurant in one of the
most scenic mountain towns in Sicily.

LAMPEDUSA—ISOLE PELAGIE

Baia Turchese ★★★
Contrada Guitgia – Via Lido Azzurro, Isola Lampedusa (AG) 92010
Tel: 39 (0922) 970-455
baiaturchese@lampedusa.to
Single 64–119 euro, double 87–134 euro, TV, air-conditioning, elevator,
bar, restaurant, private park, parking, reading room, TV room, client
transportation, babysitting, horseback riding, skin diving, private beach,
windsurfing.

La Perla ★★★
Porto Turistico – Lungomare Luigi Rizzo 1-5, Isola Lampedusa (AG) 92010
Tel: 39 (0922) 971-932
Single 44–85 euro, double 88–190 euro, TV, air-conditioning, elevator,
bar, restaurant, TV room, groups welcome, skin diving.

Martello ★★★
Piazza Medusa 1, Isola Lampedusa (AG) 92010
Tel: 39 (0922) 970-025

Single 55–69 euro, double 90–100, high season 120–130 euro, TV, air-conditioning, elevator, bar, restaurant, vegetarian menu, private park, wheelchair accessible, TV room, client transportation, babysitting, skin diving, swimming pool.

SCIACCA

Grand Hotel Delle Terme ★★★★
Via Delle Terme 1, Sciacca (AG) 92019
Tel: 39 (0925) 231-33
info@grandhoteldelleterme.com
www.grandhoteldelleterme.com
Single 61 euro, high season 77 euro, double 101 euro, high season 139 euro, TV, air-conditioning, elevator, bar, restaurant, private park, parking, wheelchair accessible, reading room, TV room, groups welcome, garage, babysitting, swimming pool, spa with thermal treatments, and baths with spectacular views.

Villa Palocla ★★★★
Contrada Raganella, Sciacca (AG) 92019
Tel: 39 (0922) 902-812
info@villapalocla.it
Single 67–80 euro, double 110–140 euro, breakfast, TV, air-conditioning, elevator, bar, restaurant, private park, parking, wheelchair accessible, reading room, TV room, groups welcome, garage, babysitting, conference facilities, private beach, swimming pool.

Alicudi ★★★
Contrada Savareto, Sciacca (AG) 92019
Tel: 39 (0925) 994-000
info@aeroviaggi.it
www.aeroviaggi.it
Single 48–81 euro, high season 79–134 euro, double 59–100 euro, high season 110–187 euro, breakfast, TV, air-conditioning, elevator, bar, restaurant, private park, parking, wheelchair accessible, reading room, TV room, groups welcome, client transportation, garage, babysitting, children's playground, conference facilities, private beach, archery, tennis, open and covered swimming pools, waterskiing, miniature golf, bocce, horseback riding, thermal treatments and baths, sauna, fitness, sailing, dancing.

Cala Regina ★★★
Contrada Savareto, Sciacca (AG) 92019
Tel: 39 (0925) 992-161
info@aeroviaggi.it

Single 53–91 euro, high season 96–162 euro, double 69–118 euro, high season 142–242 euro, breakfast, TV, air-conditioning, elevator, bar, restaurant, private park, parking, wheelchair accessible, reading room, TV room, groups welcome, client transportation, babysitting, children's playground, conference facilities, private beach, archery, tennis, open and covered swimming pools, waterskiing, miniature golf, bocce, horseback riding, thermal treatments and baths, sauna, fitness, sailing.

Torre Macauda ★★★
Contrada Macauda SS115, Sciacca (AG) 92019
Tel: 39 (0925) 968-824
info@torremacauda.com
www.torremacauda.com

Single 34–51 euro, double 51–88 euro, TV, air-conditioning, elevator, bar, restaurant, private park, parking, reading room, TV room, babysitting, conference facilities, dancing, private beach, swimming pool, horseback riding, thermal treatments, sauna, sailing, windsurfing.

Where Else to Eat

To eat well on a budget, go to the lower town of Sciacca, where you will find wonderful restaurants with excellent fish right near the port.

Hostaria del Vicolo
Vicolo Sammaritano 10, Sciacca (AG) 92019
Tel: 39 (0925) 230-71

Moderate prices. Well prepared fish and seafood with wonderful pastas.

Miramare
Piazza Scandagliato 6, Sciacca (AG) 92019
Tel: 39 (0925) 260-50

Moderate prices. Enjoy dinner on the terrace with a view of the beautiful Mediterranean. Fish is the specialty, but pizza is also served.

AGRITURISMO FARM

Montalbano
Located at Scunchipani, Sciacca (AG) 92019
Tel: 39 (0925) 801-54

Guests are housed in a modern farmhouse nestled in olive and orange groves.

Caltanissetta (CL)

CALTANISSETTA

San Michele ★★★★
Via Dei Fasci Siciliani, Caltanissetta (CL) 93100
Tel: 39 (0934) 553-750
hotelsanmichele@tin.it
www.hotelsanmichelesicilia.it
Single 40–80 euro, double 60–120 euro, breakfast, TV, air-conditioning, elevator, bar, restaurant, vegetarian cuisine available, private park, parking, wheelchair accessible, reading room, TV room, pets allowed, outdoor and covered swimming pools.

Park Hotel – Ambassador San Domenico
Contrada Grottarossa-SS 640 CL/AG Casella Postale 61-Serradifalco (CL) 93100
sita.hotel@libero.it
Single 26–32 euro, double 42–52 euro, breakfast, TV, air-conditioning, bar, restaurant, private park, parking, wheelchair accessible, reading room, TV room.

Where Else to Eat

Cortese
Viale Sicilia 158, Caltanissetta (CL) 93100
Tel: 39 (09034) 591-686
Moderate prices. Excellent Sicilian food.

Il Gattopardo
Viale Pacini 20, Caltanissetta (CL) 93100
Tel: 39 (09034) 598-384
Very affordable. Restaurant and pizzeria open for dinner only.

Bar Pasticceria Florino
Viale Candura 4/F, Caltanissetta (CL) 93100
Tel: 39 (09034) 583-109
Try their delicious bignè or cream puffs filled with hazelnut cream, chocolate, coffee custard, or dense whipped cream.

Caffè Pasticceria Rair
Corso Umberto I 163, Caltanissetta (CL) 93100
Tel: 39 (09034) 214-02

Try Sicilian cannoli and their specialty cannolicchi filled with fresh sweetened ricotta perfumed with cinnamon and covered with coarsely ground almonds and filberts.

GELA

Sileno ★★★
Contrada Giardinelli SS115bis Km 92, Gela (CL) 93912
Tel: 39 (0933) 907-236
giorgiabracchitta@virgilio.it
Single 56–62 euro, double 73–83 euro, breakfast, TV, air-conditioning, elevator, bar, restaurant, groups welcome, client transportation, reading room.

Sole ★
Via Mare 32, Gela (CL) 93012
Tel: 39 (0933) 925-292
info@hotelsole.sicilia.it
www.hotelsole.sicilia.it
Single 20–35 euro, double 30–50 euro, breakfast, TV, air-conditioning, elevator, restaurant, groups welcome, wheelchair accessible, pets allowed.

Where Else to Eat

Centrale Totò
Via Generale Cascino 39, Gela (CL) 93012
Tel: 39 (0933) 913-104
Excellent traditional Sicilian cooking. Closed Sundays.

ENNA (EN)

AIDONE

Morgantina ★★
Via Adelasia 42, Aidone (EN) 94010
Tel: 39 (0935)88088 or 88111
hotelmorgantina@tiscali.it
www.hotelmorgantina.it
Single 40–45 euro, double 55–60 euro, breakfast, TV, bar, restaurant, parking, reading room, separate TV room, conference facilities, hiking.

ENNA

Grande Albergo Sicilia ★★★
Piazza Napoleone Colajanni 7, Enna (EN) 94100
Tel: 39 (0935) 500-850
hotelsiciliaenna@vivienna.it
www.hotelsiciliaenna.it
Single 57–62 euro, double 85–91, TV, air-conditioning, elevator, bar, reading room, TV room, groups welcome, client transportation, conference facilities, dancing, tennis.

Hotel Demetra ★★★
Contrada Misericordia SS121, Enna (EN) 94100
Tel: 39 (0935) 502-300
hoteldemetra@tin.it
www.paginegialle.it/demetrahtl
Single 51–78 euro, double 83–110 euro, breakfast, TV, air-conditioning, elevator, bar, restaurant, private garden, parking, reading room, TV room, groups welcome, client transportation, conference facilities, tennis.

Masseria Mandrascate
Località Mandrascate S.P.4 Km 9,800 Valguarnera, Enna (EN) 94100
Tel: 39 (0935) 958-502
www.masseriamandrascate.it
An ancient family run homestead, where you will wine and dine in style.

Pasticceria Il Dolce
Piazza Sant'Agostino 40, Enna (EN) 94100
Tel: 39 (0935) 240-18
Try their delicious Sfoghiatelle with ricotta, traditional cannoli, and almond cookies.

Bar Pasticceria Caprice
Via Firenze 17, Enna (EN) 94100
Tel: 39 (0935) 252-81
Serves a very tempting selection of delectable sweets and snacks. Try gelati di frutta, some of the best fresh fruit ice creams, or have a coffee or tea with a ricotta tart called a cassatella.

EXCURSIONS AND TOURS

Scarlat Travel Service
Via Roma 137, Enna (EN) 94100
Tel: 39 (0935) 500-101
Tours of the archeological sites of Enna.

PERGUSA

Hotel Villa Giulia ★★★
Villaggio Pergusa, Pergusa (EN) 94100
Tel: 39 (0935) 541-043
info@hotelvillagiulia.org
www.hotelvillagiulia.it

Single 40–67 euro, double 52–93 euro, breakfast, TV, air-conditioning, elevator, bar, restaurant, vegetarian menu, parking, wheelchair accessible, reading room, TV room, groups welcome, client transportation, dancing, tennis, trekking, horseback riding.

Park Hotel La Giara ★★★
Via Nazionale 125, Pergusa (EN) 94010
Tel: 39 (0935) 541-521
info@parkhotellagiara.it
www.parkhotellagiara.it

Single 62–93 euro, double 73–109 euro, TV, air-conditioning, elevator, bar, restaurant, vegetarian menu, private garden, parking, reading room, TV room, groups welcome, client transportation, conference facilities, dancing, tennis, swimming pool, billiards, ping-pong, solarium, fitness, soccer, trekking.

Where Else to Eat

Ariston
Via Roma 353, Enna (EN) 94100
Tel: 39 (0935) 260-38

Moderate prices. A well-known local restaurant serving excellent Sicilian food. Closed Sundays.

Demetra
Contrada Misericordia, Enna (EN) 94100
Tel: 39 (0935) 502-300

Moderate prices. Delicious regional specialties with local vegetables.

La Fontana
Via Volturno 6, Enna (EN) 94100
Tel: 39 (0935) 254-65

Inexpensive and a very good trattoria.

PIAZZA ARMERINA

Park Hotel Paradiso ★★★
Contrada Romalda, Piazza Armerina (EN) 94015
Tel: 39 (0935) 680-841
parkhotelparadiso@tiscali.it
www.paginegialle.it/photelparadiso

Single 50–70 euro, double 80–110 euro, breakfast, TV, air-conditioning, elevator, bar, restaurant, vegetarian menu, groups welcome, client transportation, reading room, TV room, conference facilities, dancing, tennis, open and covered swimming pool, horseback riding, billiards, trekking, thermal treatments, sauna, solarium, fitness.

Villa Romana ★★★
Via Alcide De Gasperi 18, Piazza Armerina (EN) 94015
Tel: 39 (0935) 682-911
hotelvillaromana@piazza-armerina.it
www.piazza-armerina.it/hotelvillaromana

Single 50–60 euro, double 75–85 euro, breakfast, TV, air-conditioning, elevator, bar, restaurant, vegetarian menu, groups welcome, client transportation, reading room, TV room, conference facilities, dancing, tennis, horseback riding, trekking.

Mosaici Da Battiato ★★
Contrada Paratore, Piazza Armerina (EN) 94015
Tel: 39 (0935) 685-453

Single 35 euro, double 45 euro, TV, air-conditioning, bar, restaurant, vegetarian menu, private garden, parking, reading room, TV room, groups welcome, client transportation, conference facilities, tennis, horseback riding, trekking.

Where Else to Eat

La Ruota di Pioni Fiorella (near the Roman Villa Casale)
Contrada Paratore Casale, Piazza Armerina (EN) 94015
Tel: 39 (0935) 680-542

Moderate prices. Serves delicious pastas and other homemade traditional dishes.

Al Folgher
Contrada Bellia, Piazza Armerina (EN) 94015
Tel: 39 (0935) 684-123

Serves a wonderful selection of classic and traditional dishes with over four hundred wines. Closed Sundays. Member of the Viaggio Enogastronomico, a group of excellent restaurants that pair the gourmet food of Sicily with a vast Sicilian wine list. Visit www.lesostediulisse.it for the complete list of participating restaurants.

Mosaici
Contrada Paratore, Piazza Armerina (EN) 94015
Tel: 39 (0935) 685-453
Modest prices. Good tasty food. Call for reservations.

AGRITURISMO FARM

Azienda Agricola Savoca
Località Polleri 13, Piazza Armerina (EN) 94015
Tel: 39 (0935) 683-078
You will be housed in a beautiful estate with a renovated nineteenth-century farmhouse. A lovely stream permits fishing. Bicycles are available for guests.

BIBLIOGRAPHY

Boccaccio, Giovanni. *Decameron*. Translated by Mark Musa. New York: W.W. Norton & Company, 1982.

Camilleri, Andrea. *Un Mese Con Moltalbano*. Milan: Mondadori, 1998.

Chierichetti, Sandro. *Masterworks of Sicily*. Milan: Editrice CO.GRAF, 1981.

———. *Sicily, Garden of Europe*. Milan: Kina Italia S.p.A.

Collura, Matteo. *Musica Degli Iblei*. Palermo: Bruno Leopardi Editore, 2001.

———. *Sicilia Sconosciuta*. Edizione II. Milan: Rizzoli, 1998.

Cosentini, Gaetano, and Gianni Pirrone. *Donnafugata*. Palermo: Leopardi Editore, 1985.

Di, Pirajno, and Denti Alberto. *Siciliani a Tavola*. Milan: Longanesi & C., 1970.

Dolci, Danilo. *Report from Palermo*. New York: Viking Press, 1970.

Fernandez, Dominique. *Grand Tour in Sicilia*. Palermo: Bruno Leopardi Editore, 1998.

Ferrari-Bravo, Anna. *Sicily*. Milan: Touring Club of Italy, 2002.

Francesio, Giovanni, ed. *Sicily*. New York: DK Publishing, 2003.

Gefen, Gerard. *La Sicilia Al Tempo Dei Gattopardi*. Messina: Edizioni GBM, 2002.

Gilmour, David. *The Last Leopard*. New York: Random House, 1988.

Gramsci, Antonio. *Lettere dal Carcere*. Rome: Editori Riuniti, 1956.

Granof, Victoria. *Sweet Sicily*. New York: HarperCollins, 2001.

Hughes, Serge. *The Fall and Rise of Modern Italy*. New York: Macmillan, 1967.

243

Iacono, Giuseppe. *Pearls of Sicily*. Messina: Società Editrice Affinità Elettive, 1998.

Levi, Carlo. *Words Are Stones*. London: Hesperus Press Limited, 2005.

Maraini, Dacia, *Bagheria*. Sesta Edizione. Milan: Rizzoli, 1998.

Orlando, Leoluca. *Fighting the Mafia*. San Francisco: Encounter Books, 2001.

Phelps, Daphne. *A House in Sicily*. New York: Carroll & Graf, 1999.

Pike, Jeffrey, ed. *Insight Guide: Sicily*. New York: Langenscheidt, 2000.

Pirandello, Luigi. *Novelle Per Un Anno*. Rome: Newton Campton Editore, 1993.

Pitrolo, Giuseppe. *Mestieri Arti e Gente*. Modica: Del Mio Paese, 2003.

Quasimodo, Salvatore. *Ed È Subito Sera*. Milan: Mondadori, 1942.

Romeo, Rosario. *Il Risorgimento in Sicilia*. Bari: La Terza, 1970.

Sapienza, Teresa. *Sicily: Art, History and Natural Beauty*. Bologna: Officina Grafica Bolognese S.N.C., 1998.

Sciascia, Leonardo. *Opere 1956–1971*. Milan: Bompiani, 1996.

Sicilia, vol. 4. Milan: Touring Club Italiano, 1933.

Simeti, Mary Taylor. *Bitter Almonds*. New York: William & Morrow, 1994.

———. *On Persephone's Island*. New York: Alfred A. Knopf, 1986.

Tomasi, Gioacchino Lanza. *Giuseppe Tomasi di Lampedusa*. Palermo: Sellerio, 1998.

———. *Sicilia Sicily*. Palermo: Bruno Leopardi Editore, 2001.

Tomasi, Giuseppe di Lampedusa. *Il Gattopardo*. 79th ed. Milan: Feltrinelli, 1962.

Tornabene, Wanda & Giovanna. *La Cucina Siciliana di Gangivecchio*. New York: Alfred A. Knopf, 1996.

Trotta, Donatella. *Sicily*. New York: Rizzoli International, 2000.

Valdes, Giuliano. *Art e Storia: Sicilia*. Florence: Casa Editrice Bonechi, 2004.

Veronelli, Luigi. *Sicilia*. Milan: Garzanti, 1970.

Virgadavola, Giovanni. *Il Canto Del Carretto*. Ragusa: Self-published, 1994.

Zipelli, Cesare. *Il Barocco Interpretato da Oscar Spadola*. Ragusa Ibla: Libreria Paolino, 2004.

INDEX